P9-DFQ-976

lex & yacc

lex & yacc

John R. Levine
Tony Mason
Doug Brown

O'REILLY®

Beijing · Cambridge · Farnham · Köln · Paris · Sebastopol · Taipei · Tokyo

lex & yacc

by John R. Levine, Tony Mason and Doug Brown

Copyright © 1990, 1992 O'Reilly & Associates, Inc. All rights reserved.
Printed in the United States of America.

Editor: Dale Dougherty

Printing History:

May 1990:	First Edition.
January 1991:	Minor corrections.
October 1992:	Second Edition. Major revisions.
February 1995:	Minor corrections.

Nutshell Handbook, the Nutshell Handbook logo, and the O'Reilly logo are registered trademarks and The Java Series is a trademark of O'Reilly & Associates, Inc. Many of the designations used by manufacturers and sellers to distinguish their products are claimed as trademarks. Where those designations appear in this book, and O'Reilly and Associates, Inc. was aware of a trademark claim, the designations have been printed in caps or initial caps.

While every precaution has been taken in the preparation of this book, the publisher assumes no responsibility for errors or omissions, or for damages resulting from the use of the information contained herein.

ISBN: 1-56592-000-7
[M]

[4/03]

Table of Contents

3: Using Yacc — 51

4: A Menu Generation Language — 81

5: Parsing SQL — 109

6: A Reference for Lex Specifications   147

7: A Reference for Yacc Grammars   181

8: *Yacc Ambiguities and Conflicts*   *217*

Figures

Examples

Preface

Lex and yacc are tools designed for writers of compilers and interpreters, although they are also useful for many applications that will interest the noncompiler writer. Any application that looks for patterns in its input, or has an input or command language is a good candidate for lex and yacc. Furthermore, they allow for rapid application prototyping, easy modification, and simple maintenance of programs. To stimulate your imagination, here are a few things people have used lex and yacc to develop:

- The desktop calculator *bc*

- The tools *eqn* and *pic*, typesetting preprocessors for mathematical equations and complex pictures.

- *PCC*, the Portable C Compiler used with many UNIX systems, and *GCC*, the GNU C Compiler

- A menu compiler

- A SQL data base language syntax checker

- The *lex* program itself

What's New in the Second Edition

We have made extensive revisions in this new second edition. Major changes include:

- Completely rewritten introductory Chapters 1-3

- New Chapter 5 with a full SQL grammar

- New, much more extensive reference chapters

- Full coverage of all major MS-DOS and UNIX versions of lex and yacc, including AT&T lex and yacc, Berkeley yacc, flex, GNU bison, MKS lex and yacc, and Abraxas PCYACC

- Coverage of the new POSIX 1003.2 standard versions of lex and yacc

Scope of This Book

Chapter 1, *Lex and Yacc*, gives an overview of how and why lex and yacc are used to create compilers and interpreters, and demonstrates some small lex and yacc applications. It also introduces basic terms we use throughout the book.

Chapter 2, *Using Lex*, describes how to use lex. It develops lex applications that count words in files, analyze program command switches and arguments, and compute statistics on C programs.

Chapter 3, *Using Yacc*, gives a full example using lex and yacc to develop a fully functional desktop calculator.

Chapter 4, *A Menu Generation Language*, demonstrates how to use lex and yacc to develop a menu generator.

Chapter 5, *Parsing SQL*, develops a parser for the full SQL relational data base language. First we use the parser as a syntax checker, then extend it into a simple preprocessor for SQL embedded in C programs.

Chapter 6, *A Reference for Lex Specifications*, and Chapter 7, *A Reference for Yacc Grammars*, provide detailed descriptions of the features and options available to the lex and yacc programmer. These chapters and the two that follow provide technical information for the now experienced lex and yacc programmer to use while developing new lex and yacc applications.

Chapter 8, *Yacc Ambiguities and Conflicts*, explains yacc ambiguities and conflicts, which are problems that keep yacc from parsing a grammar correctly. It then develops methods that can be used to locate and correct such problems.

Chapter 9, *Error Reporting and Recovery*, discusses techniques that the compiler or interpreter designer can use to locate, recognize, and report errors in the compiler input.

Appendix A, *AT&T Lex*, describes the command-line syntax of AT&T lex and the error messages it reports and suggests possible solutions.

Appendix B, *AT&T Yacc*, describes the command-line syntax of AT&T yacc and lists errors reported by yacc. It provides examples of code which can cause such errors and suggests possible solutions.

Appendix C, *Berkeley Yacc*, describes the command-line syntax of Berkeley yacc, a widely used free version of yacc distributed with Berkeley UNIX, and lists errors reported by Berkeley yacc with suggested solutions.

Appendix D, *GNU Bison*, discusses differences found in bison, the Free Software Foundation's implementation of yacc.

Appendix E, *Flex*, discusses flex, a widely used free version of lex, lists differences from other versions, and lists errors reported by flex with suggested solutions.

Appendix F, *MKS Lex and Yacc*, discusses the MS-DOS and OS/2 version of lex and yacc from Mortice Kern Systems.

Appendix G, *Abraxas Lex and Yacc*, discusses PCYACC, the MS-DOS and OS/2 versions of lex and yacc from Abraxas Software.

Appendix H, *POSIX Lex and Yacc*, discusses the versions of lex and yacc defined by the IEEE POSIX 1003.2 standard.

Appendix I, *MGL Compiler Code*, provides the complete source code for the menu generation language compiler discussed in Chapter 4.

Appendix J, *SQL Parser Code*, provides the complete source code and a cross-reference for the SQL parser discussed in Chapter 5.

The *Glossary* lists technical terms language and compiler theory.

The *Bibliography* lists other documentation on lex and yacc, as well as helpful books on compiler design.

We presume the reader is familiar with C, as most examples are in C, lex, or yacc, with the remainder being in the special purpose languages developed within the text.

Availability of Lex and Yacc

Lex and yacc were both developed at Bell Laboratories in the 1970s. Yacc was the first of the two, developed by Stephen C. Johnson. Lex was designed by Mike Lesk and Eric Schmidt to work with yacc. Both lex and yacc have been standard UNIX utilities since 7th Edition UNIX. System V and older versions of BSD use the original AT&T versions, while the newest version of BSD uses flex (see below) and Berkeley yacc. The articles written by the developers remain the primary source of information on lex and yacc.

The GNU Project of the Free Software Foundation distributes *bison*, a yacc replacement; bison was written by Robert Corbett and Richard Stallman. The bison manual, written by Charles Donnelly and Richard Stallman, is excellent, especially for referencing specific features. Appendix D discusses bison.

BSD and GNU Project also distribute *flex* (*Fast Lex*ical Analyzer Generator), "a rewrite of lex intended to right some of that tool's deficiencies," according to its reference page. Flex was originally written by Jef Poskanzer; Vern Paxson and Van Jacobson have considerably improved it and Vern currently maintains it. Appendix E covers topics specific to flex.

There are at least two versions of lex and yacc available for MS-DOS and OS/2 machines. MKS (Mortice Kern Systems Inc.), publishers of the MKS Toolkit, offers lex and yacc as a separate product that supports many PC C compilers. MKS lex and yacc comes with a very good manual. Appendix F covers MKS lex and yacc. Abraxas Software publishes PCYACC, a version of lex and yacc which comes with sample parsers for a dozen widely used programming languages. Appendix G covers Abraxas' version lex and yacc.

Sample Programs

The programs in this book are available free from UUNET (that is, free except for UUNET's usual connect-time charges). If you have access to UUNET, you can retrieve the source code using UUCP or FTP. For UUCP, find a machine with direct access to UUNET, and type the following command:

```
uucp uunet\!~/nutshell/lexyacc/progs.tar.Z yourhost\!~/yourname/
```

The backslashes can be omitted if you use the Bourne shell (*sh*) instead of the C shell (*csh*). The file should appear some time later (up to a day or more) in the directory */usr/spool/uucppublic/*yourname. If you don't have an account but would like one so that you can get electronic mail, then contact UUNET at 703-204-8000.

To use *ftp*, find a machine with direct access to the Internet. Here is a sample session, with commands in boldface.

```
% ftp ftp.oreilly.com
Connected to ftp.oreilly.com.
220 FTP server (Version 5.99 Wed May 23 14:40:19 EDT 1990) ready.
Name (ftp.oreilly.com:yourname): anonymous
331 Guest login ok, send ident as password.
Password: ambar@ora.com (use your user name and host here)
230 Guest login ok, access restrictions apply.
ftp> cd published/oreilly/nutshell/lexyacc
250 CWD command successful.
ftp> binary (you must specify binary transfer for compressed files)
200 Type set to I.
ftp> get progs.tar.Z
200 PORT command successful.
150 Opening BINARY mode data connection for progs.tar.Z.
226 Transfer complete.
ftp> quit
221 Goodbye.
%
```

The file is a compressed tar archive. To extract files once you have retrieved the archive, type:

```
% zcat progs.tar.Z | tar xf -
```

System V systems require the following tar command instead:

```
% zcat progs.tar.Z | tar xof -
```

Conventions Used in This Handbook

The following conventions are used in this book:

Bold   is used for statements and functions, identifiers, and program names.

Italic   is used for file, directory, and command names when they appear in the body of a paragraph as well as for data types and to emphasize new terms and concepts when they are introduced.

Constant Width	is used in examples to show the contents of files or the output from commands.
Constant Bold	is used in examples to show command lines and options that you type literally.
Quotes	are used to identify a code fragment in explanatory text. System messages, signs, and symbols are quoted as well.
%	is the Shell prompt.
[]	surround optional elements in a description of program syntax. (Don't type the brackets themselves.)

Acknowledgments

This first edition of this book began with Tony Mason's MGL and SGL compilers. Tony developed most of the material in this book, working with Dale Dougherty to make it a "Nutshell." Doug Brown contributed Chapter 8, *Yacc Ambiguities and Conflicts*. Dale also edited and revised portions of the book. Tim O'Reilly made it a better book by withholding his editorial blessing until he found what he was looking for in the book. Thanks to Butch Anton, Ed Engler, and Mike Loukides for their comments on technical content. Thanks also to John W. Lockhart for reading a draft with an eye for stylistic issues. And thanks to Chris Reilley for his work on the graphics. Finally, Ruth Terry brought the book into print with her usual diligence and her sharp eye for every editorial detail. Though she was trying to work odd hours to also care for her family, it seemed she was caring for this book all hours of the day.

For the second edition, Tony rewrote chapters 1 and 2, and Doug updated Chapter 8. John Levine wrote Chapters 3, 5, 6, 7, and most of the appendices, and edited the rest of the text. Thanks to the technical reviewers, Bill Burke, Warren Carithers, Jon Mauney, Gary Merrill, Eugene Miya, Andy Oram, Bill Torcaso, and particularly Vern Paxson whose detailed page-by-page suggestions made the fine points much clearer. Margaret Levine Young's blue pencil (which was actually pink) tightened up the text and gave the book editorial consistency. She also compiled most of the index. Chris Reilly again did the graphics, and Donna Woonteiler did the final editing and shepherded the book through the production process.

1

Lex and Yacc

Lex and yacc help you write programs that transform structured input. This includes an enormous range of applications—anything from a simple text search program that looks for patterns in its input file to a C compiler that transforms a source program into optimized object code.

In programs with structured input, two tasks that occur over and over are dividing the input into meaningful units, and then discovering the relationship among the units. For a text search program, the units would probably be lines of text, with a distinction between lines that contain a match of the target string and lines that don't. For a C program, the units are variable names, constants, strings, operators, punctuation, and so forth. This division into units (which are usually called *tokens*) is known as *lexical analysis*, or *lexing* for short. Lex helps you by taking a set of descriptions of possible tokens and producing a C routine, which we call a *lexical analyzer*, or a *lexer*, or a *scanner* for short, that can identify those tokens. The set of descriptions you give to lex is called a *lex specification*.

The token descriptions that lex uses are known as *regular expressions*, extended versions of the familiar patterns used by the *grep* and *egrep* commands. Lex turns these regular expressions into a form that the lexer can use to scan the input text extremely fast, independent of the number of expressions that it is trying to match. A lex lexer is almost always faster than a lexer that you might write in C by hand.

As the input is divided into tokens, a program often needs to establish the relationship among the tokens. A C compiler needs to find the expressions, statements, declarations, blocks, and procedures in the program. This task is known as *parsing* and the list of rules that define the relationships that the program understands is a *grammar.* Yacc takes a concise description of a grammar and produces a C routine that can parse that grammar, a *parser.* The yacc parser automatically detects whenever a sequence of input tokens matches one of the rules in the grammar and also detects a syntax error whenever its input doesn't match any of the rules. A yacc parser is generally not as fast as a parser you could write by hand, but the ease in writing and modifying the parser is invariably worth any speed loss. The amount of time a program spends in a parser is rarely enough to be an issue anyway.

When a task involves dividing the input into units and establishing some relationship among those units, you should think of lex and yacc. (A search program is so simple that it doesn't need to do any parsing so it uses lex but doesn't need yacc. We'll see this again in Chapter 2, where we build several applications using lex but not yacc.)

By now, we hope we've whetted your appetite for more details. We do not intend for this chapter to be a complete tutorial on lex and yacc, but rather a gentle introduction to their use.

The Simplest Lex Program

This lex program copies its standard input to its standard output:

```
%%
.|\n          ECHO;
%%
```

It acts very much like the UNIX *cat* command run with no arguments.

Lex automatically generates the actual C program code needed to handle reading the input file and sometimes, as in this case, writing the output as well.

Whether you use lex and yacc to build parts of your program or to build tools to aid you in programming, once you master them they will prove their worth many times over by simplifying difficult input handling problems, providing more easily maintainable code base, and allowing for easier "tinkering" to get the right semantics for your program.

Recognizing Words with Lex

Let's build a simple program that recognizes different types of English words. We start by identifying parts of speech (noun, verb, etc.) and will later extend it to handle multiword sentences that conform to a simple English grammar.

We start by listing a set of verbs to recognize:

is	am	are	were
was	be	being	been
do	does	did	will
would	should	can	could
has	have	had	go

Example 1-1 shows a simple lex specification to recognize these verbs.

Example 1-1: Word recognizer ch1-02.l

```
%{
/*
 * this sample demonstrates (very) simple recognition:
 * a verb/not a verb.
 */

%}
%%

[\t ]+          /* ignore whitespace */ ;

is |
am |
are |
were |
was |
be |
being |
been |
do |
does |
did |
will |
would |
should |
can |
could |
has |
have |
had |
go          { printf("%s: is a verb\n", yytext); }
```

Example 1-1: Word recognizer ch1-02.l (continued)

```
[a-zA-Z]+    { printf("%s: is not a verb\n", yytext); }

.|\n         { ECHO; /* normal default anyway */ }
%%

main()
{
    yylex();
}
```

Here's what happens when we compile and run this program. What we type is in **bold**.

```
% example1
did I have fun?
did: is a verb
I: is not a verb
have: is a verb
fun: is not a verb
?
^D
%
```

To explain what's going on, let's start with the first section:

```
%{
/*
 * This sample demonstrates very simple recognition:
 * a verb/not a verb.
 */

%}
```

This first section, the *definition section*, introduces any initial C program code we want copied into the final program. This is especially important if, for example, we have header files that must be included for code later in the file to work. We surround the C code with the special delimiters "%{" and "%}." Lex copies the material between "%{" and "%}" directly to the generated C file, so you may write any valid C code here.

In this example, the only thing in the definition section is some C comments. You might wonder whether we could have included the comments without the delimiters. Outside of "%{" and "%}", comments must be indented with whitespace for lex to recognize them correctly. We've seen some amazing bugs when people forgot to indent their comments and lex interpreted them as something else.

The %% marks the end of this section.

The next section is the *rules section*. Each rule is made up of two parts: a *pattern* and an *action*, separated by whitespace. The lexer that lex generates will execute the action when it recognizes the pattern. These patterns are UNIX-style regular expressions, a slightly extended version of the same expressions used by tools such as *grep, sed,* and *ed.* Chapter 6 describes all the rules for regular expressions. The first rule in our example is the following:

```
[\t ]+              /* ignore whitespace */ ;
```

The square brackets, "[]", indicate that any one of the characters within the brackets matches the pattern. For our example, we accept either "\t" (a tab character) or " " (a space). The "+" means that the pattern matches one or more consecutive copies of the subpattern that precedes the plus. Thus, this pattern describes whitespace (any combination of tabs and spaces.) The second part of the rule, the *action*, is simply a semicolon, a do-nothing C statement. Its effect is to ignore the input.

The next set of rules uses the "|" (vertical bar) action. This is a special action that means to use the same action as the next pattern, so all of the verbs use the action specified for the last one.*

Our first set of patterns is:

```
is |
am |
are |
were |
was |
be |
being |
been |
do |
does |
did |
should |
can |
could |
has |
have |
had |
go          { printf("%s: is a verb\n", yytext); }
```

---

*You can also use a vertical bar within a pattern, e.g., **foo|bar** is a pattern that matches either the string "foo" or the string "bar." We leave some space between the pattern and the vertical bar to indicate that "bar" is the action, not part of the pattern.

Our patterns match any of the verbs in the list. Once we recognize a verb, we execute the action, a C **printf** statement. The array **yytext** contains the text that matched the pattern. This action will print the recognized verb followed by the string ": is a verb\n".

The last two rules are:

```
[a-zA-Z]+   { printf("%s: is not a verb\n", yytext); }

.|\n        { ECHO; /* normal default anyway */ }
```

The pattern "[a-zA-Z]+" is a common one: it indicates any alphabetic string with at least one character. The "–" character has a special meaning when used inside square brackets: it denotes a range of characters beginning with the character to the left of the "–" and ending with the character to its right. Our action when we see one of these patterns is to print the matched token and the string ": is not a verb\n".

It doesn't take long to realize that any word that matches any of the verbs listed in the earlier rules will match this rule as well. You might then wonder why it won't execute both actions when it sees a verb in the list. And would both actions be executed when it sees the word "island," since "island" starts with "is"? The answer is that lex has a set of simple disambiguating rules. The two that make our lexer work are:

1. Lex patterns only match a given input character or string once.
2. Lex executes the action for the longest possible match for the current input. Thus, lex would see "island" as matching our all-inclusive rule because that was a longer match than "is."

If you think about how a lex lexer matches patterns, you should be able to see how our example matches only the verbs listed.

The last line is the default case. The special character "." (period) matches any single character other than a newline, and "\n" matches a newline character. The special action ECHO prints the matched pattern on the output, copying any punctuation or other characters. We explicitly list this case although it is the default behavior. We have seen some complex lexers that worked incorrectly because of this very feature, producing occasional strange output when the default pattern matched unanticipated input characters. (Even though there is a default action for unmatched input characters, well-written lexers invariably have explicit rules to match all possible input.)

The end of the rules section is delimited by another %%.

The final section is the *user subroutines section,* which can consist of any legal C code. Lex copies it to the C file after the end of the lex generated code. We have included a **main()** program.

```
%%

main()
{
     yylex();
}
```

The lexer produced by lex is a C routine called **yylex()**, so we call it.* Unless the actions contain explicit **return** statements, **yylex()** won't return until it has processed the entire input.

We placed our original example in a file called *ch1-02.l* since it is our second example. To create an executable program on our UNIX system we enter these commands:

```
% lex ch1-02.l
% cc lex.yy.c -o first -ll
```

Lex translates the lex specification into a C source file called *lex.yy.c* which we compiled and linked with the lex library *–ll.* We then execute the resulting program to check that it works as we expect, as we saw earlier in this section. Try it to convince yourself that this simple description really does recognize exactly the verbs we decided to recognize.

Now that we've tackled our first example, let's "spruce it up." Our second example, Example 1-2, extends the lexer to recognize different parts of speech.

Example 1-2: Lex example with multiple parts of speech ch1-03.l

```
%{
/*
 * We expand upon the first example by adding recognition of some other
 * parts of speech.
 */

%}
%%

[\t ]+          /* ignore whitespace */ ;
```

---

*Actually, we could have left out the main program because the lex library contains a default main routine just like this one.

Example 1-2: Lex example with multiple parts of speech ch1-03.l (continued)

```
is  |
am  |
are  |
were  |
was  |
be  |
being  |
been  |
do  |
does  |
did  |
will  |
would  |
should  |
can  |
could  |
has  |
have  |
had  |
go          { printf("%s: is a verb\n", yytext); }

very  |
simply  |
gently  |
quietly  |
calmly  |
angrily     { printf("%s: is an adverb\n", yytext); }

to  |
from  |
behind  |
above  |
below  |
between  |
below       { printf("%s: is a preposition\n", yytext); }

if  |
then  |
and  |
but  |
or          { printf("%s: is a conjunction\n", yytext); }

their  |
my  |
your  |
his  |
her  |
its         { printf("%s: is an adjective\n", yytext); }

I  |
you  |
he  |
```

Example 1-2: Lex example with multiple parts of speech ch1-03.l (continued)

```
she |
we |
they          { printf("%s: is a pronoun\n", yytext); }


[a-zA-Z]+ {
        printf("%s:  don't recognize, might be a noun\n", yytext);
        }

.|\n          { ECHO; /* normal default anyway */ }

%%

main()
{
    yylex();
}
```

Symbol Tables

Our second example isn't really very different. We list more words than we did before, and in principle we could extend this example to as many words as we want. It would be more convenient, though, if we could build a table of words as the lexer is running, so we can add new words without modifying and recompiling the lex program. In our next example, we do just that—allow for the dynamic declaration of parts of speech as the lexer is running, reading the words to declare from the input file. Declaration lines start with the name of a part of speech followed by the words to declare. These lines, for example, declare four nouns and three verbs:

```
noun dog cat horse cow
verb chew eat lick
```

The table of words is a simple *symbol table*, a common structure in lex and yacc applications. A C compiler, for example, stores the variable and structure names, labels, enumeration tags, and all other names used in the program in its symbol table. Each name is stored along with information describing the name. In a C compiler the information is the type of symbol, declaration scope, variable type, etc. In our current example, the information is the part of speech.

Adding a symbol table changes the lexer quite substantially. Rather than putting separate patterns in the lexer for each word to match, we have a single pattern that matches any word and we consult the symbol table to decide which part of speech we've found. The names of parts of speech (noun, verb, etc.) are now "reserved words" since they introduce a declaration line. We still have a separate lex pattern for each reserved word. We also have to add symbol table maintenance routines, in this case **add_word( )**, which puts a new word into the symbol table, and **lookup_word( )**, which looks up a word which should already be entered.

In the program's code, we declare a variable **state** that keeps track of whether we're looking up words, state LOOKUP, or declaring them, in which case **state** remembers what kind of words we're declaring. Whenever we see a line starting with the name of a part of speech, we set the state to declare that kind of word; each time we see a \n we switch back to the normal lookup state.

Example 1-3 shows the definition section.

Example 1-3: Lexer with symbol table (part 1 of 3) ch1-04.l

```
%{
/*
 * Word recognizer with a symbol table.
 */

enum {
        LOOKUP = 0, /* default - looking rather than defining. */
        VERB,
        ADJ,
        ADV,
        NOUN,
        PREP,
        PRON,
        CONJ
};

int state;

int add_word(int type, char *word);
int lookup_word(char *word);
%}
```

We define an *enum* in order to use in our table to record the types of individual words, and to declare a variable **state**. We use this enumerated type both in the state variable to track what we're defining and in the symbol table to record what type each defined word is. We also declare our symbol table routines.

Example 1-4 shows the rules section.

Example 1-4: Lexer with symbol table (part 2 of 3) ch1-04.l

```
%%
\n    { state = LOOKUP; }    /* end of line, return to default state */

      /* whenever a line starts with a reserved part of speech name */
      /* start defining words of that type */
^verb { state = VERB; }
^adj  { state = ADJ; }
^adv  { state = ADV; }
^noun { state = NOUN; }
^prep { state = PREP; }
^pron { state = PRON; }
^conj { state = CONJ; }


[a-zA-Z]+ {
                /* a normal word, define it or look it up */
            if(state != LOOKUP) {
                /* define the current word */
                add_word(state, yytext);
            } else {
                switch(lookup_word(yytext)) {
                case VERB: printf("%s: verb\n", yytext); break;
                case ADJ: printf("%s: adjective\n", yytext); break;
                case ADV: printf("%s: adverb\n", yytext); break;
                case NOUN: printf("%s: noun\n", yytext); break;
                case PREP: printf("%s: preposition\n", yytext); break;
                case PRON: printf("%s: pronoun\n", yytext); break;
                case CONJ: printf("%s: conjunction\n", yytext); break;
                default:
                        printf("%s:  don't recognize\n", yytext);
                        break;
                }
            }
        }

.    /* ignore anything else */ ;

%%
```

For declaring words, the first group of rules sets the state to the type corresponding to the part of speech being declared. (The caret, ""̂", at the beginning of the pattern makes the pattern match only at the beginning of an input line.) We reset the state to LOOKUP at the beginning of each line so that after we add new words interactively we can test our table of words to determine if it is working correctly. If the state is LOOKUP when the pattern "[a-zA-Z]+" matches, we look up the word, using **lookup_word()**, and if found print out its type. If we're in any other state, we define the word with **add_word()**.

The user subroutines section in Example 1-5 contains the same skeletal **main( )** routine and our two supporting functions.

Example 1-5: Lexer with symbol table (part 3 of 3) ch1-04.l

```
main( )
{
     yylex( );
}

/* define a linked list of words and types */
struct word {
     char *word_name;
     int word_type;
     struct word *next;
};

struct word *word_list; /* first element in word list */

extern void *malloc( );

int
add_word(int type, char *word)
{
     struct word *wp;

     if(lookup_word(word) != LOOKUP) {
          printf("!!! warning: word %s already defined \n", word);
          return 0;
     }

     /* word not there, allocate a new entry and link it on the list */

     wp = (struct word *) malloc(sizeof(struct word));

     wp->next = word_list;

     /* have to copy the word itself as well */

     wp->word_name = (char *) malloc(strlen(word)+1);
     strcpy(wp->word_name, word);
     wp->word_type = type;
     word_list = wp;
     return 1;   /* it worked */
}

int
lookup_word(char *word)
{
     struct word *wp = word_list;

     /* search down the list looking for the word */
     for(; wp; wp = wp->next) {
```

Example 1-5: Lexer with symbol table (part 3 of 3) ch1-04.l (continued)

```
        if(strcmp(wp->word_name, word) == 0)
            return wp->word_type;
    }

    return LOOKUP;     /* not found */
}
```

These last two functions create and search a linked list of words. If there are a lot of words, the functions will be slow since, for each word, they might have to search through the entire list. In a production environment we would use a faster but more complex scheme, probably using a hash table. Our simple example does the job, albeit slowly.

Here is an example of a session we had with our last example:

```
verb is am are was were be being been do
is
is: verb
noun dog cat horse cow
verb chew eat lick
verb run stand sleep
dog run
dog: noun
run: verb
chew eat sleep cow horse
chew: verb
eat: verb
sleep: verb
cow: noun
horse: noun
verb talk
talk
talk: verb
```

We strongly encourage you to play with this example until you are satisfied you understand it.

Grammars

For some applications, the simple kind of word recognition we've already done may be more than adequate; others need to recognize specific sequences of tokens and perform appropriate actions. Traditionally, a description of such a set of actions is known as a *grammar*. It seems especially appropriate for our example. Suppose that we wished to recognize common sentences. Here is a list of simple sentence types:

> *noun verb.*
> *noun verb noun.*

At this point, it seems convenient to introduce some notation for describing grammars. We use the right facing arrow, "→", to mean that a particular set of tokens can be replaced by a new symbol.* For instance:

> *subject → noun | pronoun*

would indicate that the new symbol *subject* is either a noun or a pronoun. We haven't changed the meaning of the underlying symbols; rather we have built our new symbol from the more fundamental symbols we've already defined. As an added example we could define an object as follows:

> *object → noun*

While not strictly correct as English grammar, we can now define a sentence:

> *sentence → subject verb object*

Indeed, we could expand this definition of sentence to fit a much wider variety of sentences. However, at this stage we would like to build a yacc grammar so we can test our ideas out interactively. Before we introduce our yacc grammar, we must modify our lexical analyzer in order to return values useful to our new parser.

Parser-Lexer Communication

When you use a lex scanner and a yacc parser together, the parser is the higher level routine. It calls the lexer **yylex()** whenever it needs a token from the input. The lexer then scans through the input recognizing tokens. As soon as it finds a token of interest to the parser, it returns to the parser, returning the token's code as the value of **yylex()**.

Not all tokens are of interest to the parser—in most programming languages the parser doesn't want to hear about comments and whitespace,

---

*We say symbol rather than token here, because we reserve the name "token" for symbols returned from the lexer, and the symbol to the left of the arrow did not come from the lexer. All tokens are symbols, but not all symbols are tokens.

for example. For these ignored tokens, the lexer doesn't return so that it can continue on to the next token without bothering the parser.

The lexer and the parser have to agree what the token codes are. We solve this problem by letting yacc define the token codes. The tokens in our grammar are the parts of speech: **NOUN, PRONOUN, VERB, ADVERB, ADJEC-TIVE, PREPOSITION,** and **CONJUNCTION.** Yacc defines each of these as a small integer using a preprocessor *#define.* Here are the definitions it used in this example:

```
# define NOUN 257
# define PRONOUN 258
# define VERB 259
# define ADVERB 260
# define ADJECTIVE 261
# define PREPOSITION 262
# define CONJUNCTION 263
```

Token code zero is always returned for the logical end of the input. Yacc doesn't define a symbol for it, but you can yourself if you want.

Yacc can optionally write a C header file containing all of the token defini-tions. You include this file, called *y.tab.h* on UNIX systems and *ytab.h* or *yytab.h* on MS-DOS, in the lexer and use the preprocessor symbols in your lexer action code.

The Parts of Speech Lexer

Example 1-6 shows the declarations and rules sections of the new lexer.

Example 1-6: Lexer to be called from the parser ch1-05.l

```
%{
/*
 * We now build a lexical analyzer to be used by a higher-level parser.
 */

#include "y.tab.h"      /* token codes from the parser */

#define    LOOKUP 0    /* default - not a defined word type. */

int state;

%}

%%

\n    { state = LOOKUP; }

\.\n  {    state = LOOKUP;
```

Example 1-6: Lexer to be called from the parser ch1-05.l (continued)

```
              return 0; /* end of sentence */
      }

^verb { state = VERB; }
^adj  { state = ADJECTIVE; }
^adv  { state = ADVERB; }
^noun { state = NOUN; }
^prep { state = PREPOSITION; }
^pron { state = PRONOUN; }
^conj { state = CONJUNCTION; }

[a-zA-Z]+ {
              if(state != LOOKUP) {
              add_word(state, yytext);
              } else {
              switch(lookup_word(yytext)) {
              case VERB:
                return(VERB);
              case ADJECTIVE:
                return(ADJECTIVE);
              case ADVERB:
                return(ADVERB);
              case NOUN:
                return(NOUN);
              case PREPOSITION:
                return(PREPOSITION);
              case PRONOUN:
                return(PRONOUN);
              case CONJUNCTION:
                return(CONJUNCTION);
              default:
                printf("%s:  don't recognize\n", yytext);
                /* don't return, just ignore it */
              }
              }
          }

.     ;

%%
```

... same add_word( ) and lookup_word( ) as before ...

There are several important differences here. We've changed the part of speech names used in the lexer to agree with the token names in the parser. We have also added **return** statements to pass to the parser the token codes for the words that it recognizes. There aren't any **return** statements for the tokens that define new words to the lexer, since the parser doesn't care about them.

These return statements show that **yylex()** acts like a coroutine. Each time the parser calls it, it takes up processing at the exact point it left off. This allows us to examine and operate upon the input stream incrementally. Our first programs didn't need to take advantage of this, but it becomes more useful as we use the lexer as part of a larger program.

We added a rule to mark the end of a sentence:

```
\.\n  {     state = LOOKUP;
            return 0; /* end of sentence */
      }
```

The backslash in front of the period quotes the period, so this rule matches a period followed by a newline. The other change we made to our lexical analyzer was to omit the **main()** routine as it will now be provided within the parser.

A Yacc Parser

Finally, Example 1-7 introduces our first cut at the yacc grammar.

Example 1-7: Simple yacc sentence parser ch1-05.y

```
%{
/*
 * A lexer for the basic grammar to use for recognizing English sentences.
 */
#include <stdio.h>
%}

%token NOUN PRONOUN VERB ADVERB ADJECTIVE PREPOSITION CONJUNCTION

%%
sentence: subject VERB object{ printf("Sentence is valid.\n"); }
        ;

subject:    NOUN
        |   PRONOUN
        ;

object:         NOUN
        ;
%%

extern FILE *yyin;

main()
{
    do
      {
        yyparse();
      }
```

17

Example 1-7: Simple yacc sentence parser ch1-05.y (continued)

```
        while(!feof(yyin));
}

yyerror(s)
char *s;
{
    fprintf(stderr, "%s\n", s);
}
```

The structure of a yacc parser is, not by accident, similar to that of a lex lexer. Our first section, the definition section, has a literal code block, enclosed in "%{" and "%}". We use it here for a C comment (as with lex, C comments belong inside C code blocks, at least within the definition section) and a single include file.

Then come definitions of all the tokens we expect to receive from the lexical analyzer. In this example, they correspond to the eight parts of speech. The name of a token does not have any intrinsic meaning to yacc, although well-chosen token names tell the reader what they represent. Although yacc lets you use any valid C identifier name for a yacc symbol, universal custom dictates that token names be all uppercase and other names in the parser mostly or entirely lowercase.

The first %% indicates the beginning of the rules section. The second %% indicates the end of the rules and the beginning of the user subroutines section. The most important subroutine is **main()** which repeatedly calls **yyparse()** until the lexer's input file runs out. The routine **yyparse()** is the parser generated by yacc, so our main program repeatedly tries to parse sentences until the input runs out. (The lexer returns a zero token whenever it sees a period at the end of a line; that's the signal to the parser that the input for the current parse is complete.)

The Rules Section

The rules section describes the actual grammar as a set of *production rules* or simply *rules.* (Some people also call them *productions.*) Each rule consists of a single name on the left-hand side of the ":" operator, a list of symbols and action code on the right-hand side, and a semicolon indicating the end of the rule. By default, the first rule is the highest-level rule. That is, the parser attempts to find a list of tokens which match this initial rule, or more commonly, rules found from the initial rule. The expression on the right-hand side of the rule is a list of zero or more names. A typical simple rule has a single symbol on the right-hand side as in the **object** rule which is defined to be a NOUN. The symbol on the left-hand side of the rule can then be used like a token in other rules. From this, we build complex grammars.

In our grammar we use the special character "|", which introduces a rule with the same left-hand side as the previous one. It is usually read as "or," e.g., in our grammar a subject can be either a NOUN or a PRONOUN. The *action* part of a rule consists of a C block, beginning with "{" and ending with "}". The parser executes an action at the end of a rule as soon as the rule matches. In our **sentence** rule, the action reports that we've successfully parsed a sentence. Since **sentence** is the top-level symbol, the entire input must match a **sentence**. The parser returns to its caller, in this case the main program, when the lexer reports the end of the input. Subsequent calls to **yyparse()** reset the state and begin processing again. Our example prints a message if it sees a "subject VERB object" list of input tokens. What happens if it sees "subject subject" or some other invalid list of tokens? The parser calls **yyerror()**, which we provide in the user subroutines section, and then recognizes the special rule **error**. You can provide error recovery code that tries to get the parser back into a state where it can continue parsing. If error recovery fails or, as is the case here, there is no error recovery code, **yyparse()** returns to the caller after it finds an error.

The third and final section, the user subroutines section, begins after the second %%. This section can contain any C code and is copied, verbatim, into the resulting parser. In our example, we have provided the minimal set of functions necessary for a yacc-generated parser using a lex-generated lexer to compile: **main()** and **yyerror()**. The main routine keeps calling the parser until it reaches the end-of-file on **yyin**, the lex input file. The only other necessary routine is **yylex()** which is provided by our lexer.

In our final example of this chapter, Example 1-8, we expand our earlier grammar to recognize a richer, although by no means complete, set of sentences. We invite you to experiment further with this example—you will see how difficult English is to describe in an unambiguous way.

Example 1-8: Extended English parser ch1-06.y

```
%{
#include <stdio.h>
%}

%token NOUN PRONOUN VERB ADVERB ADJECTIVE PREPOSITION CONJUNCTION

%%

sentence: simple_sentence    { printf("Parsed a simple sentence.\n"); }
```

Example 1-8: Extended English parser ch1-06.y (continued)

```
        | compound_sentence { printf("Parsed a compound sentence.\n"); }
        ;

simple_sentence: subject verb object
        |       subject verb object prep_phrase
        ;

compound_sentence: simple_sentence CONJUNCTION simple_sentence
        |       compound_sentence CONJUNCTION simple_sentence
        ;

subject:    NOUN
        |       PRONOUN
        |       ADJECTIVE subject
        ;

verb:       VERB
        |       ADVERB VERB
        |       verb VERB
        ;

object:         NOUN
        |       ADJECTIVE object
        ;

prep_phrase:        PREPOSITION NOUN
        ;

%%

extern FILE *yyin;

main()
{
        do
          {
                yyparse();
          }
          while(!feof(yyin));
}

yyerror(s)
char *s;
{
    fprintf(stderr, "%s\n", s);
}
```

We have expanded our **sentence** rule by introducing a traditional grammar formulation from elementary school English class: a sentence can be either a simple sentence or a compound sentence which contains two or more independent clauses joined with a coordinating conjunction. Our current lexical analyzer does not distinguish between a coordinating conjunction e.g., "and," "but," "or," and a subordinating conjunction (e.g., "if").

We have also introduced *recursion* into this grammar. Recursion, in which a rule refers directly or indirectly to itself, is a powerful tool for describing grammars, and we use the technique in nearly every yacc grammar we write. In this instance the **compound_sentence** and **verb** rules introduce the recursion. The former rule simply states that a **compound_sentence** is two or more simple sentences joined by a conjunction. The first possible match,

```
simple_sentence CONJUNCTION simple_sentence
```

defines the "two clause" case while

```
compound_sentence CONJUNCTION simple_sentence
```

defines the "more than two clause case." We will discuss recursion in greater detail in later chapters.

Although our English grammar is not particularly useful, the techniques for identifying words with lex and then for finding the relationship among the words with yacc are much the same as we'll use in the practical applications in later chapters. For example, in this C language statement,

```
if( a == b ) break; else func(&a);
```

a compiler would use lex to identify the tokens **if**, **(**, **a**, **==**, and so forth, and then use yacc to establish that "a == b" is the expression part of an **if** statement, the **break** statement was the "true" branch, and the function call its "false" branch.

Running Lex and Yacc

We conclude by describing how we built these tools on our system.

We called our various lexers *ch1-N.l*, where *N* corresponded to a particular lex specification example. Similarly, we called our parsers *ch1-M.y*, where again *M* is the number of an example. Then, to build the output, we did the following in UNIX:

```
% lex ch1-n.1
% yacc -d ch1-m.y
% cc -c lex.yy.c y.tab.c
% cc -o example-m.n lex.yy.o y.tab.o -11
```

The first line runs lex over the lex specification and generates a file, *lex.yy.c*, which contains C code for the lexer. In the second line, we use yacc to generate both *y.tab.c* and *y.tab.h* (the latter is the file of token definitions created by the *–d* switch.) The next line compiles each of the two C files. The final line links them together and uses the routines in the lex library *libl.a*, normally in */usr/lib/libl.a* on most UNIX systems. If you are not using AT&T lex and yacc, but one of the other implementations, you may be able to simply substitute the command names and little else will change. (In particular, Berkeley yacc and flex will work merely by changing the *lex* and *yacc* commands to *byacc* and *flex*, and removing the *–ll* linker flag.) However, we know of far too many differences to assure the reader that this is true. For example, if we use the GNU replacement bison instead of yacc, it would generate two files called *ch1-M.tab.c* and *ch1-M.tab.h*. On systems with more restrictive naming, such as MS-DOS, these names will change (typically *ytab.c* and *ytab.h*.) See Appendices A through H for details on the various lex and yacc implementations.

Lex vs. Hand-written Lexers

People have often told us that writing a lexer in C is so easy that there is no point in going to the effort to learn lex. Maybe and maybe not. Example 1-9 shows a lexer written in C suitable for a simple command language that handles commands, numbers, strings, and new lines, ignoring white space and comments. Example 1-10 is an equivalent lexer written in lex. The lex version is a third the length of the C lexer. Given the rule of thumb that the number of bugs in a program is roughly proportional to its length, we'd expect the C version of the lexer to take three times as long to write and debug.

Example 1-9: A lexer written in C

```
#include <stdio.h>
#include <ctype.h>
char *progname;

#define NUMBER 400
#define COMMENT 401
#define TEXT 402
#define COMMAND 403

main(argc,argv)
int argc;

char *argv[];
{
int val;
```

Example 1-9: A lexer written in C (continued)

```
while(val = lexer()) printf("value is %d\n",val);
}

lexer()
{
    int c;

    while ((c=getchar()) == ' ' || c == '\t')
        ;
    if (c == EOF)
        return 0;
    if (c == '.' || isdigit(c)) {    /* number */
        while ((c = getchar()) != EOF && isdigit(c));
    if (c == '.') while ((c = getchar()) != EOF && isdigit(c));
        ungetc(c, stdin);
        return NUMBER;
    }
    if ( c == '#' ) { /* comment */
        while ((c = getchar()) != EOF && c != '\n');
        ungetc(c,stdin);
        return COMMENT;
    }
    if ( c == '"' ) { /* literal text */
        while ((c = getchar()) != EOF &&
        c != '"' && c != '\n');
        if(c == '\n') ungetc(c,stdin);
        return TEXT;
    }
    if ( isalpha(c)) { /* check to see if it is a command */
        while ((c = getchar()) != EOF && isalnum(c));
        ungetc(c, stdin);
        return COMMAND;
    }
    return c;
}
```

Example 1-10: The same lexer written in lex

```
%{
#define NUMBER 400
#define COMMENT 401
#define TEXT 402
#define COMMAND 403
%}
%%
[ \t]+                   ;
[0-9]+                   |
[0-9]+\.[0-9]+           |
\.[0-9]+                 { return NUMBER; }
#.*                      { return COMMENT; }
```

Example 1-10: The same lexer written in lex (continued)

```
\"[^\"\n]*\"              { return TEXT; }
[a-zA-Z][a-zA-Z0-9]+      { return COMMAND; }
\n                        { return '\n'; }
%%
#include <stdio.h>

main(argc,argv)
int argc;
char *argv[];
{
int val;

while(val = yylex()) printf("value is %d\n",val);
}
```

Lex handles some subtle situations in a natural way that are difficult to get right in a hand written lexer. For example, assume that you're skipping a C language comment. To find the end of the comment, you look for a "*", then check to see that the next character is a "/". If it is, you're done, if not you keep scanning. A very common bug in C lexers is not to consider the case that the next character is itself a star, and the slash might follow that. In practice, this means that some comments fail:

```
/** comment **/
```

(We've seen this exact bug in a sample, hand-written lexer distributed with one version of yacc!)

Once you get comfortable with lex, we predict that you'll find, as we did, that it's so much easier to write in lex that you'll never write another hand-written lexer.

In the next chapter we delve into the workings of lex more deeply. In the chapter following we'll do the same for yacc. After that we'll consider several larger examples which describe many of the more complex issues and features of lex and yacc.

Exercises

1. Extend the English-language parser to handle more complex syntax: prepositional phrases in the subject, adverbs modifying adjectives, etc.

2. Make the parser handle compound verbs better, e.g., "has seen." You might want to add new word and token types AUXVERB for auxiliary verbs.

3. Some words can be more than one part of speech, e.g., "watch," "fly," "time," or "bear." How could you handle them? Try adding a new word and token type NOUN_OR_VERB, and add it as an alternative to the rules for **subject**, **verb**, and **object**. How well does this work?

4. When people hear an unfamiliar word, they can usually guess from the context what part of speech it is. Could the lexer characterize new words on the fly? For example, a word that ends in "ing" is probably a verb, and one that follows "a" or "the" is probably a noun or an adjective.

5. Are lex and yacc good tools to use for building a realistic English-language parser? Why not?

2

Using Lex

In the first chapter we demonstrated how to use lex and yacc. We now show how to use lex by itself, including some examples of applications for which lex is a good tool. We're not going to explain every last detail of lex here; consult Chapter 6, *A Reference for Lex Specifications.*

Lex is a tool for building *lexical analyzers* or *lexers.* A lexer takes an arbitrary input stream and tokenizes it, i.e., divides it up into lexical tokens. This tokenized output can then be processed further, usually by yacc, or it can be the "end product." In Chapter 1 we demonstrated how to use it as an intermediate step in our English grammar. We now look more closely at the details of a lex specification and how to use it; our examples use lex as the final processing step rather than as an intermediate step which passes information on to a yacc-based parser.

When you write a *lex specification,* you create a set of patterns which lex matches against the input. Each time one of the patterns matches, the lex program invokes C code that you provide which does something with the matched text. In this way a lex program divides the input into strings which we call tokens. Lex itself doesn't produce an executable program; instead it translates the lex specification into a file containing a C routine called **yylex( )**. Your program calls **yylex( )** to run the lexer.

Using your regular C compiler, you compile the file that lex produced along with any other files and libraries you want. (Note that lex and the C compiler don't even have to run on the same computer. The authors have often taken the C code from UNIX lex to other computers where lex is not available but C is.)

Regular Expressions

Before we describe the structure of a lex specification, we need to describe regular expressions as used by lex. Regular expressions are widely used within the UNIX environment, and lex uses a rich regular expression language.

A *regular expression* is a pattern description using a "meta" language, a language that you use to describe particular patterns of interest. The characters used in this metalanguage are part of the standard ASCII character set used in UNIX and MS-DOS, which can sometimes lead to confusion. The characters that form regular expressions are:

.   Matches any single character except the newline character ("\n").

*   Matches zero or more copies of the preceding expression.

[]   A *character class* which matches any character within the brackets. If the first character is a circumflex ("^") it changes the meaning to match any character *except* the ones within the brackets. A dash inside the square brackets indicates a character range, e.g., "[0–9]" means the same thing as "[0123456789]". A "–" or "]" as the first character after the "[" is interpreted literally, to let you include dashes and square brackets in character classes. POSIX introduces other special square bracket constructs useful when handling non-English alphabets. See Appendix H, *POSIX Lex and Yacc*, for details. Other metacharacters have no special meaning within square brackets except that C escape sequences starting with "\" are recognized.

^   Matches the beginning of a line as the first character of a regular expression. Also used for negation within square brackets.

$ Matches the end of a line as the last character of a regular expression.

{}   Indicates how many times the previous pattern is allowed to match when containing one or two numbers. For example:

     A{1,3}

matches one to three occurrences of the letter A. If they contain a name, they refer to a substitution by that name.

\\   Used to escape metacharacters, and as part of the usual C escape sequences, e.g., "\n" is a newline character, while "*" is a literal asterisk.

+   Matches one or more occurrence of the preceding regular expres-
        sion. For example:

        [0-9]+

        matches "1", "111", or "123456" but not an empty string. (If the plus
        sign were an asterisk, it would also match the empty string.)

?   Matches zero or one occurrence of the preceding regular expression.
        For example:

        -?[0-9]+

        matches a signed number including an optional leading minus.

| Matches either the preceding regular expression or the following
        regular expression. For example:

        cow | pig | sheep

        matches any of the three words.

"..."   Interprets everything within the quotation marks literally—meta-
        characters other than C escape sequences lose their meaning.

/   Matches the preceding regular expression but only if followed by
        the following regular expression. For example:

        0/1

        matches "0" in the string "01" but would not match anything in the
        strings "0" or "02". The material matched by the pattern following
        the slash is not "consumed" and remains to be turned into subse-
        quent tokens. Only one slash is permitted per pattern.

()   Groups a series of regular expressions together into a new regular
        expression. For example:

        (01)

        represents the character sequence 01. Parentheses are useful when
        building up complex patterns with *, +, and |.

Note that some of these operators operate on single characters (e.g., [])
while others operate on regular expressions. Usually, complex regular
expressions are built up from simple regular expressions.

Examples of Regular Expressions

We are ready for some examples. First, we've already shown you a regular expression for a "digit":

```
[0-9]
```

We can use this to build a regular expression for an integer:

```
[0-9]+
```

We require at least one digit. This would have allowed no digits at all:

```
[0-9]*
```

Let's add an optional unary minus:

```
-?[0-9]+
```

We can then expand this to allow decimal numbers. First we will specify a decimal number (for the moment we insist that the last character always be a digit):

```
[0-9]*\.[0-9]+
```

Notice the "\" before the period to make it a literal period rather than a wild card character. This pattern matches "0.0", "4.5", or ".31415". But it won't match "0" or "2". We'd like to combine our definitions to match them as well. Leaving out our unary minus, we could use:

```
([0-9]+)|([0-9]*\.[0-9]+)
```

We use the grouping symbols "()" to specify what the regular expressions are for the "|" operation. Now let's add the unary minus:

```
-?(([0-9]+)|([0-9]*\.[0-9]+))
```

We can expand this further by allowing a float-style exponent to be specified as well. First, let's write a regular expression for an exponent:

```
[eE][-+]?[0-9]+
```

This matches an upper- or lowercase letter E, then an optional plus or minus sign, then a string of digits. For instance, this will match "e12" or "E-3". We can then use this expression to build our final expression, one that specifies a real number:

```
-?((([0-9]+)|([0-9]*\.[0-9]+))([eE][-+]?[0-9]+)?)
```

Our expression makes the exponent part optional. Let's write a real lexer that uses this expression. Nothing fancy, but it examines the input and tells us each time it matches a number according to our regular expression.

Example 2-1 shows our program.

Example 2-1: Lex specification for decimal numbers

```
%%
[\n\t ]      ;

-?(([0-9]+)|([0-9]*\.[0-9]+)([eE][-+]?[0-9]+)?) { printf("number\n"); }

.       ECHO;
%%
main()
{
      yylex();
}
```

Our lexer ignores whitespace and echoes any characters it doesn't recognize as parts of a number to the output. For instance, here are the results with something close to a valid number:

```
.65ea12
number
eanumber
```

We encourage you to play with this and all our examples until you are satisfied you understand how they work. For instance, try changing the expression to recognize a unary plus as well as a unary minus.

Another common regular expression is one used by many scripts and simple configuration files, an expression that matches a comment starting with a sharp sign, "#".* We can build this regular expression as:

```
#.*
```

The "." matches any character except newline and the "*" means match zero or more of the preceding expression. This expression matches anything on the comment line up to the newline which marks the end of the line.

Finally, here is a regular expression for matching quoted strings:

```
\"[^"\n]*["\n]
```

It might seem adequate to use a simpler expression such as:

```
\".*\"
```

---

*Also known as a hash mark, pound sign, and by some extremists as an octothorpe.

Unfortunately, this causes lex to match incorrectly if there are two strings on the same input line. For instance:

```
"how" to "do"
```

would match as a single pattern since "*" matches as much as possible. Knowing this, we then might try:

```
\"[^"]*\"
```

This regular expression can cause lex to overflow its internal input buffer if the trailing quotation mark is not present, because the expression "[^"]*" matches any character except a quote, including "\n". So if the user leaves out a quote by mistake, the pattern could potentially scan through the entire input file looking for another quote. Since the token is stored in a fixed size buffer,* sooner or later the amount read will be bigger than the buffer and the lexer will crash. For example:

```
"How", she said, "is it that I cannot find it.
```

would match the second quoted string continuing until it saw another quotation mark. This might be hundreds or thousands of characters later. So we add the new rule that a quoted string must not extend past one line and end up with the complex (but safer) regular expression shown above. Lex can handle longer strings, but in a different way. See the section on **yymore** in Chapter 6, *A Reference for Lex Specifications.*

A Word Counting Program

Let's look at the actual structure of a lex specification. We will use a basic word count program (similar to the UNIX program *wc*).

A lex specification consists of three sections: a definition section, a rules section, and a user subroutines section. The first section, the definition section, handles options lex will be using in the lexer, and generally sets up the execution environment in which the lexer operates.

---

*The size of the buffer varies a lot from one version to the next, sometimes being as small as 100 bytes or as large as 8K. For more details, see the section on **yytext** in Chapter 6.

The definition section for our word count example is:

```
%{
unsigned charCount = 0, wordCount = 0, lineCount = 0;
%}

word  [^ \t\n]+
eol   \n
```

The section bracketed by "%{" and "%}" is C code which is copied verbatim into the lexer. It is placed early on in the output code so that the data definitions contained here can be referenced by code within the rules section. In our example, the code block here declares three variables used within the program to track the number of characters, words, and lines encountered.

The last two lines are *definitions*. Lex provides a simple substitution mechanism to make it easier to define long or complex patterns. We have added two definitions here. The first provides our description of a word: any non-empty combination of characters except space, tab, and newline. The second describes our end-of-line character, newline. We use these definitions in the second section of the file, the *rules section*.

The rules section contains the patterns and actions that specify the lexer. Here is our sample word count's rules section:

```
%%
{word}      { wordCount++; charCount += yyleng; }
{eol} { charCount++; lineCount++; }
.     charCount++;
```

The beginning of the rules section is marked by a "%%". In a pattern, lex replaces the name inside the braces {} with *substitution*, the actual regular expression in the definition section. Our example increments the number of words and characters after the lexer has recognized a complete word.

The actions which consist of more than one statement are enclosed in braces to make a C language compound statement. Most versions of lex take everything after the pattern to be the action, while others only read the first statement on the line and silently ignore anything else. To be safe, and to make the code clearer, always use braces if the action is more than one statement or more than one line long.

It is worth repeating that lex always tries to match the longest possible string. Thus, our sample lexer would recognize the string "well-being" as a single word.

Our sample also uses the lex internal variable **yyleng** which contains the length of the string our lexer recognized. If it matched well-being, **yyleng** would be 10.

When our lexer recognizes a newline, it will increment both the character count and the line count. Similarly, if it recognizes any other character it increments the character count. For this lexer, the only "other characters" it could recognize would be space or tab; anything else would match the first regular expression and be counted as a word.

The lexer always tries to match the longest possible string, but when there are two possible rules that match the same length, the lexer uses the earlier rule in the lex specification. Thus, the word "I" would be matched by the {word} rule, not by the . rule. Understanding and using this principle will make your lexers clearer and more bug free.

The third and final section of the lex specification is the user subroutines section. Once again, it is separated from the previous section by "%%". The user subroutines section can contain any valid C code. It is copied verbatim into the generated lexer. Typically this section contains support routines. For this example our "support" code is the main routine:

```
%%
main()
{
        yylex();
        printf("%d %d %d\n",lineCount, wordCount, charCount);
}
```

It first calls the lexer's entry point **yylex()** and then calls **printf()** to print the results of this run. Note that our sample doesn't do anything fancy; it doesn't accept command-line arguments, doesn't open any files, but uses the lex default to read from the standard input. We will stick with this for most of our sample programs as we assume you know how to build C programs which do such things. However, it is worthwhile to look at one way to reconnect lex's input stream, as shown in Example 2-2.

Example 2-2: User subroutines for word count program cb2-02.l

```
main(argc,argv)
int argc;
char **argv;
{
        if (argc > 1) {
                FILE *file;

                file = fopen(argv[1], "r");
                if (!file) {
```

Example 2-2: User subroutines for word count program ch2-02.l (continued)

```
                fprintf(stderr,"could not open %s\n",argv[1]);
                exit(1);
        }
        yyin = file;
    }
    yylex();
    printf("%u %u %u\n",charCount, wordCount, lineCount);
    return 0;
}
```

This example assumes that the second argument the program is called with is the file to open for processing.* A lex lexer reads its input from the standard I/O file **yyin**, so you need only change **yyin** as needed. The default value of **yyin** is **stdin**, since the default input source is standard input.

We stored this example in ch2-02.l, since it's the second example in Chapter 2, and lex source files traditionally end with .l. We ran it on itself, and obtained the following results:

```
% ch2-02 ch2-02.l
467 72 30
```

One big difference between our word count example and the standard UNIX word count program is that ours handles only a single file. We'll fix this by using lex's end-of-file processing handler.

When **yylex()** reaches the end of its input file, it calls **yywrap()**, which returns a value of 0 or 1. If the value is 1, the program is done and there is no more input. If the value is 0, on the other hand, the lexer assumes that **yywrap()** has opened another file for it to read, and continues to read from **yyin**. The default **yywrap()** always returns 1. By providing our own version of **yywrap()**, we can have our program read all of the files named on the command line, one at a time.

Handling multiple files requires considerable code changes. Example 2-3 shows our final word counter in its entirety.

---

*Traditionally, the first name is that of the program, but if it differs in your environment you might have to adjust our example to get the right results.

Example 2-3: Multi-file word count program ch2-03.l

```
%{
/*
 * ch2-03.1
 *
 * The word counter example for multiple files
 *
 */

unsigned long charCount = 0, wordCount = 0, lineCount = 0;

#undef yywrap       /* sometimes a macro by default */

%}

word [^ \t\n]+
eol  \n
%%
{word}      { wordCount++; charCount += yyleng; }
{eol} { charCount++; lineCount++; }
.       charCount++;
%%

char **fileList;
unsigned currentFile = 0;
unsigned nFiles;
unsigned long totalCC = 0;
unsigned long totalWC = 0;
unsigned long totalLC = 0;

main(argc,argv)
int argc;
char **argv;
{
        FILE *file;

        fileList = argv+1;
        nFiles = argc-1;

        if (argc == 2) {
            /*
             * we handle the single file case differently from
             * the multiple file case since we don't need to
             * print a summary line
             */
            currentFile = 1;
            file = fopen(argv[1], "r");
            if (!file) {
                    fprintf(stderr,"could not open %s\n",argv[1]);
                    exit(1);
            }
            yyin = file;
```

Example 2-3: Multi-file word count program ch2-03.l (continued)

```
        }
        if (argc > 2)
            yywrap();   /* open first file */

    yylex();
        /*
         * once again, we handle zero or one file
        * differently from multiple files.
         */
        if (argc > 2) {
            printf("%8lu %8lu %8lu %s\n", lineCount, wordCount,
                    charCount, fileList[currentFile-1]);
            totalCC += charCount;
            totalWC += wordCount;
            totalLC += lineCount;
            printf("%8lu %8lu %8lu total\n",totalLC, totalWC, totalCC);
        } else
            printf("%8lu %8lu %8lu\n",lineCount, wordCount, charCount);

        return 0;
}


/*
 * the lexer calls yywrap to handle EOF conditions (e.g., to
 * connect to a new file, as we do in this case.)
 */

yywrap()
{
    FILE *file = NULL;

    if ((currentFile != 0) && (nFiles > 1) && (currentFile < nFiles)) {
        /*
         * we print out the statistics for the previous file.
         */
        printf("%8lu %8lu %8lu %s\n", lineCount, wordCount,
                charCount, fileList[currentFile-1]);
        totalCC += charCount;
        totalWC += wordCount;
        totalLC += lineCount;
        charCount = wordCount = lineCount = 0;
        fclose(yyin);      /* done with that file */
    }

    while (fileList[currentFile] != (char *)0) {
        file = fopen(fileList[currentFile++], "r");
        if (file != NULL) {
            yyin = file;
            break;
        }
        fprintf(stderr,
            "could not open %s\n",
```

Example 2-3: Multi-file word count program cb2-03.l (continued)

```
                fileList[currentFile-1]);
    }
    return (file ? 0 : 1); /* 0 means there's more input */
}
```

Our example uses **yywrap()** to perform the continuation processing. There are other possible ways, but this is the simplest and most portable. Each time the lexer calls **yywrap()** we try to open the next filename from the command line and assign the open file to **yyin**, returning 0 if there was another file and 1 if not.

Our example reports both the sizes for the individual files as well as a cumulative total for the entire set of files at the end; if there is only one file the numbers for the specified file are reported once.

We ran our final word counter on both the lex file, *cb2-03.l,* then on both the lex file and the generated C file *cb2-03.c.*

```
% ch2-03.pgm ch2-03.1
    107       337      2220
% ch2-03.pgm ch2-03.1 ch2-03.c
    107       337      2220 ch2-03.1
    405      1382      9356 ch2-03.c
    512      1719     11576 total
```

The results will vary from system to system, since different versions of lex produce different C code. We didn't devote much time to beautifying the output; that is left as an exercise for the reader.

Parsing a Command Line

Now we turn our attention to another example using lex to parse command input. Normally a lex program reads from a file, using the predefined macro **input()**, which gets the next character from the input, and **unput()**, which puts a character back in the logical input stream. Lexers sometimes need to use **unput()** to peek ahead in the input stream. For example, a lexer can't tell that it's found the end of a word until it sees the punctuation after the end of the word, but since the punctuation isn't part of the word, it has to put the punctuation back in the input stream for the next token.

In order to scan the command line rather than a file, we must rewrite **input()** and **unput()**. The implementation we use here only works in AT&T lex, because other versions for efficiency reasons don't let you redefine the two routines. (Flex, for example, reads directly from the input buffer and never uses **input( )**.) If you are using another version of lex, see the section "Input from Strings" in Chapter 6 to see how to accomplish the same thing.

We will take the command-line arguments our program is called with, and recognize three distinct classes of argument: **help**, **verbose**, and a **filename**. Example 2-4 creates a lexer that reads the standard input, much as we did for our earlier word count example.

Example 2-4: Lex specification to parse command-line input ch2-04.l

```
%{
unsigned verbose;
char *progName;
%}

%%

-h      |
"-?"    |
-help { printf("usage is: %s [-help | -h | -? ] [-verbose | -v] "
        "[(-file| -f) filename]\n", progName);
      }
-v      |
-verbose { printf("verbose mode is on\n"); verbose = 1; }

%%

main(argc, argv)
int argc;
char **argv;
{
    progName = *argv;
    yylex();
}
```

The definition section includes a code literal block. The two variables, **verbose** and **progName**, are variables used later within the rules section.

In our rules section the first rules recognize the keyword *–help* as well as abbreviated versions *–h* and *–?*. Note the action following this rule which simply prints a usage string.* Our second set of rules recognize the keyword *–verbose* and the short variant *–v*. In this case we set the global variable **verbose**, which we defined above, to the value 1.

---

*Since the string doesn't fit on one line we've used the ANSI C technique of splitting the string into two strings catenated at compile time. If you have a pre-ANSI C compiler you'll have to paste the two strings together yourself.

In our user subroutines section the **main( )** routine stores the program name, which is used in our help command's usage string, and then calls **yylex( )**.

This example does not parse the command-line arguments, as the lexer is still reading from the standard input, not from the command line. Example 2-5 adds code to replace the standard **input( )** and **unput( )** routines with our own. (This example is specific to AT&T lex. See Appendix E for the equivalent in flex.)

Example 2-5: Lex specification to parse a command line ch2-05.l

```
%{
#undef input
#undef unput
int input(void);
void unput(int ch);
unsigned verbose;
char *progName;
%}

%%

-h      |
"-?"    |
-help { printf("usage is: %s [-help | -h | -? ] [-verbose | -v]"
          " [(-file| -f) filename]\n", progName);
      }
-v      |
-verbose { printf("verbose mode is on\n"); verbose = 1; }

%%
char **targv;     /* remembers arguments */
char **arglim;    /* end of arguments */

main(int argc, char **argv)
{
      progName = *argv;
      targv = argv+1;
      arglim = argv+argc;
      yylex();
}

static unsigned offset = 0;

int
input(void)
{
      char c;

      if (targv >= arglim)
            return(0);  /* EOF */
```

Example 2-5: Lex specification to parse a command line ch2-05.l (continued)

```
        /* end of argument, move to the next */
        if ((c = targv[0][offset++]) != '\0')
                return(c);
        targv++;
        offset = 0;
        return(' ');
}

/* simple unput only backs up, doesn't allow you to */
/* put back different text */
void
unput(int ch)
{

        /* AT&T lex sometimes puts back the EOF ! */
        if(ch == 0)
                return;         /* ignore, can't put back EOF */
        if (offset) {           /* back up in current arg */
                offset--;
                return;
        }

        targv--;        /* back to previous arg */
        offset = strlen(*targv);
}
```

In the definition section we **#undef** both **input** and **unput** since AT&T lex by default defines them as macros, and we redefine them as C functions.

Our rules section didn't change in this example. Instead, most of the changes are in the user subroutines section. In this new section we've added three variables—**targv**, which tracks the current argument, **arglim**, which marks the end of the arguments, and **offset**, which tracks the position in the current argument. These are set in **main()** to point at the argument vector passed from the command line.

The **input()** routine handles calls from the lexer to obtain characters. When the current argument is exhausted it moves to the next argument, if there is one, and continues scanning. If there are no more arguments, we treat it as the lexer's end-of-file condition and return a zero byte.

The **unput()** routine handles calls from the lexer to "push back" characters into the input stream. It does this by reversing the pointer's direction, moving backwards in the string. In this case we assume that the characters pushed back are the same as the ones that were there in the first place, which will always be true unless action code explicitly pushes back something else. In the general case, an action routine can push back anything it wants and a private version of **unput**() must be able to handle that.

Our resulting example still echoes input it doesn't recognize and prints out the two messages for the inputs it does understand. For instance, here is a sample run:

```
% ch2-05 -verbose foo
verbose mode is on
 foo %
```

Our input now comes from the command line and unrecognized input is echoed. Any text which is not recognized by the lexer "falls through" to the default rule, which echoes the unrecognized text to the output.

Start States

Finally, we add a *–file* switch and recognize a filename. To do this we use a *start state*, a method of capturing context sensitive information within the lexer. Tagging rules with start states tells the lexer only to recognize the rules when the start state is in effect. In this case, to recognize a filename after a *–file* argument, we use a start state to note that it's time to look for the filename, as shown in Example 2-6.

Example 2-6: Lex command scanner with filenames ch2-06.l

```
%{
#undef input
#undef unput
unsigned verbose;
unsigned fname;
char *progName;
%}

%s FNAME

%%
[ ]+        /* ignore blanks */ ;

-h      |
"-?"    |
-help { printf("usage is: %s [-help | -h | -? ] [-verbose | -v]"
        " (-file| -f) filename\n", progName);
      }
-v      |
-verbose { printf("verbose mode is on\n"); verbose = 1; }
```

Example 2-6: Lex command scanner with filenames ch2-06.l (continued)

```
-f      |
-file { BEGIN FNAME; fname = 1; }

<FNAME>[^ ]+ { printf("use file %s\n", yytext); BEGIN 0; fname = 2;}

[^ ]+   ECHO;
%%
char **targv;      /* remembers arguments */
char **arglim;     /* end of arguments */

main(int argc, char **argv)
{
        progName = *argv;
        targv = argv+1;
        arglim = argv+argc;
        yylex();
        if(fname < 2)
                printf("No filename given\n");
}
```

... same input( ) and unput( ) as Example 2-5 ...

In the definition section we have added the line "%s FNAME" which creates a new start state in the lexer. In the rules section we have added rules which begin with "<FNAME>". These rules are only recognized when the lexer is in state FNAME. Any rule which does not have an explicit state will match no matter what the current start state is. The *–file* argument switches to FNAME state, which enables the pattern that matches the filename. Once it's matched the filename, it switches back to the regular state.

Code within the actions of the rules section change the current state. You enter a new state with a BEGIN statement. For instance, to change to the FNAME state we used the statement "BEGIN FNAME;". To change back to the default state, we use "BEGIN 0". (The default, state zero, is also known as INITIAL.)

In addition to changing the lex state we also added a separate variable, **fname**, so that our example program can recognize if the argument is missing; note that the main routine prints an error message if **fname's** value hasn't been changed to 2.

Other changes to this example simply handle the filename argument. Our version of **input( )** returns a blank space after each command-line argument. The rules ignore whitespace, yet without that blank space, the arguments *-f ile* and *-file* would appear identical to the lexer.

We mentioned that a rule without an explicit start state will match regardless of what start state is active (Example 2-7).

Example 2-7: Start state example ch2-07.l

```
%s MAGIC

%%
<MAGIC>.+   { BEGIN 0; printf("Magic:"); ECHO; }
magic       BEGIN MAGIC;
%%

main( )
{
     yylex( );
}
```

We switch into state MAGIC when we see the keyword "magic." Otherwise we simply echo the input. If we are in state MAGIC, we prepend the string "Magic:" to the next token echoed. We created an input file with three words in it: "magic," "two," and "three," and ran it through this lexer.

```
% ch2-07 < magic.input

Magic:two
three
```

Now, we change the example slightly, so that the rule with the start state follows the one without, as shown in Example 2-8.

Example 2-8: Broken start state example ch2-08.l

```
%{
     /* This example deliberately doesn't work! */
%}

%s MAGIC

%%
magic       BEGIN MAGIC;
.+          ECHO;
<MAGIC>.+   { BEGIN 0; printf("Magic:"); ECHO; }
%%

main( )
{
     yylex( );
}
```

With the same input we get very different results:

```
% ch2-08 < magic.input

two
three
```

Think of rules without a start state as implicitly having a "wild card" start state—they match all start states. This is a frequent source of bugs. Flex and other more recent versions of lex have "exclusive start states" which fix the wild card problem. See "Start States" in Chapter 6 for details.

A C Source Code Analyzer

Our final example examines a C source file and counts the number of different types of lines we see that contain code, that just contain comments, or are blank. This is a little tricky to do since a single line can contain both comments and code, so we have to decide how to count such lines.

First, we describe a line of whitespace. We will consider any line with nothing more than a newline as whitespace. Similarly, a line with any number of blank spaces or tabs, but nothing else, is whitespace. The regular expression describing this is:

```
^[ \t]*\n
```

The "^" operator denotes that the pattern must start at the beginning of a line. Similarly, we require that the entire line be only whitespace by requiring a newline, "\n", at the end.

Now, we can complement this with the description of what a line of code or comments is—any line which isn't entirely whitespace!

```
^[ \t]*\n
\n    /* whitespace lines matched by previous rule */
.     /* anything else */
```

We use the new rule "\n" to count the number of lines we see which aren't all whitespace. The second new rule we use to discard characters in which we aren't interested. Here is the rule we add to describe a comment:

```
^[ \t]*"/*".**"*/"[ \t]*\n
```

This describes a single, self contained comment on a single line, with optional text between the "/*" and the "*/". Since "*" and "/" are both special pattern characters, we have to quote them when they occur literally. Actually this pattern isn't quite right, since something like this:

```
/* comment */ /* comment
```

won't match it. Comments might span multiple lines and the "." operator excludes the "\n" character. Indeed, if we were to allow the "\n" character we would probably overflow the internal lex buffer on a long comment. Instead, we circumvent the problem by adding a start state, COMMENT, and by entering that state when we see only the beginning of a comment. When we see the end of a comment we return to the default start state. We don't need to use our start state for one-line comments. Here is our rule for recognizing the beginning of a comment:

```
^[ \t]*"/*"
```

Our action has a BEGIN statement in it to switch to the COMMENT state. It is important to note that we are requiring that a comment begin on a line by itself. Not doing so would incorrectly count cases such as:

```
int counter; /* this is
    a strange comment */
```

because the first line isn't on a line alone. We need to count the first line as a line of code and the second line as a line of comment. Here are our rules to accomplish this:

```
.+"/*".*"*/".*\n
.*"/*".*"*/".+\n
```

The two expressions describe an overlapping set of strings, but they are not identical. The following expression matches the first rule, but not the second:

```
int counter; /* comment */
```

because the second requires there be text following the comment. Similarly, this next expression matches the second but not the first:

```
/* comment */ int counter;
```

They both would match the expression:

```
/* comment # 1 */  int counter; /* comment # 2 */
```

Finally, we need to finish up our regular expressions for detecting comments. We decided to use a start state, so while we are in the COMMENT state, we merely look for newlines:

```
<COMMENT>\n
```

and count them. When we detect the "end of comment" character, we either count it as a comment line, if there is nothing else on the line after the comment ends, or we continue processing:

```
<COMMENT>"*/"[ \t]*\n
<COMMENT>"*/"
```

The first one will be counted as a comment line; the second will continue processing. As we put these rules together, there is a bit of gluing to do because we need to cover some cases in both the default start state and in the COMMENT start state. Example 2-9 shows our final list of regular expressions, along with their associated actions.

Example 2-9: C source analyzer ch2-09.l

```
%{
int comments, code, whiteSpace;
%}

%x COMMENT
%%
^[ \t]*"/*" { BEGIN COMMENT; /* enter comment eating state */ }
^[ \t]*"/*".***/"[ \t]*\n {
            comments++;     /* self-contained comment */
            }

<COMMENT>"*/"[ \t]*\n   { BEGIN 0;  comments++;}
<COMMENT>"*/"          { BEGIN 0; }
<COMMENT>\n { comments++; }
<COMMENT>.\n      { comments++; }

^[ \t]*\n   { whiteSpace++; }

.+"/*".***/".*\n { code++; }
.*"/*".***/".+\n { code++; }
.+"/*".*\n       { code++; BEGIN COMMENT; }
.\n              { code++; }

.              ; /* ignore everything else */
%%
main()
```

Example 2-9: C source analyzer cb2-09.l (continued)

```
{
    yylex();
    printf("code: %d, comments %d, whitespace %d\n",
        code, comments, whiteSpace);
}
```

We added the rules "<COMMENT>\n" and "<COMMENT>.\n" to handle the case of a blank line in a comment, as well as any text within a comment. Forcing them to match an end-of-line character means they won't match something like

```
/* this is the beginning of a comment
   and this is the end */ int counter;
```

as two lines of comments. Instead, this will count as one line of comment and one line of code.

Summary

In this chapter we covered the fundamentals of using lex. Even by itself, lex is often sufficient for writing simpler applications such as the word count and lines-of-code count utilities we developed in this chapter.

Lex uses a number of special characters to describe regular expressions. When a regular expression matches an input string, it executes the corresponding action, which is a piece of C code you specify. Lex matches these expressions first by determining the longest matching expression, and then, if two matches are the same length, by matching the expression which appears first in the lex specification. By judiciously using start states, you can further refine when specific rules are active, just as we did for the line-of-code count utility.

We also discussed special purpose routines used by the lex-generated state machines, such as **yywrap()**, which handles end-of-file conditions and lets you handle multiple files in sequence. We used this to allow our word count example to examine multiple files.

This chapter focused upon using lex alone as a processing language. Later chapters will concentrate on how lex can be integrated with yacc to build other types of tools. But lex, by itself, is capable of handling many otherwise tedious tasks without needing a full-scale yacc parser.

Exercises

1. Make the word count program smarter about what a word is, distinguishing real words which are strings of letters (perhaps with a hyphen or apostrophe) from blocks of punctuation. You shouldn't need to add more than ten lines to the program.

2. Improve the C code analyzer: count braces, keywords, etc. Try to identify function definitions and declarations, which are names followed by "(" outside of any braces.

3. Is lex really as fast as we say? Race it against *egrep, awk, sed*, or other pattern matching programs you have. Write a lex specification that looks for lines containing some string and prints the lines out. (For a fair comparison, be sure to print the whole line.) Compare the time it takes to scan a set of files to that taken by the other programs. If you have more than one version of lex, do they run at noticably different speeds?

3

Using Yacc

The previous chapter concentrated on lex alone. In this chapter we turn our attention to yacc, although we use lex to generate our lexical analyzers. Where lex recognizes regular expressions, yacc recognizes entire grammars. Lex divides the input stream into pieces (tokens) and then yacc takes these pieces and groups them together logically.

In this chapter we create a desk calculator, starting with simple arithmetic, then adding built-in functions, user variables, and finally user-defined functions.

Grammars

Yacc takes a grammar that you specify and writes a parser that recognizes valid "sentences" in that grammar. We use the term "sentence" here in a fairly general way—for a C language grammar the sentences are syntactically valid C programs.*

---

* Programs can be syntactically valid but semantically invalid, e.g., a C program that assigns a string to an *int* variable. Yacc only handles the syntax; other validation is up to you.

As we saw in Chapter 1, a grammar is a series of *rules* that the parser uses to recognize syntactically valid input. For example, here is a version of the grammar we'll use later in this chapter to build a calculator.

statement → NAME = expression

expression → NUMBER + NUMBER | NUMBER – NUMBER

The vertical bar, "|", means there are two possibilities for the same symbol, i.e., an *expression* can be either an addition or a subtraction. The symbol to the left of the → is known as the *left-hand side* of the rule, often abbreviated LHS, and the symbols to the right are the *right-hand side*, usually abbreviated RHS. Several rules may have the same left-hand side; the vertical bar is just a short hand for this. Symbols that actually appear in the input and are returned by the lexer are *terminal* symbols or *tokens*, while those that appear on the left-hand side of some rule are *non-terminal* symbols or non-terminals. Terminal and non-terminal symbols must be different; it is an error to write a rule with a token on the left side.

The usual way to represent a parsed sentence is as a tree. For example, if we parsed the input "fred = 12 + 13" with this grammar, the tree would look like Figure 3-1. "12 + 13" is an *expression*, and "fred = *expression*" is a *statement*. A yacc parser doesn't actually create this tree as a data structure, although it is not hard to do so yourself.

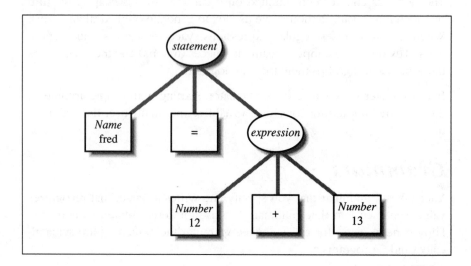

Figure 3-1: A parse tree

Every grammar includes a *start* symbol, the one that has to be at the root of the parse tree. In this grammar, *statement* is the start symbol.

Recursive Rules

Rules can refer directly or indirectly to themselves; this important ability makes it possible to parse arbitrarily long input sequences. Let's extend our grammar to handle longer arithmetic expressions:

> *expression* → *NUMBER*
> | *expression* + *NUMBER*
> | *expression* − *NUMBER*

Now we can parse a sequence like "fred = 14 + 23 − 11 + 7" by applying the expression rules repeatedly, as in Figure 3-2. Yacc can parse recursive rules very efficiently, so we will see recursive rules in nearly every grammar we use.

Shift/Reduce Parsing

A yacc parser works by looking for rules that might match the tokens seen so far. When yacc processes a parser, it creates a set of *states* each of which reflects a possible position in one or more partially parsed rules. As the parser reads tokens, each time it reads a token that doesn't complete a rule it pushes the token on an internal stack and switches to a new state reflecting the token it just read. This action is called a *shift*. When it has found all the symbols that constitute the right-hand side of a rule, it pops the right-hand side symbols off the stack, pushes the left-hand side symbol onto the stack, and switches to a new state reflecting the new symbol on the stack. This action is called a *reduction*, since it usually reduces the number of items on the stack. (Not always, since it is possible to have rules with empty right-hand sides.) Whenever yacc reduces a rule, it executes user code associated with the rule. This is how you actually do something with the material that the parser parses.

Let's look how it parses the input "fred = 12 + 13" using the simple rules in Figure 3-1. The parser starts by shifting tokens on to the internal stack one at a time:

```
fred
fred =
fred = 12
fred = 12 +
fred = 12 + 13
```

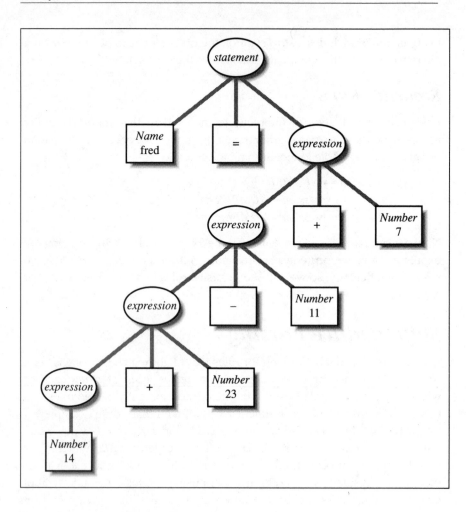

Figure 3-2: A parse using recursive rules

At this point it can reduce the rule "expression → NUMBER + NUMBER" so it pops the 12, the plus, and the 13 from the stack and replaces them with *expression*:

```
fred = expression
```

Now it reduces the rule "statement → NAME = expression", so it pops fred, =, and *expression* and replaces them with *statement*. We've reached the end of the input and the stack has been reduced to the start symbol, so the input was valid according to the grammar.

What Yacc Cannot Parse

Although yacc's parsing technique is general, you can write grammars which yacc cannot handle. It cannot deal with ambiguous grammars, ones in which the same input can match more than one parse tree.* It also cannot deal with grammars that need more than one token of lookahead to tell whether it has matched a rule. Consider this extremely contrived example:

> *phrase* → *cart_animal AND CART*
> | *work_animal AND PLOW*
>
> *cart_animal* → *HORSE* | *GOAT*
>
> *work_animal* → *HORSE* | *OX*

This grammar isn't ambiguous, since there is only one possible parse tree for any valid input, but yacc can't handle it because it requires two symbols of lookahead. In particular, in the input "HORSE AND CART" it cannot tell whether HORSE is a **cart_animal** or a **work_animal** until it sees CART, and yacc cannot look that far ahead.

If we changed the first rule to this:

> *phrase* → *cart_animal CART*
> | *work_animal PLOW*

yacc would have no trouble, since it can look one token ahead to see whether an input of HORSE is followed by CART, in which case the horse is a **cart_animal** or by PLOW in which case it is a **work_animal**.

In practice, these rules are not as complex and confusing as they may seem here. One reason is that yacc knows exactly what grammars it can parse and what it cannot. If you give it one that it cannot handle it will tell you, so there is no problem of overcomplex parsers silently failing. Another reason is that the grammars that yacc can handle correspond pretty well to ones that people really write. As often as not, a grammatical construct that confuses yacc will confuse people as well, so if you have some latitude in your language design you should consider changing the language to make it both more understandable to yacc and to its users.

---

*Actually, yacc can deal with a limited but useful set of ambiguous grammars, as we'll see later.

For more information on shift/reduce parsing, see Chapter 8. For a discussion of what yacc has to do to turn your specification into a working C program, see the classic compiler text by Aho, Sethi, and Ullman, *Compilers: Principles, Techniques, and Tools,* Addison-Wesley, 1986, often known as the "dragon book" because of the cover illustration.

A Yacc Parser

A yacc grammar has the same three-part structure as a lex specification. (Lex copied its structure from yacc.) The first section, the definition section, handles control information for the yacc-generated parser (from here on we will call it the parser), and generally sets up the execution environment in which the parser will operate. The second section contains the rules for the parser, and the third section is C code copied verbatim into the generated C program.

We'll first write parser for the simplest grammar, the one in Figure 3-1, then extend it to be more useful and realistic.

The Definition Section

The definition section includes declarations of the tokens used in the grammar, the types of values used on the parser stack, and other odds and ends. It can also include a literal block, C code enclosed in %{ %} lines. We start our first parser by declaring two symbolic tokens.

```
%token NAME NUMBER
```

You can use single quoted characters as tokens without declaring them, so we don't need to declare "=", "+", or "−".

The Rules Section

The rules section simply consists of a list of grammar rules in much the same format as we used above. Since ASCII keyboards don't have a → key, we use a colon between the left- and right-hand sides of a rule, and we put a semicolon at the end of each rule:

```
%token NAME NUMBER
%%
statement: NAME '=' expression
    |       expression
    ;
```

```
expression: NUMBER '+' NUMBER
     |      NUMBER '-' NUMBER
     ;
```

Unlike lex, yacc pays no attention to line boundaries in the rules section, and you will find that a lot of whitespace makes grammars easier to read. We've added one new rule to the parser: a statement can be a plain expression as well as an assignment. If the user enters a plain expression, we'll print out its result.

The symbol on the left-hand side of the first rule in the grammar is normally the start symbol, though you can use a **%start** declaration in the definition section to override that.

Symbol Values and Actions

Every symbol in a yacc parser has a *value*. The value gives additional information about a particular instance of a symbol. If a symbol represents a number, the value would be the particular number. If it represents a literal text string, the value would probably be a pointer to a copy of the string. If it represents a variable in a program, the value would be a pointer to a symbol table entry describing the variable. Some tokens don't have a useful value, e.g., a token representing a close parenthesis, since one close parenthesis is the same as another.

Non-terminal symbols can have any values you want, created by code in the parser. Often the action code builds a parse tree corresponding to the input, so that later code can process a whole statement or even a whole program at a time.

In the current parser, the value of a *NUMBER* or an *expression* is the numerical value of the number or expression, and the value of a *NAME* will be a symbol table pointer.

In real parsers, the values of different symbols use different data types, e.g., *int* and *double* for numeric symbols, *char ** for strings, and pointers to structures for higher level symbols. If you have multiple value types, you have to list all the value types used in a parser so that yacc can create a C *union* typedef called *YYSTYPE* to contain them. (Fortunately, yacc gives you a lot of help ensuring that you use the right value type for each symbol.)

In the first version of the calculator, the only values of interest are the numerical values of input numbers and calculated expressions. By default yacc makes all values of type *int*, which is adequate for our first version of the calculator.

Whenever the parser reduces a rule, it executes user C code associated with the rule, known as the rule's *action*. The action appears in braces after the end of the rule, before the semicolon or vertical bar. The action code can refer to the values of the right-hand side symbols as **$1**, **$2**, . . . , and can set the value of the left-hand side by setting **$$**. In our parser, the value of an *expression* symbol is the value of the expression it represents. We add some code to evaluate and print expressions, bringing our grammar up to that used in Figure 3-2.

```
%token NAME NUMBER
%%
statement:  NAME '=' expression
        |   expression        { printf("= %d\n", $1); }
        ;

expression: expression '+' NUMBER  { $$ = $1 + $3; }
        |   expression '-' NUMBER  { $$ = $1 - $3; }
        |   NUMBER                 { $$ = $1; }
        ;
```

The rules that build an expression compute the appropriate values, and the rule that recognizes an expression as a statement prints out the result. In the expression building rules, the first and second numbers' values are **$1** and **$3**, respectively. The operator's value would be **$2**, although in this grammar the operators do not have interesting values. The action on the last rule is not strictly necessary, since the default action that yacc performs after every reduction, before running any explicit action code, assigns the value **$1** to **$$**.

The Lexer

To try out our parser, we need a lexer to feed it tokens. As we mentioned in Chapter 1, the parser is the higher level routine, and calls the lexer **yylex()** whenever it needs a token from the input. As soon as the lexer finds a token of interest to the parser, it returns to the parser, returning the token code as the value. Yacc defines the token names in the parser as C preprocessor names in *y.tab.h* (or some similar name on MS-DOS systems) so the lexer can use them.

Here is a simple lexer to provide tokens for our parser:

```
%{
#include "y.tab.h"
extern int yylval;
%}

%%
[0-9]+      { yylval = atoi(yytext); return NUMBER; }
[ \t] ;             /* ignore whitespace */
\n    return 0;     /* logical EOF */
.     return yytext[0];
%%
```

Strings of digits are numbers, whitespace is ignored, and a newline returns an end of input token (number zero) to tell the parser that there is no more to read. The last rule in the lexer is a very common catch-all, which says to return any character otherwise not handled as a single character token to the parser. Character tokens are usually punctuation such as parentheses, semicolons, and single-character operators. If the parser receives a token that it doesn't know about, it generates a syntax error, so this rule lets you handle all of the single-character tokens easily while letting yacc's error checking catch and complain about invalid input.

Whenever the lexer returns a token to the parser, if the token has an associated value, the lexer must store the value in **yylval** before returning. In this first example, we explicitly declare **yylval**. In more complex parsers, yacc defines **yylval** as a *union* and puts the definition in *y.tab.h*.

We haven't defined NAME tokens yet, just NUMBER tokens, but that is OK for the moment.

Compiling and Running a Simple Parser

On a UNIX system, yacc takes your grammar and creates *y.tab.c*, the C language parser, and *y.tab.h*, the include file with the token number definitions. Lex creates *lex.yy.c*, the C language lexer. You need only compile them together with the yacc and lex libraries. The libraries contain usable default versions of all of the supporting routines, including a **main()** that calls the parser **yyparse()** and exits.

```
% yacc -d ch3-01.y   # makes y.tab.c and "y.tab.h
% lex ch3-01.1       # makes lex.yy.c
% cc -o ch3-01 y.tab.c lex.yy.c -ly -ll   # compile and link C files
% ch3-01
99+12
= 111
% ch3-01
```

```
2 + 3-14+33
= 24
% ch3-01
100 + -50
syntax error
```

Our first version seems to work. In the third test, it correctly reports a syntax error when we enter something that doesn't conform to the grammar.

Arithmetic Expressions and Ambiguity

Let's make the arithmetic expressions more general and realistic, extending the *expression* rules to handle multiplication and division, unary negation, and parenthesized expressions:

```
expression: expression '+' expression { $$ = $1 + $3; }
    |       expression '-' expression { $$ = $1 - $3; }
    |       expression '*' expression { $$ = $1 * $3; }
    |       expression '/' expression
            {      if($3 == 0)
                            yyerror("divide by zero");
                   else
                        $$ = $1 / $3;
            }
    |       '-' expression           { $$ = -$2; }
    |       '(' expression ')'       { $$ = $2; }
    |       NUMBER                   { $$ = $1; }
    ;
```

The action for division checks for division by zero, since in many implementations of C a zero divide will crash the program. It calls **yyerror()**, the standard yacc error routine, to report the error.

But this grammar has a problem: it is extremely ambiguous. For example, the input 2+3*4 might mean (2+3)*4 or 2+(3*4), and the input 3-4-5-6 might mean 3-(4-(5-6)) or (3-4)-(5-6) or any of a lot of other possibilities. Figure 3-3 shows the two possible parses for 2+3*4.

If you compile this grammar as it stands, yacc will tell you that there are 16 shift/reduce conflicts, states where it cannot tell whether it should shift the token on the stack or reduce a rule first.

For example, when parsing "2+3*4", the parser goes through these steps (we abbreviate *expression* as *E* here):

2	shift NUMBER
E	reduce E → NUMBER
E +	shift +
E + 3	shift NUMBER
E + E	reduce E → NUMBER

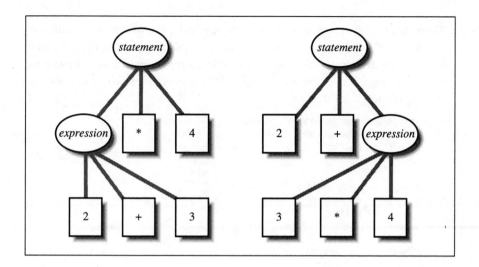

*Figure 3-3: Ambiguous input 2+3*4*

At this point, the parser looks at the "*", and could either reduce "2+3" using:

```
expression:                          expression '+' expression
```

to an *expression*, or shift the "*" expecting to be able to reduce:

```
expression:                          expression '*' expression
```

later on.

The problem is that we haven't told yacc about the precedence and associativity of the operators. *Precedence* controls which operators to execute first in an expression. Mathematical and programming tradition (dating back past the first Fortran compiler in 1956) says that multiplication and division take precedence over addition and subtraction, so a+b*c means a+(b*c) and d/e–f means (d/e)–f. In any expression grammar, operators are grouped into levels of precedence from lowest to highest. The total number of levels depends on the language. The C language is notorious for having too many precedence levels, a total of fifteen levels.

Associativity controls the grouping of operators at the same precedence level. Operators may group to the left, e.g., a–b–c in C means (a–b)–c, or to the right, e.g., a=b=c in C means a=(b=c). In some cases operators do not group at all, e.g., in Fortran A.LE.B.LE.C is invalid.

There are two ways to specify precedence and associativity in a grammar, implicitly and explicitly. To specify them *implicitly*, rewrite the grammar using separate non-terminal symbols for each precedence level. Assuming the usual precedence and left associativity for everything, we could rewrite our expression rules this way:

```
expression: expression '+' mulexp
    |       expression '-' mulexp
    |       mulexp
    ;

mulexp:             mulexp '*' primary
    |       mulexp '/' primary
    |       primary
    ;

primary:    '(' expression ')'
    |       '-' primary
    |       NUMBER
    ;
```

This is a perfectly reasonable way to write a grammar, and if yacc didn't have explicit precedence rules, it would be the only way.

But yacc also lets you specify precedences *explicitly*. We can add these lines to the definition section, resulting in the grammar in Example 3-1.

```
%left '+' '-'
%left '*' '/'
%nonassoc UMINUS
```

Each of these declarations defines a level of precedence. They tell yacc that "+" and "−" are left associative and at the lowest precedence level, "*" and "/" are left associative and at a higher precedence level, and UMINUS, a pseudo-token standing for unary minus, has no associativity and is at the highest precedence. (We don't have any right associative operators here, but if we did they'd use %**right**.) Yacc assigns each rule the precedence of the rightmost token on the right-hand side; if the rule contains no tokens with precedence assigned, the rule has no precedence of its own. When yacc encounters a shift/reduce conflict due to an ambiguous grammar, it consults the table of precedences, and if all of the rules involved in the conflict include a token which appears in a precedence declaration, it uses precedence to resolve the conflict.

In our grammar, all of the conflicts occur in the rules of the form *expression OPERATOR expression*, so setting precedences for the four operators allows it to resolve all of the conflicts. This parser using precedences is slightly smaller and faster than the one with the extra rules for implicit precedence, since it has fewer rules to reduce.

Example 3-1: The calculator grammar with expressions and precedence ch3-02.y

```
%token NAME NUMBER
%left '-' '+'
%left '*' '/'
%nonassoc UMINUS

%%

statement: NAME '=' expression
    |      expression        { printf("= %d\n", $1); }
    ;

expression: expression '+' expression { $$ = $1 + $3; }
    |       expression '-' expression { $$ = $1 - $3; }
    |       expression '*' expression { $$ = $1 * $3; }
    |       expression '/' expression
                    {     if($3 == 0)
                                yyerror("divide by zero");
                          else
                                $$ = $1 / $3;
                    }
    |       '-' expression %prec UMINUS  { $$ = -$2; }
    |       '(' expression ')'     { $$ = $2; }
    |       NUMBER                 { $$ = $1; }
    ;
%%
```

The rule for negation includes "%prec UMINUS". The only operator this rule includes is "−", which has low precedence, but we want unary minus to have higher precedence than multiplication rather than lower. The **%prec** tells yacc to use the precedence of UMINUS for this rule.

When Not to Use Precedence Rules

You can use precedence rules to fix any shift/reduce conflict that occurs in the grammar. This is usually a terrible idea. In expression grammars the cause of the conflicts is easy to understand, and the effect of the precedence rules is clear. In other situations precedence rules fix shift/reduce problems, but it is usually difficult to understand just what effect they have on the grammar.

We recommend that you use precedence in only two situations: in expression grammars, and to resolve the "dangling else" conflict in grammars for if-then-else language constructs. (See Chapter 7 for examples of the latter.)

Otherwise, if you can, you should fix the grammar to remove the conflict. Remember that conflicts mean that yacc can't properly parse a grammar, probably because it's ambiguous, which means there are multiple possible parses for the same input. Except in the two cases above, this usually points to a mistake in your language design. If a grammar is ambiguous to yacc, it's almost certainly ambiguous to humans, too. See Chapter 8 for more information on finding and repairing conflicts.

Variables and Typed Tokens

Next we extend our calculator to handle variables with single letter names. Since there are only 26 single letters (lowercase only for the moment) we can simply store the variables in a 26 entry array, which we call **vbltable**. To make the calculator more useful, we also extend it to handle multiple expressions, one per line, and to use floating point values, as shown in Examples 3-2 and 3-3.

Example 3-2: Calculator grammar with variables and real values ch3-03.y

```
%{
double vbltable[26];
%}

%union {
        double dval;
        int vblno;
}

%token <vblno> NAME
%token <dval> NUMBER
%left '-' '+'
%left '*' '/'
%nonassoc UMINUS

%type <dval> expression
%%
statement_list:    statement '\n'
        |    statement_list statement '\n'
        ;

statement: NAME '=' expression     { vbltable[$1] = $3; }
        |    expression          { printf("= %g\n", $1); }
        ;

expression: expression '+' expression { $$ = $1 + $3; }
        |    expression '-' expression { $$ = $1 - $3; }
        |    expression '*' expression { $$ = $1 * $3; }
        |    expression '/' expression
                      {    if($3 == 0.0)
```

Example 3-2: Calculator grammar with variables and real values ch3-03.y (continued)

```
                                yyerror("divide by zero");
                       else
                                $$ = $1 / $3;
                  }
     |    '-' expression %prec UMINUS  { $$ = -$2; }
     |    '(' expression ')'     { $$ = $2; }
     |    NUMBER
     |    NAME                { $$ = vbltable[$1]; }
     ;
%%
```

Example 3-3: Lexer for calculator with variables and real values ch3-03.l

```
%{
#include "y.tab.h"
#include <math.h>
extern double vbltable[26];
%}

%%
([0-9]+|([0-9]*\.[0-9]+)([eE][-+]?[0-9]+)?) {
     yylval.dval = atof(yytext); return NUMBER;
     }

[ \t] ;              /* ignore whitespace */

[a-z] { yylval.vblno = yytext[0] - 'a'; return NAME; }

"$"   { return 0; /* end of input */ }

\n    |
.     return yytext[0];
%%
```

Symbol Values and %union

We now have multiple types of symbol values. Expressions have *double* values, while the value for variable references and **NAME** symbols are integers from 0 to 25 corresponding to the slot in **vbltable**. Why not have the lexer return the value of the variable as a *double*, to make the parser simpler? The problem is that there are two contexts where a variable name can occur: as part of an expression, in which case we want the *double* value, and to the left of an equal sign, in which case we need to remember which variable it is so we can update **vbltable**.

To define the possible symbol types, in the definition section we add a **%union** declaration:

```
%union {
        double dval;
        int vblno;
}
```

The contents of the declaration are copied verbatim to the output file as the contents of a C **union** declaration defining the type **YYSTYPE** as a C typedef. The generated header file *y.tab.h* includes a copy of the definition so that you can use it in the lexer. Here is the *y.tab.h* generated from this grammar:

```
#define NAME 257
#define NUMBER 258
#define UMINUS 259
typedef union {
        double dval;
        int vblno;
} YYSTYPE;
extern YYSTYPE yylval;
```

The generated file also declares the variable **yylval**, and defines the token numbers for the symbolic tokens in the grammar.

Now we have to tell the parser which symbols use which type of value. We do that by putting the appropriate field name from the union in angle brackets in the lines in the definition section that defines the symbol:

```
%token <vblno> NAME
%token <dval> NUMBER

%type <dval> expression
```

The new declaration **%type** sets the type for non-terminals which otherwise need no declaration. You can also put bracketed types in **%left**, **%right**, or **%nonassoc**. In action code, yacc automatically qualifies symbol value references with the appropriate field name, e.g., if the third symbol is a **NUMBER**, a reference to **$3** acts like **$3.dval**.

The new, expanded parser was shown in Example 3-2. We've added a new start symbol **statement_list** so that the parser can accept a list of statements, each ended by a newline, rather than just one statement. We've also added an action for the rule that sets a variable, and a new rule at the end that turns a **NAME** into an **expression** by fetching the value of the variable.

We have to modify the lexer a little (Example 3-3). The literal block in the lexer no longer declares **yylval**, since its declaration is now in *y.tab.h*. The lexer doesn't have any automatic way to associate types with tokens, so you have to put in explicit field references when you set **yylval**. We've used the real number pattern from Chapter 2 to match floating point numbers. The action code uses **atof( )** to read the number, then assigns the value to **yylval.dval**, since the parser expects the number's value in the **dval** field. For variables, we return the index of the variable in the variable table in **yylval.vblno**. Finally, we've made "\n" a regular token, so we use a dollar sign to indicate the end of the input.

A little experimentation shows that our modified calculator works:

```
% ch3-03
2/3
= 0.666667
a = 2/7
a
= 0.285714
z = a+1
z
= 1.28571
a/z
= 0.222222
$
```

Symbol Tables

Few users will be satisfied with single character variable names, so now we add the ability to use longer variable names. This means we need a *symbol table*, a structure that keeps track of the names in use. Each time the lexer reads a name from the input, it looks the name up in the symbol table, and gets a pointer to the corresponding symbol table entry. Elsewhere in the program, we use symbol table pointers rather than name strings, since pointers are much easier and faster to use than looking up a name each time we need it.

Since the symbol table requires a data structure shared between the lexer and parser, we created a header file *ch3hdr.h* (see Example 3-4). This symbol table is an array of structures each containing the name of the variable and its value. We also declare a routine **symlook( )** which takes a name as a text string and returns a pointer to the appropriate symbol table entry, adding it if it is not already there.

Example 3-4: Header for parser with symbol table ch3hdr.h

```
#define NSYMS 20  /* maximum number of symbols */

struct symtab {
     char *name;
     double value;
} symtab[NSYMS];

struct symtab *symlook();
```

The parser changes only slightly to use the symbol table, as shown in Example 3-5. The value for a **NAME** token is now a pointer into the symbol table rather than an index as before. We change the **%union** and call the pointer field **symp**. The **%token** declaration for **NAME** changes appropriately, and the actions that assign to and read variables now use the token value as a pointer so they can read or write the value field of the symbol table entry.

The new routine **symlook( )** is defined in the user subroutines section of the yacc specification, as shown in Example 3-6. (There is no compelling reason for this; it could as easily have been in the lex file or in a file by itself.) It searches through the symbol table sequentially to find the entry corresponding to the name passed as its argument. If an entry has a **name** string and it matches the one that **symlook( )** is searching for, it returns a pointer to the entry, since the name has already been put into the table. If the **name** field is empty, we've looked at all of the table entries that are in use, and haven't found this symbol, so we enter the name into the heretofore empty table entry.

We use **strdup( )** to make a permanent copy of the name string. When the lexer calls **symlook( )**, it passes the name in the token buffer **yytext**. Since each subsequent token overwrites **yytext**, we need to make a copy ourselves here. (This is a common source of errors in lex scanners; if you need to use the contents of **yytext** after the scanner goes on to the next token, always make a copy.) Finally, if the current table entry is in use but doesn't match, **symlook( )** goes on to search the next entry.

This symbol table routine is perfectly adequate for this simple example, but more realistic symbol table code is somewhat more complex. Sequential search is too slow for symbol tables of appreciable size, so use hashing or some other faster search function. Real symbol tables tend to carry considerably more information per entry, e.g., the type of a variable, whether it is a simple variable, an array or structure, and how many dimensions if it is an array.

Example 3-5: Rules for parser with symbol table ch3-04.y

```
%{
#include "ch3hdr.h"
#include <string.h>
%}

%union {
      double dval;
      struct symtab *symp;
}
%token <symp> NAME
%token <dval> NUMBER
%left '-' '+'
%left '*' '/'
%nonassoc UMINUS

%type <dval> expression
%%
statement_list:  statement '\n'
      |       statement_list statement '\n'
      ;

statement: NAME '=' expression    { $1->value = $3; }
      |      expression        { printf("= %g\n", $1); }
      ;

expression: expression '+' expression { $$ = $1 + $3; }
      |      expression '-' expression { $$ = $1 - $3; }
      |      expression '*' expression { $$ = $1 * $3; }
      |      expression '/' expression
                        {    if($3 == 0.0)
                                    yyerror("divide by zero");
                             else
                                    $$ = $1 / $3;
                        }
      |      '-' expression %prec UMINUS  { $$ = -$2; }
      |      '(' expression ')'    { $$ = $2; }
      |      NUMBER
      |      NAME                { $$ = $1->value; }
      ;
%%
```

Example 3-6: Symbol table routine ch3-04.pgm

```
/* look up a symbol table entry, add if not present */
struct symtab *
symlook(s)
char *s;
{
      char *p;
      struct symtab *sp;
```

Example 3-6: Symbol table routine ch3-04.pgm (continued)

```
        for(sp = symtab; sp < &symtab[NSYMS]; sp++) {
            /* is it already here? */
            if(sp->name && !strcmp(sp->name, s))
                    return sp;

            /* is it free */
            if(!sp->name) {
                    sp->name = strdup(s);
                    return sp;
            }
            /* otherwise continue to next */
        }
        yyerror("Too many symbols");
        exit(1);       /* cannot continue */
} /* symlook */
```

The lexer also changes only slightly to accommodate the symbol table (Example 3-7). Rather than declaring the symbol table directly, it now also includes *ch3hdr.h*. The rule that recognizes variable names now matches "[A-Za-z][A-Za-z0-9]*", any string of letters and digits starting with a letter. Its action calls **symlook( )** to get a pointer to the symbol table entry, and stores that in **yylval.symp**, the token's value.

Example 3-7: Lexer with symbol table ch3-04.l

```
%{
#include "y.tab.h"
#include "ch3hdr.h"
#include <math.h>
%}

%%
([0-9]+|([0-9]*\.[0-9]+)([eE][-+]?[0-9]+)?) {
            yylval.dval = atof(yytext);
            return NUMBER;
      }

[ \t] ;              /* ignore whitespace */

[A-Za-z][A-Za-z0-9]*   {     /* return symbol pointer */
            yylval.symp = symlook(yytext);
            return NAME;
      }
"$"    { return 0; }
\n     |
.      return yytext[0];
%%
```

There is one minor way in which our symbol table routine is better than those in most programming languages: since we allocate string space dynamically, there is no fixed limit on the length of variable names:*

```
% ch3-04
foo = 12
foo /5
= 2.4
thisisanextremelylongvariablenamewhichnobodywouldwanttotype = 42
3 * thisisanextremelylongvariablenamewhichnobodywouldwanttotype
= 126
$
%
```

Functions and Reserved Words

The next addition we make to the calculator adds mathematical functions for square root, exponential, and logarithm. We want to handle input like this:

```
s2 = sqrt(2)
s2
= 1.41421
s2*s2
= 2
```

The brute force approach makes the function names separate tokens, and adds separate rules for each function:

```
%token SQRT LOG EXP
    . . .
%%
expression: . . .
    |       SQRT '(' expression ')'{ $$ = sqrt($3); }
    |       LOG '(' expression ')' { $$ = log($3); }
    |       EXP '(' expression ')' { $$ = exp($3); }
```

In the scanner, we have to return a **SQRT** token for "sqrt" input and so forth:

```
sqrt    return SQRT;
log     return LOG;
exp     return EXP;

[A-Za-z][A-Za-z0-9]*    {    . . .
```

---

*Actually, there is a limit due to the maximum token size that lex can handle, but you can make that rather large. See "yytext" in Chapter 6, *A Reference for Lex Specifications.*

(The specific patterns come first so they match before than the general symbol pattern.)

This works, but it has problems. One is that you must hard-code every function into the parser and the lexer, which is tedious and makes it hard to add more functions. Another is that function names are *reserved words*, i.e., you cannot use **sqrt** as a variable name. This may or may not be a problem, depending on your intentions.

Reserved Words in the Symbol Table

First we'll take the specific patterns for function names out of the lexer and put them in the symbol table. We add a new field to each symbol table entry: **funcptr**, a pointer to the C function to call if this entry is a function name.

```
struct symtab {
      char *name;
      double (*funcptr)();
      double value;
} symtab[NSYMS];
```

We have to put the function names in the symbol table before the parser starts, so we wrote our own **main()** which calls the new routine **addfunc()** to add each of the function names to the symbol table, then calls **yyparse()**. The code for **addfunc()** merely gets the symbol table entry for a name and sets the **funcptr** field.

```
main()
{
      extern double sqrt(), exp(), log();

      addfunc("sqrt", sqrt);
      addfunc("exp", exp);
      addfunc("log", log);
      yyparse();
}

addfunc(name, func)
char *name;
double (*func)();
{
      struct symtab *sp = symlook(name);
      sp->funcptr = func;
}
```

We define a token FUNC to represent function names. The lexer will return FUNC when it sees a function name and NAME when it sees a variable name. The value for either is the symbol table pointer.

In the parser, we replace the separate rules for each function with one general function rule:

```
%token <symp> NAME FUNC
%%
expression: ...
        |    FUNC '(' expression ')' { $$ = ($1->funcptr)($3); }
```

When the parser sees a function reference, it can consult the symbol table entry for the function to find the actual internal function reference.

In the lexer, we take out the patterns that matched the function names explicitly, and change the action code for names to return FUNC if the symbol table entry says that a name is a function name:

```
[A-Za-z][A-Za-z0-9]*    {
            struct symtab *sp = symlook(yytext);

            yylval.symp = sp;
            if(sp->funcptr)    /* is it a function? */
                return FUNC;
            else
                return NAME;
      }
```

These changes produce a program that works the same as the one above, but the function names are in the symbol table. The program can, for example, enter new function names as the parse progresses.

Interchangeable Function and Variable Names

A final change is technically minor, but changes the language significantly. There is no reason why function and variable names have to be disjoint! The parser can tell a function call from a variable reference by the syntax.

So we put the lexer back the way it was, always returning a **NAME** for any kind of name. Then we change the parser to accept a **NAME** in the function position:

```
%token <symp> NAME
%%
expression: ...
        |    NAME '(' expression ')' { ... }
```

The entire program is in Examples 3-8 through 3-11. As you can see in Example 3-9, we had to add some error checking to make sure that when the user calls a function, it's a real function.

Now the calculator operates as before, except that the names of functions and variables can overlap.

```
% ch3-05
sqrt(3)
= 1.73205
foo(3)
foo not a function
= 0
sqrt = 5
sqrt(sqrt)
= 2.23607
```

Whether you want to allow users to use the same name for two things in the same program is debatable. On the one hand it can make programs harder to understand, but on the other hand users are otherwise forced to invent names that do not conflict with the reserved names.

Either can be taken to extremes. COBOL has over 300 reserved words, so nobody can remember them all, and programmers resort to strange conventions like starting every variable name with a digit to be sure they don't conflict. On the other hand, PL/I has no reserved words at all, so you can write:

```
IF IF = THEN THEN ELSE = THEN; ELSE ELSE = IF;
```

Example 3-8: Final calculator header ch3hdr2.h

```
#define NSYMS 20  /* maximum number of symbols */

struct symtab {
      char *name;
      double (*funcptr)();
      double value;
} symtab[NSYMS];

struct symtab *symlook();
```

Example 3-9: Rules for final calculator parser ch3-05.y

```
%{
#include "ch3hdr2.h"
#include <string.h>
#include <math.h>
%}

%union {
      double dval;
      struct symtab *symp;
}
%token <symp> NAME
```

Example 3-9: Rules for final calculator parser cb3-05.y (continued)

```
%token <dval> NUMBER
%left '-' '+'
%left '*' '/'
%nonassoc UMINUS

%type <dval> expression
%%
statement_list:   statement '\n'
       |      statement_list statement '\n'
       ;

statement: NAME '=' expression      { $1->value = $3; }
       |      expression          { printf("= %g\n", $1); }
       ;

expression: expression '+' expression { $$ = $1 + $3; }
       |      expression '-' expression { $$ = $1 - $3; }
       |      expression '*' expression { $$ = $1 * $3; }
       |      expression '/' expression
                      {    if($3 == 0.0)
                                   yyerror("divide by zero");
                           else
                                   $$ = $1 / $3;
                      }
       |      '-' expression %prec UMINUS  { $$ = -$2; }
       |      '(' expression ')'     { $$ = $2; }
       |      NUMBER
       |      NAME                 { $$ = $1->value; }
       |      NAME '(' expression ')'{
                      if($1->funcptr)
                           $$ = ($1->funcptr)($3);
                      else {
                           printf("%s not a function\n", $1->name);
                           $$ = 0.0;
                      }
              }
       ;
%%
```

Example 3-10: User subroutines for final calculator parser cb3-05.y

```
/* look up a symbol table entry, add if not present */
struct symtab *
symlook(s)
char *s;
{
      char *p;
      struct symtab *sp;

      for(sp = symtab; sp < &symtab[NSYMS]; sp++) {
           /* is it already here? */
```

Example 3-10: User subroutines for final calculator parser ch3-05.y (continued)

```
        if(sp->name && !strcmp(sp->name, s))
            return sp;

        /* is it free */
        if(!sp->name) {
            sp->name = strdup(s);
            return sp;
        }
        /* otherwise continue to next */
    }
    yyerror("Too many symbols");
    exit(1);    /* cannot continue */
} /* symlook */

addfunc(name, func)
char *name;
double (*func)();
{
    struct symtab *sp = symlook(name);
    sp->funcptr = func;
}

main()
{
    extern double sqrt(), exp(), log();

    addfunc("sqrt", sqrt);
    addfunc("exp", exp);
    addfunc("log", log);
    yyparse();
}
```

Example 3-11: Final calculator lexer ch3-05.l

```
%{
#include "y.tab.h"
#include "ch3hdr2.h"
#include <math.h>
%}

%%
([0-9]+|([0-9]*\.[0-9]+)([eE][-+]?[0-9]+)?) {
            yylval.dval = atof(yytext);
            return NUMBER;
    }

[ \t] ;              /* ignore whitespace */

[A-Za-z][A-Za-z0-9]*   {   /* return symbol pointer */
            struct symtab *sp = symlook(yytext);
```

Example 3-11: Final calculator lexer ch3-05.l (continued)

```
            yylval.symp = sp;
            return NAME;
        }

"$"    { return 0; }

\n     |
.      return yytext[0];
%%
```

Building Parsers with Make

About the third time you recompile this example, you will probably decide that some automation in the recompilation process is in order, using the UNIX *make* program. The *Makefile* that controls the process is shown in Example 3-12.

Example 3-12: Makefile for the calculator

```
#LEX = flex -I
#YACC = byacc

CC = cc -DYYDEBUG=1

ch3-05: y.tab.o lex.yy.o
        $(CC) -o ch3-05 y.tab.o lex.yy.o -ly -ll -lm

lex.yy.o:   lex.yy.c y.tab.h

lex.yy.o y.tab.o:  ch3hdr2.h

y.tab.c y.tab.h: ch3-05.y
        $(YACC) -d ch3-05.y

lex.yy.c : ch3-05.l
        $(LEX) ch3lex.l
```

At the top are two commented assignments that substitute flex for lex and Berkeley yacc for AT&T yacc. Flex needs the *−I* flag to tell it to generate an interactive scanner, one that doesn't try to look ahead past a newline. The CC macro sets the preprocessor symbol **YYDEBUG** which compiles in some debugging code useful in testing the parser.

The rule for compiling everything together into *ch3* refers to three libraries: the yacc library *−ly*, the lex library *−ll*, and the math library *−lm*. The yacc library provides **yyerror()** and, in early versions of the calculator, **main()**. The lex library provides some internal support routines that a lex scanner needs. (Scanners generated by flex don't need the library, but it does no harm to leave it in.) The math library provides **sqrt()**, **exp()**, and **log()**.

If we were to use bison, the GNU version of yacc, we'd have to change the rule that generates *y.tab.c* because bison uses different default filenames:

```
y.tab.c y.tab.h: ch3yac.y
        bison -d ch3yac.y
        mv ch3yac.tab.c y.tab.c
        mv ch3yac.tab.h "y.tab.h
```

(Or we could change the rest of the *Makefile* and the code to use bison's more memorable names, or else use *−y* which tells bison to use the usual yacc filenames.)

For more details on *make*, see Steve Talbott's *Managing Projects with Make*, published by O'Reilly & Associates.

Summary

In this chapter, we've seen how to create a yacc grammar specification, put it together with a lexer to produce a working calculator, and extended the calculator to handle symbolic variable and function names. In the next two chapters, we'll work out larger and more realistic applications, a menu generator and a processor for the SQL database language.

Exercises

1. Add more functions to the calculator. Try adding two argument functions, e.g., modulus or arctangent, with a rule like this:

   ```
   expression: NAME '(' expression ',' expression ')'
   ```

   You should probably put a separate field in the symbol table for the two-argument functions, so you can call the appropriate version of **atan()** for one or two arguments.

2. Add a string data type, so you can assign strings to variables and use them in expressions or function calls. Add a STRING token for quoted literal strings. Change the value of an **expression** to a structure containing a tag for the type of value along with the value. Alternatively, extend the grammar with a **stringexp** non-terminal for a string expression with a string (*char **) value.

3. If you added a **stringexp** non-terminal, what happens if the user types this?

```
42 + "grapefruit"
```

How hard is it to modify the grammar to allow mixed type expressions?

4. What do you have to do to handle assigning string values to variables?

5. How hard is it to overload operators, e.g., using "+" to mean catenation if the arguments are strings?

6. Add commands to the calculator to save and restore the variables to and from disk files.

7. Add user-defined functions to the calculator. The hard part is storing away the definition of the function in a way that you can re-execute when the user calls the function. One possibility is to save the stream of tokens that define the function. For example:

```
statement: NAME '(' NAME ')' '=' { start_save($1, $3); }
    expression
    { end_save(); define_func($1, $3); }
```

The functions **start_save()** and **end_save()** tell the lexer to save a list of all of the tokens for the expression. You need to identify references within the defining expression to the dummy argument **$3**.

When the user calls the function, you play the tokens back:

```
expression: USERFUNC '(' expression ')' { start_replay($1, $3); }
    expression/* replays the function */
    { $$ = $6; }/* use its value */
```

While playing back the function, insert the argument value **$3** into the replayed expression in place of the dummy argument.

8. If you keep adding features to the calculator, you'll eventually end up with your own unique programming language. Would that be a good idea? Why or why not?

4

A Menu Generation Language

The previous chapter provided a simple example of an interpreter, a desk-top calculator. In this chapter, we turn our attention to compiler design by developing a *menu generation language* (*MGL*) and its associated com-piler. We begin with a description of the language that we are going to cre-ate. Then we look at several iterations of developing the lex and yacc specifications. Lastly, we create the actions associated with our grammar and which implement the features of the MGL.

Overview of the MGL

We'll develop a language that can be used to generate custom menu inter-faces. It will take as input a description file and produce a C program that can be compiled to create this output on a user's terminal, using the stan-dard *curses* library to draw the menus on the screen.*

In many cases when an application requires a lot of tedious and repetitive code, it is faster and easier to design a special purpose language and write a little compiler that translates your language into C or something else your computer can already handle. Curses programming is tedious, because you have to position all of the data on the screen yourself. MGL automates most of the layout, greatly easing the job.

---

*For more information on curses, see *Programming with Curses* by John Strang, published by O'Reilly & Associates.

The menu description consists of the following:

1. A name for the menu screen
2. A title or titles
3. A list of menu items, each consisting of:

   item
   [command]
   action
   [attribute]

   where *item* is the text string that appears on the menu, *command* is the mnemonic used to provide command-line access to the functions of the menu system, *action* is the procedure that should be performed when a menu item is chosen, and *attribute* indicates how this item should be handled. The bracketed items are optional.
4. A terminator

Since a useful application usually has several menus, a description file can contain several different named menus.

A sample menu description file is:

```
screen myMenu
title "My First Menu"
title "by Tony Mason"

item "List Things to Do"
command "to-do"
action execute list-things-todo
attribute command

item "Quit"
command "quit"
action quit

end myMenu
```

The MGL compiler reads this description and produces C code, which must itself be compiled. When the resulting program is executed, it creates the following menu:

```
        My First Menu
        by Tony Mason

1) List Things to Do
2) Quit
```

When the user presses the "1" key or enters the command "to-do", the procedure "list-things-todo" is executed.

A more general description of this format is:

> *screen <name>*
> *title <string>*
>
> *item <string>*
> *[command <string>]*
> *action {execute | menu | quit | ignore} [<name>]*
> *[attribute {visible | invisible}]*
>
> *end <name>*

As we develop this language, we will start with a subset of this functionality and add features to it until we implement the full specification. This approach shows you how easy it is to modify the lex-generated lexer and the yacc-generated parser as we change the language.

Developing the MGL

Let's look at the design process that led to the grammar above. Menus provide a simple, clean interface for inexperienced users. For these users, the rigidity and ease of use provided by a menu system is ideal.

A major disadvantage of menus is that they keep experienced users from moving directly into the desired application. For these people, a command-driven interface is more desirable. However, all but the most experienced users occasionally want to fall back into the menu to access some seldom used function.

Our MGL should be designed with both of these design goals in mind. Initially, suppose we start with the keyword *command*, which indicates a menu choice or command that a user can issue to access some function.

This hardly constitutes a usable language. Nevertheless, we can sketch out a lexical specification for it:

```
ws      [ \t]+
nl      \n
%%
{ws}    ;
command     { return COMMAND; }
{nl}    { lineno++; }
.       { return yytext[0];}
```

and its corresponding yacc grammar:

```
%{
#include <stdio.h>
%}

%token COMMAND
%%
start:     COMMAND
      ;
```

Our lexer merely looks for our keyword and returns the appropriate token when it recognizes one. If the parser sees the token **COMMAND**, then the **start** rule will be matched, and **yyparse( )** will return successfully.

Each item on a menu should have an action associated with it. We can introduce the keyword **action**. One action might be to ignore the item (for unimplemented or unavailable commands), and another might be to execute a program; we can add the keywords **ignore** and **execute**.

Thus, a sample item using our modified vocabulary might be:

```
command action execute
```

We must tell it what to execute, so we add our first noncommand argument, a string. Because program names can contain punctuation, we will presume that a program name is a quoted string. Now our sample item becomes:

```
command action execute "/bin/sh"
```

Example 4-1 demonstrates that we can modify our lex specification to support the new keywords, as well as the new token type.

Example 4-1: First version of MGL lexer

```
ws        [ \t]+
qstring   \"[^\"\n]*[\"\n]
nl        \n
%%
{ws}      ;
{qstring} { yylval.string = strdup(yytext+1); /* skip open quote */
            if(yylval.string[yyleng-2] != '"')
                warning("Unterminated character string",(char *)0);
          else
                yylval.string[yyleng-2] = '\0'; /* remove close quote */
            return QSTRING;
          }
action    { return ACTION; }
execute   { return EXECUTE; }
```

Example 4-1: First version of MGL lexer (continued)

```
command     { return COMMAND; }
ignore      { return IGNORE; }
{nl}        { lineno++; }
.           { return yytext[0]; }
```

Our complex definition of a **qstring** is necessary to prevent lex from matching a line like:

```
"apples" and "oranges"
```

as a single token. The "`[^\"\n]*`" part of the pattern says to match against every character that is not a quotation mark or a newline. We do not want to match beyond a newline because a missing closing quotation mark could cause the lexical analyzer to plow through the rest of the file, which is certainly not what the user wants, and may overflow internal lex buffers and make the program fail. With this method, we can report the error condition to the user in a more polite manner. When we copy the string, we remove the opening and closing quotes, because it's easier to handle the string without quotes in the rest of the code.

We also need to modify our yacc grammar (Example 4-2).

Example 4-2: First version of MGL parser

```
%{
#include <stdio.h>
%}

%union {
        char *string;          /* string buffer */
}

%token COMMAND ACTION IGNORE EXECUTE
%token <string> QSTRING
%%
start:      COMMAND action
      ;

action:   ACTION IGNORE
        | ACTION EXECUTE QSTRING
        ;
%%
```

We defined a **%union** including the "string" type and the new token **QSTRING**, which represents a quoted string.

We need to group information for a single command and choice combination together as a *menu item*. We introduce each new item as an item, using the keyword **item**. If there is an associated command, we indicate that using the keyword **command**. We add the new keyword to the lexer:

```
    . . .
%%
    . . .
item          { return ITEM; }
```

Although we have changed the fundamental structure of the language, there is little change in the lexical analyzer. The change shows up in the yacc grammar, as shown in Example 4-3.

Example 4-3: Grammar with items and actions

```
%{
#include <stdio.h>
%}

%union {
        char *string;          /* string pointer */
}

%token COMMAND ACTION IGNORE EXECUTE ITEM
%token <string> QSTRING
%%
item:    ITEM command action
      ;

command:   /* empty */
         | COMMAND
         ;

action:   ACTION IGNORE
        | ACTION EXECUTE QSTRING
        ;
%%
```

Since each menu item need not have a corresponding command, one of the **command** rules has an empty right-hand side. Surprisingly, yacc has no trouble with such rules, so long as the rest of the grammar makes it possible to tell unambiguously that the optional elements are not there.

We still have not given any meaning to the keyword **command**. Indeed, it is often a good idea to try writing the yacc grammar alone, because it can indicate "holes" in the language design. Fortunately, this is quickly

remedied. We will restrict commands to strings of alphanumeric characters. We add an **ID** for "identifier" token to our lexical analyzer:

```
  . . .
id        [a-zA-Z][a-zA-Z0-9]*
%%
  . . .
{id}      { yylval.string = strdup(yytext);
            return ID;
          }
```

The value of an **ID** is a pointer to the name of the identifier. In general, it is
a poor idea to pass back a pointer to **yytext** as the value of a symbol,
because as soon as the lexer reads the next token it may overwrite **yytext**.
(Failure to copy **yytext** is a common lexer bug, often producing strange
symptoms as strings and identifiers mysteriously seem to change their
names.) We copy the token using **strdup()** and pass back a pointer to the
copy. The rules that use an **ID** must be careful to free the copy when they
are done with it.

In Example 4-4 we add the **ID** token to our yacc grammar.

Example 4-4: Grammar with command identifiers

```
%{
#include <stdio.h>
%}

%union {
        char *string;          /* string buffer */
}

%token COMMAND ACTION IGNORE EXECUTE ITEM
%token <string> QSTRING ID
%%
item:     ITEM command action
          ;

command:   /* empty */
          | COMMAND ID
          ;

action:   ACTION IGNORE
          | ACTION EXECUTE QSTRING
          ;
%%
```

The grammar does not provide for more than a single line in a menu. We add some rules for **items** that support multiple **items**:

```
   . . .
%%
items:  /* empty */
        | items item
        ;

item:    ITEM command action
         ;
   . . .
```

Unlike all our previous rules, these rely upon recursion. Because yacc prefers left-recursive grammars, we wrote "items item" rather than the right-recursive version "item items." (See the section "Recursive Rules" in Chapter 7 for why left-recursion is better.)

One of the rules for **items** has an empty right-hand side. For any recursive rule, there must be a terminating condition, a rule that matches the same non-terminal non-recursively. If a rule is purely recursive with no non-recursive alternative, most versions of yacc will halt with a fatal error since it is impossible to construct a valid parser under those circumstances. We will use left-recursion many times in many grammars.

In addition to being able to specify items within the menu, you may want to have a title at the top of the menu. Here is a grammar rule that describes a title:

```
title:        TITLE       QSTRING
         ;
```

The keyword **title** introduces a title. We require that the title be a quoted string. We add the new token **TITLE** to our lex specification:

```
   . . .
%%
title       { return TITLE; }
   . . .
```

We might want more than a single title line. Our addition to the grammar is:

```
titles:   /* empty */
        | titles title
        ;

title:        TITLE       QSTRING
         ;
```

A recursive definition allows multiple title lines.

The addition of title lines does imply that we must add a new, higher-level rule to consist of either items or titles. Titles will come before items, so Example 4-5 adds a new rule, **start**, to our grammar.

Example 4-5: Grammar with titles

```
%{
#include <stdio.h>
%}

%union {
        char *string;          /* string buffer */
}

%token COMMAND ACTION IGNORE EXECUTE ITEM TITLE
%token <string> QSTRING ID
%%
start: titles items
        ;

titles:   /* empty */
        | titles title
        ;

title:          TITLE          QSTRING
        ;

items:  /* empty */
        | items item
        ;

item:    ITEM command action
        ;

command:   /* empty */
        | COMMAND ID
        ;

action:   ACTION IGNORE
        | ACTION EXECUTE QSTRING
        ;
%%
```

After we'd used the MGL a little bit, we found that one menu screen wasn't enough. We wanted multiple screens and the ability to refer to one screen from another to allow multi-level menus.

We defined a new rule *screen*, to contains a complete menu with both titles and items. To add the handling of multiple screens, we can, once again, use a recursive rule to build a new **screens** rule. We wanted to allow for empty screens, so we added a total of five new sets of rules:

```
screens:  /* empty */
        | screens screen
        ;

screen:  screen_name screen_contents screen_terminator
       | screen_name screen_terminator
       ;

screen_name:  SCREEN ID
           | SCREEN
           ;

screen_terminator:  END ID
                 | END
                 ;

screen_contents: titles lines
```

We provide each screen with a unique name. When we wish to reference a particular menu screen, say, "first," we can use a line such as:

```
item "first" command first action menu first
```

When we name screens, we must also indicate when a screen ends, so we need a **screen_terminator** rule. Thus, a sample screen specification might be something like this:

```
screen main
title "Main screen"
item "fruits" command fruits action menu fruits
item "grains" command grains action menu grains
item "quit" command quit action quit
end main

screen fruits
title "Fruits"
item "grape" command grape action execute "/fruit/grape"
item "melon" command melon action execute "/fruit/melon"
item "main" command main action menu main
end fruits

screen grains
title "Grains"
item "wheat" command wheat action execute "/grain/wheat"
item "barley" command barley action execute "/grain/barley"
item "main" command main action menu main
end grains
```

Our rule *does* provide for the case when no name is given; hence, the two cases for **screen_name** and **screen_terminator**. When we actually write actions for the specific rules, we will check that the names are consistent, to detect inconsistent editing of a menu description buffer, for instance.

After some thought, we decided to add one more feature to our menu generation language. For each item, we wish to indicate if it is *visible* or *invisible*. Since of this is an attribute of the individual item, we precede the choice of visible or invisible with the new keyword **attribute**. Here is the portion of our new grammar that describes an attribute:

```
attribute: /* empty */
         | ATTRIBUTE VISIBLE
         | ATTRIBUTE INVISIBLE
         ;
```

We allow the attribute field to be empty to accept a default, probably *visible*. Example 4-6 is our workable grammar.

Example 4-6: Complete MGL grammar

```
screens:  /* empty */
        | screens screen
        ;

screen:   screen_name screen_contents screen_terminator
        | screen_name screen_terminator
        ;

screen_name:  SCREEN ID
            | SCREEN
            ;

screen_terminator:  END ID
                  | END
                  ;

screen_contents: titles lines
               ;

titles:  /* empty */
       | titles title
       ;

title: TITLE QSTRING
     ;

lines: line
     | lines line
     ;
```

Example 4-6: Complete MGL grammar (continued)

```
line: ITEM QSTRING command ACTION action attribute
        ;


command:  /* empty */
        | COMMAND ID
        ;

action:   EXECUTE QSTRING
        | MENU ID
        | QUIT
        | IGNORE
        ;

attribute:  /* empty */
          | ATTRIBUTE VISIBLE
          | ATTRIBUTE INVISIBLE
          ;
```

We have replaced the **start** rule of previous examples with the **screens** rule as the top-level rule. If there is no %**start** line in the declarations section, it simply uses the first rule.

Building the MGL

Now that we have a basic grammar, the work of building the compiler begins. First, we must finish modifying our lexical analyzer to cope with the new keywords we introduced in our last round of grammar changes. Our modified lex specification is shown in Example 4-7.

Example 4-7: MGL lex specification

```
ws        [ \t]+
comment   #.*
qstring   \"[^\"\n]*[\"\n]
id        [a-zA-Z][a-zA-Z0-9]*
nl        \n

%%

{ws}      ;
{comment} ;
{qstring} { yylval.string = strdup(yytext+1);
            if(yylval.string[yyleng-2] != '"')
              warning("Unterminated character string",(char *)0);
          else
              yylval.string[yyleng-2] = '\0'; /* remove close quote */
            return QSTRING;
          }
```

Example 4-7: MGL lex specification (continued)

```
screen     { return SCREEN; }
title      { return TITLE; }
item       { return ITEM; }
command    { return COMMAND; }
action     { return ACTION; }
execute    { return EXECUTE; }
menu       { return MENU; }
quit       { return QUIT; }
ignore     { return IGNORE; }
attribute  { return ATTRIBUTE; }
visible    { return VISIBLE; }
invisible  { return INVISIBLE; }
end        { return END; }
{id}       { yylval.string = strdup(yytext);
             return ID;
           }
{nl}       { lineno++; }
.          { return yytext[0]; }
%%
```

An alternative way to handle keywords is demonstrated in Example 4-8.

Example 4-8: Alternative lex specification

```
 . . .
id         [a-zA-Z][a-zA-Z0-9]*
%%
 . . .
{id}       { if(yylval.cmd = keyword(yytext)) return yylval.cmd;
             yylval.string = strdup(yytext);
             return ID;
           }
%%
/*
 * keyword: Take a text string and determine if it is, in fact,
 * a valid keyword.  If it is, return the value of the keyword;
 * if not, return zero.  N.B.:  The token values must be nonzero.
 */

static struct keyword {
char *name;     /* text string */
int value;      /* token */
} keywords[] =
{
"screen",   SCREEN,
"title",    TITLE,
"item",     ITEM,
"command",  COMMAND,
"action",   ACTION,
"execute",  EXECUTE,
"menu",     MENU,
"quit",     QUIT,
```

Example 4-8: Alternative lex specification (continued)

```
"ignore",     IGNORE,
"attribute",  ATTRIBUTE,
"visible",    VISIBLE,
"invisible",  INVISIBLE,
"end",        END,
NULL, 0,
};

int keyword(string)
   char *string;
   {
   struct keyword *ptr = keywords;

   while(ptr->name != NULL)
      if(strcmp(ptr->name,string) == 0)
        {
   return ptr->value;
}
   else
       ptr++;

   return 0; /* no match */
}
```

The alternate implementation in Example 4-8 uses a static table to identify keywords. The alternative version is invariably slower, since a lex lexer's speed is independent of the number or complexity of the patterns. We chose to include it here simply because it demonstrates a useful technique we could use if we wished to make the language's vocabulary extensible. In that case, we would use a single lookup mechanism for all keywords, and add new keywords to the table as needed.

Logically, we can divide the work in processing an MGL specification file into several parts:

Initialization   Initialize all internal data tables, emit any preambles needed for the generated code.

Start-of-screen processing   Set up a new screen table entry, add the name of the screen to the name list, and emit the initial screen code.

Screen processing   As we encounter each individual item, we deal with it; when we see title lines, we add them to the title list, and when we see new menu items, we add them to the item list.

End-of-screen processing　　　When we see the **end** statement, we process the data structures we have built
while reading the screen description and
emit code for the screen.

Termination　　　We "clean up" the internal state, emit any
final code, and assure that this termination
is OK; if there is a problem, we report it to
the user.

Initialization

A certain amount of work must be performed when any compiler begins
operation. For instance, internal data structures must be initialized; recall
that Example 4-8 uses a keyword lookup scheme rather than the hardcoded
keyword recognition scheme used earlier in Example 4-7. In a more complex application with a symbol table as part of initialization we would
insert the keywords into the symbol table as we did in Example 3-10.

Our **main()** routine starts out simply:

```
main()
{
    yyparse();
}
```

We must also be able to invoke our compiler by giving it a filename.
Because lex reads from **yyin** and writes to **yyout**, which are assigned to the
standard input and standard output by default, we can reattach the input
and output files to obtain the appropriate action. To change the input or
output, we open the desired files using *fopen()* from the standard I/O
library and assign the result to **yyin** or **yyout**.

If the user invokes the program with no arguments, we write out to a
default file, *screen.out*, and read from the standard input, *stdin.* If the user
invokes the program with one argument, we still write to *screen.out* and
use the named file as the input. If the user invokes the program with two
arguments, we use the first arguemnt as the input file and the second argument as the output file.

After we return from **yyparse()**, we perform post-processing and then
check to assure we are terminating with no error condition. We then clean
up and exit.

Example 4-9 shows our resulting **main()** routine.

Example 4-9: MGL main() routine

```
char *progname = "mgl";
int lineno = 1;

#define DEFAULT_OUTFILE "screen.out"

char *usage = "%s: usage [infile] [outfile]\n";

main(int argc, char **argv)
{
    char *outfile;
    char *infile;
    extern FILE *yyin, *yyout;

    progname = argv[0];

    if(argc > 3)
    {
        fprintf(stderr,usage, progname);
        exit(1);
    }
    if(argc > 1)
    {
        infile = argv[1];
        /* open for read */
        yyin = fopen(infile,"r");
        if(yyin == NULL) /* open failed */
        {
            fprintf(stderr,"%s: cannot open %s\n",
                    progname, infile);
            exit(1);
        }
    }

    if(argc > 2)
    {
        outfile = argv[2];
    }
    else
    {
        outfile = DEFAULT_OUTFILE;
    }

    yyout = fopen(outfile,"w");
    if(yyout == NULL) /* open failed */
    {
        fprintf(stderr,"%s: cannot open %s\n",
                progname, outfile);
        exit(1);
    }
```

Example 4-9: MGL main() routine (continued)

```
        /* normal interaction on yyin and
           yyout from now on */

        yyparse();

        end_file(); /* write out any final information */

        /* now check EOF condition */
        if(!screen_done) /* in the middle of a screen */
        {
                warning("Premature EOF",(char *)0);
                unlink(outfile); /* remove bad file */
                exit(1);
        }
        exit(0); /* no error */
}

warning(char *s, char *t) /* print warning message */
{
        fprintf(stderr, "%s: %s", progname, s);
        if (t)
                fprintf(stderr, " %s", t);
        fprintf(stderr, " line %d\n", lineno);
}
```

Screen Processing

Once we have initialized the compiler and opened the files, we turn our attention to the real work of the menu generator—processing the menu descriptions. Our first rule, **screens**, requires no actions. Our **screen** rule decomposes into the parts **screen_name**, **screen_contents**, and **screen_terminator**. **screen_name** interests us first:

```
screen_name:  SCREEN ID
            | SCREEN
            ;
```

We insert the specified name into our list of names duplicates; in case no name is specified, we will use the name "default." Our rule becomes:

```
screen_name:  SCREEN ID   { start_screen($2); }
            | SCREEN       { start_screen(strdup("default")); }
            ;
```

(We need the call to **strdup()** to be consistent with the first rule which passes a string dynamically allocated by the lexer.) The **start_screen** routine enters the name into our list of screens and begin to generate the code.

For instance, if our input file said "screen first", the **start_screen** routine would produce the following code:

```
/* screen first */
menu_first()
{
        extern struct item menu_first_items[];

        if(!init) menu_init();

        clear();
        refresh();
```

When processing our menu specification, the next object is a title line:

```
title: TITLE QSTRING
     ;
```

We call **add_title()**, which computes the positioning for the title line:

```
title: TITLE QSTRING { add_title($2); }
     ;
```

Our sample output for title lines looks like this:

```
        move(0,37);
        addstr("First");
        refresh();
```

We add a title line by positioning the cursor and printing out the given quoted string (with some rudimentary centering as well). This code can be repeated for each title line we encounter; the only change is to the line number used to generate the **move()** call.

To demonstrate this, we make a menu description with an extra title line:

```
screen first
title "First"
title "Copyright 1992"

item "first" command first action ignore
     attribute visible
item "second" command second action execute "/bin/sh"
     attribute visible
end first

screen second
title "Second"
item "second" command second action menu first
     attribute visible
item "first" command first action quit
     attribute invisible
end second
```

Our sample output for title lines is:

```
move(0,37);
addstr("First");
refresh();
move(1,32);
addstr("Copyright 1992");
refresh();
```

Once we see a list of item lines, we take the individual entries and build an internal table of the associated actions. This continues until we see the statement **end first** when we perform post-processing and finish building the screen. To build a table of menu items, we add the following actions to the **item** rule:

```
line: ITEM qstring command ACTION action attribute
        {
        item_str = $2;
        add_line($5, $6);
          $$ = ITEM;
          }
        ;
```

The rules for **command, action,** and **attribute** primarily store the token values for later use:

```
command: /* empty */ { cmd_str = strdup(""); }
       | COMMAND id  { cmd_str = $2; }
       ;
```

A **command** can be null or a specific command. In the first case we save a null string for the command name (using **strdup()** to be consistent with the next rule), and in the second we save the identifier given for the command in **cmd_str**.

The **action** rules and the associated actions are more complex, partially because of the larger number of variations possible:

```
action: EXECUTE qstring
          { act_str = $2;
          $$ = EXECUTE;
          }
      | MENU id
          { /* make "menu_" $2 */
          act_str = malloc(strlen($2) + 6);
          strcpy(act_str,"menu_");
            strcat(act_str, $2);
          free($2);
          $$ = MENU;
        }
      | QUIT   { $$ = QUIT; }
      | IGNORE { $$ = IGNORE; }
      ;
```

Finally, the **attribute** rule is simpler, as the only semantic value is represented by the token:

```
attribute:  /* empty */               { $$ = VISIBLE; }
          | ATTRIBUTE VISIBLE         { $$ = VISIBLE; }
          | ATTRIBUTE INVISIBLE       { $$ = INVISIBLE; }
          ;
```

The return values of the **action** rule and the **attribute** rule were passed to the **add_line** routine; this call takes the contents of the various static string pointers, plus the two return values, and creates an entry in the internal state table.

Upon seeing the **end first** statement, we must the final processing of the screen. From our sample output, we finish the **menu_first** routine:

```
        menu_runtime(menu_first_items);
}
```

The actual menu items are written into the array **menu_first_items**:

```
/* end first */
struct item menu_first_items[]={
     {"first","first",271,"",0,273},
     {"second","second",267,"/bin/sh",0,273},
     {(char *)0, (char *)0, 0, (char *)0, 0, 0},
};
```

The run-time routine **menu_runtime** will display the individual items; this will be included in the generated file as part of the code at the end.

Termination

The final stage of dealing with a single screen is to see the termination of that screen. Recall our **screen** rule:

```
screen:   screen_name screen_contents screen_terminator
        | screen_name screen_terminator
        ;
```

The grammar expects to see the **screen_terminator** rule:

```
screen_terminator:  END ID
                  | END
                  ;
```

We add a call to our post-processing routine for end-of-screen post-processing (not the end-of-file post-processing which we will discuss later in this section). The resulting rule is:

```
screen_terminator: END id { end_screen($2); }
               | END { end_screen(strdup("default")); }
               ;
```

It calls the routine **end_screen** with the name of the screen or "default" if no name is provided. This routine validates the screen name. Example 4-10 shows the code that implements it.

Example 4-10: Screen end code

```
/*
 * end_screen:
 * Finish screen, print out postamble.
 */

end_screen(char *name)
{
        fprintf(yyout, "menu_runtime(menu_%s_items);\n",name);

        if(strcmp(current_screen,name) != 0)
        {
                warning("name mismatch at end of screen",
                        current_screen);
        }
        fprintf(yyout, "}\n");
        fprintf(yyout, "/* end %s */\n",current_screen);

        process_items();

        /* write initialization code out to file */
        if(!done_end_init)
        {
                done_end_init = 1;
                dump_data(menu_init);
        }

        current_screen[0] = '\0';    /* no current screen */

        screen_done = 1;

        return 0;
}
```

This routine handles a screen name mismatch as a *nonfatal* error. Since the mismatch does not cause problems within the compiler, it can be reported to the user without termination.

This routine processes the data generated by our **add_item( )** call by processing individual item entries with **process_items( )**. Then it calls **dump_data** to write out some initialization routines; these initialization routines are really a static array of strings that are built into the MGL compiler. We call **dump_data( )** in several places to dump different code fragments to the output file. An alternative approach is to simply copy these code fragments from a "skeleton" file containing the boiler-plate code, as some versions of lex and yacc do.

Post-processing occurs after all input has been read and parsed. This is done by the **main( )** routine by calling **end_file( )** after **yyparse( )** has completed successfully. Our implementation is:

```
/*
 * this routine writes out the run-time support
 */

end_file()
{
        dump_data(menu_runtime);
}
```

This routine contains a single call to **dump_data( )** to write the runtime routines, which are stored in a static array in the compiler as the initialization code was. All our routines that handle the boiler-plate code are sufficiently modular in design that these could be rewritten to use skeleton files.

Once this routine has been called, the **main** routine terminates by checking to determine if the end of input was detected at a valid point, i.e., at a screen boundary, and is not generating an error message.

Sample MGL Code

Now that we have built a simple compiler, let's demonstrate the basic workings of it. Our implementation of the MGL consists of three parts: the yacc grammar, the lex specification, and our supporting code routines. The final version of our yacc grammar, lex lexer, and supporting code is shown in Appendix I, *MGL Compiler Code*.

We do not consider the sample code to be robust enough for serious use; our attention was given to developing a first-stage implementation. The resulting compiler will, however, generate a fully functional menu compiler. Here is our sample input file:

```
screen first
title "First"

item "dummy line" command dummy action ignore
     attribute visible
item "run shell" command shell action execute "/bin/sh"
     attribute visible

end first

screen second

title "Second"

item "exit program" command exit action quit
     attribute invisible
item "other menu" command first action menu first
     attribute visible

end second
```

When that description file was processed by our compiler, we got the following output file:

```
/*
 * Generated by MGL: Thu Aug 27 18:03:33 1992
 */

/* initialization information */
static int init;

#include <curses.h>
#include <sys/signal.h>
#include <ctype.h>
#include "mglyac.h"

/* structure used to store menu items */
struct item {
     char *desc;
     char *cmd;
     int  action;
     char    *act_str;     /* execute string */
     int (*act_menu)();    /* call appropriate function */
     int  attribute;
};

/* screen first */
menu_first()
{
     extern struct item menu_first_items[];
```

```
        if(!init) menu_init();

        clear();
        refresh();
        move(0,37);
        addstr("First");
        refresh();
        menu_runtime(menu_first_items);
}
/* end first */
struct item menu_first_items[]={
{"dummy line","dummy",269,"",0,271},
{"run shell","shell",265,"/bin/sh",0,271},
{(char *)0, (char *)0, 0, (char *)0, 0, 0},
};

menu_init()
{
        void menu_cleanup();

        signal(SIGINT, menu_cleanup);
        initscr();
        crmode();
}



menu_cleanup()
{
        mvcur(0, COLS - 1, LINES - 1, 0);
        endwin();
}

/* screen second */
menu_second()
{
        extern struct item menu_second_items[];

        if(!init) menu_init();

        clear();
        refresh();
        move(0,37);
        addstr("Second");
        refresh();
        menu_runtime(menu_second_items);
}
/* end second */
struct item menu_second_items[]={
{"exit program","exit",268,"",0,272},
{"other menu","first",267,"",menu_first,271},
{(char *)0, (char *)0, 0, (char *)0, 0, 0},
};

/* runtime */
```

```
menu_runtime(items)
struct item *items;
{
        int visible = 0;
        int choice = 0;
        struct item *ptr;
        char buf[BUFSIZ];

        for(ptr = items; ptr->desc != 0; ptr++) {
                addch('\n'); /* skip a line */
                if(ptr->attribute == VISIBLE) {
                        visible++;
                        printw("\t%d) %s",visible,ptr->desc);
                }
        }

        addstr("\n\n\t"); /* tab out so it looks nice */
        refresh();

        for(;;)
        {
                int i, nval;

                getstr(buf);

                /* numeric choice? */
                nval = atoi(buf);

                /* command choice ? */
                i = 0;
                for(ptr = items; ptr->desc != 0; ptr++) {
                        if(ptr->attribute != VISIBLE)
                                continue;
                        i++;
                        if(nval == i)
                                break;
                        if(!casecmp(buf, ptr->cmd))
                                break;
                }

                if(!ptr->desc)
                        continue;   /* no match */

                switch(ptr->action)
                {
                case QUIT:
                        return 0;
                case IGNORE:
                        refresh();
                        break;
                case EXECUTE:
                        refresh();
                        system(ptr->act_str);
                        break;
```

```
        case MENU:
                refresh();
                (*ptr->act_menu)();
                break;
        default:
                printw("default case, no action\n");
                refresh();
                break;
        }
        refresh();
    }
}

casecmp(char *p, char *q)
{
    int pc, qc;

    for(; *p != 0; p++, q++) {
        pc = tolower(*p);
        qc = tolower(*q);

        if(pc != qc)
            break;
    }
    return pc-qc;
}
```

In turn, we compiled this code, generated by our compiler and written to *first.c*, with the following command:

```
$ cat >> first.c
main()
{
menu_second();
menu_cleanup();
}
^D
$ cc -o first first.c -lcurses -ltermcap
$
```

We had to add a **main()** routine to the generated code; in a revision of the MGL, it might be desirable to include a command-line option or a specification option to provide the name of a routine to call from within the main loop; this a typical possible enhancement. Because we wrote our grammar in yacc, this modification would be easy. For example, we might modify the **screens** rule to read:

```
screens:  /* nothing */
        | preamble screens screen
        | screens screen
        ;
```

```
preamble: START ID
        | START DEFAULT
        ;
```

where we add appropriate keywords for **START** and **DEFAULT**.

Running our MGL-generated screen code, we see with the following menu screen:

```
                        Second

  1) other menu
```

We see the one visible menu entry, and when we enter "1" or "first" move to the first menu:

```
                        First
  1) dummy line
  2) run shell
```

Exercises

1. Add a command to identify the main screen and generate a main routine, as outlined previously.

2. Improve the screen handling: read characters in CBREAK mode rather than a line at a time, allow more flexible command handling, e.g., accept unique prefixes of commands rather than requiring the whole command, allow application code to set and clear the invisible attribute, etc.

3. Extend the screen definition language to let titles and command names come from variables in the host program, e.g.:

```
screen sample
title $titlevar

item $label1 command $cmd1 action ignore
    attribute visible

end sample
```

where **titlevar** and **label1** are character arrays or pointers in the host program.

4. (Term project) Design a language to specify pulldown or pop-up menus. Implement several translators based on the same parser so you can use the same menu specification to create menus that run in different environments, e.g., a terminal with curses, Motif, and Open Look.

5. Yacc is often used to implement "little languages" that are specific to an application area and translate into lower-level, more general languages. The MGL turns a menu specification into C, *eqn* turns an equation language into raw troff. What are some other application areas that would benefit from a little language? Design and implement a few of them with lex and yacc.

5

Parsing SQL

SQL (which stands for Structured Query Language and is usually pronounced *sequel*) is the most common language used to handle relational data bases.* First we'll develop a SQL parser that checks the syntax of its input but doesn't do anything else with it. Then we'll turn that into a preprocessor for SQL embedded in C programs.

This parser is based on the definition of SQL in C. J. Date, *A Guide to the SQL Standard*, Second Edition, Addison-Wesley, 1989. Date's description is written in *Backus-Naur Form* or *BNF*, a standard form used to write formal language descriptions. Yacc input syntax is similar to BNF except for the punctuation, so in many places it was sufficient to transliterate the BNF to get the corresponding yacc rules. In most cases we use the same symbol names Date did, although in a few places we've deviated from his usage in order to make the grammar suitable for yacc.

The ultimate definitions for SQL are the standards documents, ANSI X3.135-1989 (which defines SQL itself) and ANSI X3.168-1989 (which defines the way to embed SQL in other programming languages).

A Quick Overview of SQL

SQL is a special purpose language for relational data bases. Rather than manipulating data in memory, it manipulates data in data base tables, referring to memory only incidentally.

---

*SQL is the Fortran of data bases—nobody likes it much, the language is ugly and ad hoc, every data base supports it, and we all use it.

Relational Data Bases

A *data base* is a collection of *tables*, which are analogous to files. Each table contains *rows* and *columns*, which are analogous to records and fields. The rows in a table are not kept in any particular order. You create a set of tables by giving the name and type of each column:

```
CREATE SCHEMA
AUTHORIZATION JOHNL

CREATE TABLE Foods (
      name  CHAR(8) NOT NULL,
      type  CHAR(5),
      flavor      CHAR(6),
      PRIMARY KEY ( name )
)

CREATE TABLE Courses (
      course      CHAR(8) NOT NULL PRIMARY KEY,
      flavor      CHAR(6),
      sequence INTEGER
)
```

The syntax is completely free-format and there are often several different syntactic ways to write the same thing—notice the two different ways we gave the PRIMARY KEY specifier. (The *primary key* in a table is a column or set of columns that uniquely specify a row.) Figure 5-1 shows the two tables we just created after loading in data.

Foods

name	type	flavor
peach	fruit	sweet
tomato	fruit	savory
lemon	fruit	sour
lard	fat	bland
cheddar	fat	savory

Courses

course	flavor	sequence
salad	savory	1
main	savory	2
dessert	sweet	3

Figure 5-1: Two relational tables

To use a data base, you tell the data base what you want from your tables. It's up to the data base to figure out how to get it. The specification of a set of desired data is a *query*. For example, using the two tables in Figure 5-1, to get a list of fruits, you would say:

```
SELECT      Foods.name, Foods.flavor
FROM  Foods
WHERE Foods.type = "fruit"
```

The response is:

name   *flavor*

peach	sweet
tomato	savory
lemon	sour

You can also ask questions spanning more than one table. To get a list of foods suitable to each course of the meal, you say:

```
SELECT  course, name, Foods.flavor, type
FROM    Courses, Foods
WHERE   Courses.flavor = Foods.flavor
```

The response is:

course   *name*   *flavor*   *type*

course	name	flavor	type
salad	tomato	savory	fruit
salad	cheddar	savory	fat
main	tomato	savory	fruit
main	cheddar	savory	fat
dessert	peach	sweet	fruit

When listing the column names we can leave out the table name if the column name is unambiguous.

Manipulating Relations

SQL has a rich set of table manipulation commands. You can read and write individual rows with SELECT, INSERT, UPDATE, and DELETE commands. More commonly, you need to do something to each of a group of rows. In that case a different variant of SELECT defines a *cursor*, a sort of file pointer that can step through a set of rows to let you handle the rows one at a time. You then use OPEN and CLOSE commands to find the relevant rows and FETCH, UPDATE CURRENT, and DELETE CURRENT to do things to them. The COMMIT and ROLLBACK commands complete or abort a set of commands as a transaction.

The SELECT statement has a very complex syntax that lets you look for values in columns, compare columns to each other, do arithmetic, and compute minimum, maximum, average, and group totals.

Three Ways to Use SQL

In the original version of SQL, users typed commands into a file or directly at the terminal and received responses immediately. People still sometimes use it this way for creating tables and for debugging, but for the vast majority of applications, SQL commands come from inside programs and the results are returned to those programs.

The first approach to combining SQL with conventional languages was the SQL module language, which let you define little routines in SQL that you could call from conventional languages. Example 5-1 defines a cursor and three procedures that use it.

Example 5-1: Example of SQL module language

```
MODULE LANGUAGE C AUTHORIZATION JOHNL

DECLARE flav CURSOR FOR
        SELECT      Foods.name, Foods.type
        FROM   Foods
        WHERE Foods.flavor = myflavor
        -- myflavor is defined below

PROCEDURE open_flav
        SQLCODE
        myflavor CHAR(6) ;
        OPEN flav

PROCEDURE close_flav
        SQLCODE ;
        CLOSE flav

PROCEDURE get_flav
        SQLCODE
        myname CHAR(8)
        mytype CHAR(5) ;
        FETCH flav INTO myname, mytype
```

Within a C program one could use the routines in the module by writing:

```
char flavor[6], name[8], type[5];

main()
{
      int icode;

      scanf("%s", flavor);
      open_flav(&icode, flavor);
      for(;;) {
            get_flav(&icode, name, type);
            if(icode != 0)
                  break;
            printf("%8.8s %5.5s\n", name, type);
      }
      close_flav(&icode);
}
```

This works, but it is a pain in the neck to use, because every SQL statement you write has to be wrapped in a little routine. The approach people really use is *embedded SQL,* which lets you put chunks of SQL right in your program. Each SQL statement is introduced by "EXEC SQL" and ends with a semicolon. References to host language variables are preceded by a colon. Example 5-2 shows the same program written as embedded SQL.

Example 5-2: Example of embedded SQL

```
char flavor[6], name[8], type[5];
int SQLCODE;      /* global status variable */

EXEC SQL DECLARE flav CURSOR FOR
      SELECT      Foods.name, Foods.type
      FROM  Foods
      WHERE Foods.flavor = :flavor ;

main()
{
      scanf("%s", flavor);
      EXEC SQL OPEN flav ;
      for(;;) {
            EXEC SQL FETCH flav INTO :name, :type ;
            if(SQLCODE != 0)
                  break;
            printf("%8.8s %5.5s\n", name, type);
      }
      EXEC SQL CLOSE flav ;
}
```

To compile this, you run it through a SQL preprocessor which turns the SQL code into calls to C routines, then compile the pure C program. Later in this chapter, we'll write a simple version of such a preprocessor.

The Syntax Checker

Writing a syntax checker in yacc is easy. You parse something, and if the parse worked, the syntax must have been OK. (If we put some error recovery into the parser, things wouldn't be quite this simple. See Chapter 9 for details.) We'll build a syntax checker for SQL, a task which consists almost entirely of writing a yacc grammar for SQL. Since the syntax of SQL is so large, we have reproduced the entire yacc grammar in one place in Appendix J, with a cross-reference for all of the symbols in the grammar.

The Lexer

First we need a lexer for the tokens that SQL uses. The syntax is free format, with whitespace ignored except to separate words. There is a fairly long but fixed set of reserved words. The other tokens are conventional: names, strings, numbers, and punctuation. Comments are Ada-style, from a pair of dashes to the end of the line. Example 5-3 shows the SQL lexer.

Example 5-3: The first SQL lexer

```
%{
#include "sql1.h"
#include <string.h>

int lineno = 1;
void yyerror(char *s);
%}

%e 1200
%%
        /* literal keyword tokens */

ADA             { return ADA; }
ALL             { return ALL; }
AND             { return AND; }
AVG             { return AMMSC; }
MIN             { return AMMSC; }
MAX             { return AMMSC; }
SUM             { return AMMSC; }
COUNT           { return AMMSC; }
ANY             { return ANY; }
AS              { return AS; }
ASC             { return ASC; }
AUTHORIZATION       { return AUTHORIZATION; }
BETWEEN             { return BETWEEN; }
BY              { return BY; }
C               { return C; }
CHAR(ACTER)?        { return CHARACTER; }
CHECK           { return CHECK; }
```

Example 5-3: The first SQL lexer (continued)

```
CLOSE       { return CLOSE; }
COBOL       { return COBOL; }
COMMIT          { return COMMIT; }
CONTINUE    { return CONTINUE; }
CREATE          { return CREATE; }
CURRENT         { return CURRENT; }
CURSOR          { return CURSOR; }
DECIMAL         { return DECIMAL; }
DECLARE         { return DECLARE; }
DEFAULT         { return DEFAULT; }
DELETE          { return DELETE; }
DESC        { return DESC; }
DISTINCT    { return DISTINCT; }
DOUBLE          { return DOUBLE; }
ESCAPE          { return ESCAPE; }
EXISTS          { return EXISTS; }
FETCH       { return FETCH; }
FLOAT       { return FLOAT; }
FOR         { return FOR; }
FOREIGN         { return FOREIGN; }
FORTRAN         { return FORTRAN; }
FOUND       { return FOUND; }
FROM        { return FROM; }
GO[ \t]*TO  { return GOTO; }
GRANT       { return GRANT; }
GROUP       { return GROUP; }
HAVING          { return HAVING; }
IN          { return IN; }
INDICATOR   { return INDICATOR; }
INSERT          { return INSERT; }
INT(EGER)?  { return INTEGER; }
INTO        { return INTO; }
IS          { return IS; }
KEY         { return KEY; }
LANGUAGE    { return LANGUAGE; }
LIKE        { return LIKE; }
MODULE          { return MODULE; }
NOT         { return NOT; }
NULL        { return NULLX; }
NUMERIC         { return NUMERIC; }
OF          { return OF; }
ON          { return ON; }
OPEN        { return OPEN; }
OPTION          { return OPTION; }
OR          { return OR; }
ORDER       { return ORDER; }
PASCAL          { return PASCAL; }
PLI         { return PLI; }
PRECISION   { return PRECISION; }
PRIMARY         { return PRIMARY; }
PRIVILEGES  { return PRIVILEGES; }
PROCEDURE   { return PROCEDURE; }
```

Example 5-3: The first SQL lexer (continued)

```
PUBLIC              { return PUBLIC; }
REAL        { return REAL; }
REFERENCES  { return REFERENCES; }
ROLLBACK    { return ROLLBACK; }
SCHEMA              { return SCHEMA; }
SELECT              { return SELECT; }
SET         { return SET; }
SMALLINT    { return SMALLINT; }
SOME        { return SOME; }
SQLCODE             { return SQLCODE; }
TABLE       { return TABLE; }
TO          { return TO; }
UNION       { return UNION; }
UNIQUE              { return UNIQUE; }
UPDATE              { return UPDATE; }
USER        { return USER; }
VALUES              { return VALUES; }
VIEW        { return VIEW; }
WHENEVER    { return WHENEVER; }
WHERE       { return WHERE; }
WITH        { return WITH; }
WORK        { return WORK; }

     /* punctuation */

"="   |
"<>"  |
"<"   |
">"   |
"<="  |
">="        { return COMPARISON; }

[-+*/:(),.;]    { return yytext[0]; }


     /* names */
[A-Za-z][A-Za-z0-9_]*   { return NAME; }

     /* numbers */

[0-9]+      |
[0-9]+"."[0-9]* |
"."[0-9]*   { return INTNUM; }

[0-9]+[eE][+-]?[0-9]+   |
[0-9]+"."[0-9]*[eE][+-]?[0-9]+ |
"."[0-9]*[eE][+-]?[0-9]+        { return APPROXNUM; }

     /* strings */

'[^'\n]*'   {
            int c = input();
```

Example 5-3: The first SQL lexer (continued)

```
                unput(c);   /* just peeking */
                if(c != '\'')
                        return STRING;
                else
                        yymore();
        }

'[^'\n]*$   { yyerror("Unterminated string"); }

        /* whitespace */
\n              lineno++;

[ \t\r]+   ;    /* whitespace */

"--".*          ;       /* comment */

        /* anything else */
.               yyerror("invalid character);
%%

void
yyerror(char *s)
{
        printf("%d: %s at %s\n", lineno, s, yytext);
}

main(int ac, char **av)
{
        if(ac > 1 && (yyin = fopen(av[1], "r")) == NULL) {
                perror(av[1]);
                exit(1);
        }

        if(!yyparse())
                printf("SQL parse worked\n");
        else
                printf("SQL parse failed\n");
} /* main */
```

The lexer starts with a few include files, notably *sql1.h*, the token name definition file generated by yacc. (We renamed it from the default *y.tab.h*.) All of the reserved words are separate tokens in the parser, because it is the easiest thing to do. Notice that CHARACTER and INTEGER can be abbreviated to CHAR and INT, and GOTO can be written as one word or two. The reserved words AVG, MIN, MAX, SUM, and COUNT all turn into a **AMMSC** token; in the SQL preprocessor we'll use the token value to remember which of the words it was.

Next come the punctuation tokens, including the usual trick to match all of the single-character operators with the same pattern. Names start with a letter and are composed of letters, digits, and underscores. This pattern has to follow all of the reserved words so the reserved word patterns take precedence.

SQL defines exact numbers, which may have a decimal point (but no explicit exponent), and approximate numbers, which do have exponents. Separate patterns distinguish the two.

SQL strings are enclosed in single quotes, using a pair of quotes to represent a single quote in the string. The first string pattern matches a quoted string that contains no embedded quotes. Its action routine uses **input( )** and **unput( )** to peek at the next character and see if it's another quote (meaning that it found a doubled quote, not the end of the string). If so it uses **yymore( )** to append the next quoted string to the token. The next pattern catches unterminated strings and prints a diagnostic when it sees one.

The last few patterns skip whitespace, counting lines when the whitespace is a newline, skip comments, and complain if any invalid character appears in the input.

Error and Main Routines

This version of **yyerror( )** reports the current line number, current token, and an error message. This simple routine is often all you need for useful error reports. For maximum portability we've put it in with the lexer because it needs to refer to **yytext**, and only in the lexer's source file is **yytext** already defined. (Different versions of lex define **yytext** as an array or a pointer, so you can't portably write references to it anywhere else.)

The **main( )** routine opens a file named on the command line, if any, and then calls the parser. When the parser returns, the return value reports whether the parse succeeded or failed. We put **main( )** here because **yyin** is already defined here, though putting **main( )** in a file of its own and declaring **yyin** an external "*FILE* *" would have worked equally well.

The Parser

The SQL parser is larger than any of the parsers we've seen up to this point, but we can understand it in pieces.

Definitions

Example 5-4: Definition section of first SQL parser

```
%union {
        int intval;
        double floatval;
        char *strval;
        int subtok;
}

%token NAME
%token STRING
%token INTNUM APPROXNUM

        /* operators */

%left OR
%left AND
%left NOT
%left COMPARISON /* = <> < > <= >= */
%left '+' '-'
%left '*' '/'
%nonassoc UMINUS

        /* literal keyword tokens */

%token ALL AMMSC ANY AS ASC AUTHORIZATION BETWEEN BY
%token CHARACTER CHECK CLOSE COMMIT CONTINUE CREATE CURRENT
%token CURSOR DECIMAL DECLARE DEFAULT DELETE DESC DISTINCT DOUBLE
%token ESCAPE EXISTS FETCH FLOAT FOR FOREIGN FOUND FROM GOTO
%token GRANT GROUP HAVING IN INDICATOR INSERT INTEGER INTO
%token IS KEY LANGUAGE LIKE MODULE NULLX NUMERIC OF ON
%token OPEN OPTION ORDER PRECISION PRIMARY PRIVILEGES PROCEDURE
%token PUBLIC REAL REFERENCES ROLLBACK SCHEMA SELECT SET
%token SMALLINT SOME SQLCODE SQLERROR TABLE TO UNION
%token UNIQUE UPDATE USER VALUES VIEW WHENEVER WHERE WITH WORK
%token COBOL FORTRAN PASCAL PLI C ADA
```

Example 5-4 shows the definition section of the parser. First comes the definition of the value union. The fields **intval** and **floatval** handle integer and floating point numbers. (Actually, since SQL's exact numbers can include decimals, we'll end up storing all the numeric values as **floatval** s.) Strings can be returned as **strval**, although in this version of the parser we don't bother to do so. Finally, **subtok** holds sub-token codes for the tokens that represent multiple input tokens, e.g., AVG, MIN, MAX, SUM, and COUNT, although again we don't bother to do so in the syntax checker.

Next come definitions of the tokens used in the grammar. There are tokens for NAME, STRING, INTNUM, and APPROXNUM, all of which we saw in the lexer. Then all the operators appear in **%left** declarations to set their precedence and associativity. We declare the literal + – * / tokens since we need to set their precedence and the pseudo-token UMINUS which is used only in **%prec** clauses later.

Finally come the token definitions for all of SQL's reserved words.

Top Level Rules

Example 5-5: Top level rules in first SQL parser

```
sql_list:
            sql ';'
     |      sql_list sql ';'
     ;
     . . .
     /* schema definition language */
     /* Note: other "sql:" rules appear later in the grammar */
sql:        schema
     ;
     . . .
     /* module language */
sql:        module_def
     ;
     . . .
     /* manipulative statements */

sql:        manipulative_statement
     ;
```

Example 5-5 shows the top-level rules for the parser. The start rule is **sql_list**, a list of **sql** rules, each of which is one kind of statement. There are three different kinds of statements, a **schema** which defines tables, a **module_def** module definition, and a **manipulative_statement** which encompasses all of the statements such as OPEN, CLOSE, and SELECT that actually manipulate a data base. We've put a **sql** rule at the beginning of each of the sections of the grammar. (Yacc doesn't care if all of the rules with the same left-hand side appear together in the specification, and in cases like this it is easier if they don't. If you do this, be sure to include comments explaining what you've done.)

The Schema Sublanguage

Example 5-6: Schema sublanguage, top part

```
schema:
            CREATE SCHEMA AUTHORIZATION user opt_schema_element_list
        ;

user:       NAME
        ;

opt_schema_element_list:
            /* empty */
        |   schema_element_list
        ;

schema_element_list:
            schema_element
        |   schema_element_list schema_element
        ;

schema_element:
            base_table_def
        |   view_def
        |   privilege_def
        ;
```

The schema sublanguage defines data base tables. As in the example above, it starts with CREATE SCHEMA AUTHORIZATION "user", followed by an optional list of schema elements. Example 5-6 shows the top-level schema definition rules. We have a rule saying that a **user** is a NAME. Syntactically, we could have used NAME directly in the **schema** rule, but this separate rule provides a convenient place for action code that verifies that the name given is a plausible user name.

The schema element list syntax uses a lot of rules, but they're not complex. An **opt_schema_element_list** is either a **schema_element_list** or nothing, a **schema_element_list** is a list of **schema_elements**, and a **schema_element** is one of three kinds of definitions. We could have simplified these rules considerably to this:

```
opt_schema_element_list:
            /* empty */
        |   opt_schema_element_list base_table_def
        |   opt_schema_element_list view_def
        |   opt_schema_element_list privilege_def
        ;
```

although the more complex version turns out to be easier to use when we add action code.

Base Tables

Example 5-7: Schema sublanguage, base tables

```
base_table_def:
        CREATE TABLE table '(' base_table_element_commalist ')'
    ;

table:
        NAME
    |   NAME '.' NAME
    ;

base_table_element_commalist:
        base_table_element
    |   base_table_element_commalist ',' base_table_element
    ;

base_table_element:
        column_def
    |   table_constraint_def
    ;

column_def:
        column data_type column_def_opt_list
    ;

data_type:
        CHARACTER
    |   CHARACTER '(' INTNUM ')'
    |   NUMERIC
    |   NUMERIC '(' INTNUM ')'
    |   NUMERIC '(' INTNUM ',' INTNUM ')'
    |   DECIMAL
    |   DECIMAL '(' INTNUM ')'
    |   DECIMAL '(' INTNUM ',' INTNUM ')'
    |   INTEGER
    |   SMALLINT
    |   FLOAT
    |   FLOAT '(' INTNUM ')'
    |   REAL
    |   DOUBLE PRECISION
    ;

column_def_opt_list:
        /* empty */
    |   column_def_opt_list column_def_opt
    ;

column_def_opt:
        NOT NULLX
    |   NOT NULLX UNIQUE
    |   NOT NULLX PRIMARY KEY
```

Example 5-7: Schema sublanguage, base tables (continued)

```
    |       DEFAULT literal
    |       DEFAULT NULLX
    |       DEFAULT USER
    |       CHECK '(' search_condition ')'
    |       REFERENCES table
    |       REFERENCES table '(' column_commalist ')'
    ;

table_constraint_def:
            UNIQUE '(' column_commalist ')'
    |       PRIMARY KEY '(' column_commalist ')'
    |       FOREIGN KEY '(' column_commalist ')'
                REFERENCES table
    |       FOREIGN KEY '(' column_commalist ')'
                REFERENCES table '(' column_commalist ')'
    |       CHECK '(' search_condition ')'
    ;


column_commalist:
            column
    |       column_commalist ',' column
    ;

column:         NAME
    ;

literal:
            STRING
    |       INTNUM
    |       APPROXNUM
    ;
```

Example 5-7 shows the base table language. Again there is a lot of syntax, but it isn't complicated once you look at the parts. A base table definition **base_table_def** is "CREATE TABLE," the table name which may be a simple name or a name qualified by a user name, and a comma-separated list of base table elements in parentheses. Each **base_table_element** is a column definition or a table constraint definition.

A column definition **column_def** is a column name, its data type, and an optional list of column definition options. There are long lists of possible data types and of column definition options. Each column has exactly one data type, since there is one reference to **data_type**. Some of these tokens are reserved words and some are numbers, so that a type like NUMERIC(5,2) matches the fifth **data_type** rule. For the column definition options, **column_def_opt_list** allows zero or more options in any order. These options state whether a column may contain null (undefined) values, state whether values must be unique, set default values, or set validity check conditions or inter-table consistency (REFERENCES) conditions. The **search_condition** is defined later, since it is syntactically part of the manipulation language.

We represent the reserved word NULL by the token **NULLX**, because yacc defines all of the tokens as C preprocessor symbols, and the symbol NULL already means something in C. For the same reason, avoid the token names FILE, BUFSIZ, and EOF, all names preempted by symbols in the standard I/O library.

Base table elements can also be table constraints in one of several forms. SQL syntax is redundant here; these two forms are equivalent:

```
thing CHAR(3) NOT NULL UNIQUE

thing CHAR(3),
      UNIQUE ( some_name )
```

The first form is parsed as a **column_def** with "NOT NULL" and "UNIQUE" each being a **column_def_opt** in a **column_def_opt_list**. The second form is a **column_def** followed by a **table_constraint_def**, with each then being a **base_table_element** and the two combined in a **base_table_element_list**.

The SQL definition prohibits NULLs in unique columns, but is inconsistent about whether you have to say so explicitly. It is up to the action code to recognize that these two forms are equivalent, since syntactically they are different and that's all yacc knows about.

View Definition

A *view* is a virtual table defined by a query, whose contents are the result of executing the query each time an application opens the view.* For example, we could create a view of fruits in our food table:

```
CREATE VIEW fruits (frname, frflavor)
       AS SELECT Foods.name, Foods.flavor
       FROM Foods
       WHERE Foods.type = "fruit"
```

Example 5-8 shows the syntax for a schema view definition.

---

*This is a slight oversimplification, since in many cases you can write rows into a view and the data base updates the underlying tables appropriately.

Example 5-8: Schema view definitions

```
view_def:
            CREATE VIEW table opt_column_commalist
            AS query_spec opt_with_check_option
      ;

opt_with_check_option:
            /* empty */
      |     WITH CHECK OPTION
      ;

opt_column_commalist:
            /* empty */
      |     '(' column_commalist ')'
      ;
```

A view definition is "CREATE VIEW," the table name, an optional list of column names (the default being to use the names in the base table), the keyword "AS," a query specification (defined later), and an optional check option that controls the amount of error checking when new rows are written into the view.

Privilege Definitions

Example 5-9: Schema privilege definitions

```
privilege_def:
            GRANT privileges ON table TO grantee_commalist
            opt_with_grant_option
      ;

opt_with_grant_option:
            /* empty */
      |     WITH GRANT OPTION
      ;

privileges:
            ALL PRIVILEGES
      |     ALL
      |     operation_commalist
      ;

operation_commalist:
            operation
      |     operation_commalist ',' operation
      ;

operation:
            SELECT
```

Example 5-9: Schema privilege definitions (continued)

```
        |     INSERT
        |     DELETE
        |     UPDATE opt_column_commalist
        |     REFERENCES opt_column_commalist
        ;

grantee_commalist:
        grantee
        |     grantee_commalist ',' grantee
        ;

grantee:
        PUBLIC
        |     user
        ;
```

Example 5-9 shows the privilege definition sublanguage, the last of the view definition sublanguages. The owner of a table or view can give other users the authority to perform various operations on their tables, e.g.:

```
GRANT SELECT, UPDATE (address, telephone)
      ON employees TO PUBLIC

GRANT ALL ON foods TO tony, dale WITH GRANT OPTION

GRANT REFERENCES (flavor) ON Foods TO PUBLIC
```

WITH GRANT OPTION allows the grantees to re-grant their authority to other users. **REFERENCES** is the authority needed to create a table keyed to a column in an existing table. Otherwise both the syntax and meaning of the **GRANT** statement are fairly straightforward.

The Module Sublanguage

Since the module language is for practical purposes obsolete, we don't cover it in detail here. You can find its yacc definition in the complete listing of the SQL grammar in Appendix J.

Cursor Definitions

Example 5-10: Cursor definition

```
cursor_def:
        DECLARE cursor CURSOR FOR query_exp opt_order_by_clause
        ;

opt_order_by_clause:
        /* empty */
        |     ORDER BY ordering_spec_commalist
```

Example 5-10: Cursor definition (continued)

```
        ;

ordering_spec_commalist:      /* define sort order */
        ordering_spec
    |   ordering_spec_commalist ',' ordering_spec
        ;


ordering_spec:
        INTNUM opt_asc_desc      /* by column number */
    |   column_ref opt_asc_desc /* by column name */
        ;

opt_asc_desc:
        /* empty */
    |   ASC
    |   DESC
        ;

cursor:         NAME
        ;

column_ref:
        NAME         /* column name */
    |   NAME '.' NAME      /* table.col or range.col */
    |   NAME '.' NAME '.' NAME /* user.table.col */
        ;
```

We do need the cursor definition statements from the module language for use in embedded SQL. Example 5-10 shows the syntax for cursor definitions. A typical cursor definition is:

```
DECLARE course_cur CURSOR FOR
    SELECT      ALL
    FROM  Courses
    ORDER BY sequence ASC
```

Cursor definitions look a lot like view definitions, since both associate a name with a SELECT query. The difference is that a view is a permanent object that lives in the data base, while a cursor is a temporary object that lives in an application program. Practically, views can have their own privileges different from the tables on which they are built. (This is the main reason to create a view.) You need a cursor to read or write data in a program; to read or write a view you need a cursor on the view. Also, the query expression used to define a cursor is more general than the query specification used to define a view. We'll see both in connection with the SELECT statement, in the following section.

The Manipulation Sublanguage

The heart of SQL is the *manipulation sublanguage*, the commands that search, read, insert, delete, and update rows and tables.

Example 5-11: Manipulation sublanguage, top part

```
sql:        manipulative_statement
    ;

manipulative_statement:
            close_statement
    |       commit_statement
    |       delete_statement_positioned
    |       delete_statement_searched
    |       fetch_statement
    |       insert_statement
    |       open_statement
    |       rollback_statement
    |       select_statement
    |       update_statement_positioned
    |       update_statement_searched
    ;
```

There are 11 different kinds of manipulative statements, listed in the rules in Example 5-11. SQL statements are executed one at a time although some statements, particularly SELECT statements, can involve a lot of work on the part of the data base.

Simple Statements

Example 5-12: Simple manipulative statements

```
open_statement:
            OPEN cursor
    ;

close_statement:
            CLOSE cursor
    ;

commit_statement:
            COMMIT WORK
    ;

rollback_statement:
            ROLLBACK WORK
    ;

delete_statement_positioned:
            DELETE FROM table WHERE CURRENT OF cursor
    ;
```

Most manipulative statements are quite simple, so Example 5-12 shows them all. OPEN and CLOSE are analogous to opening and closing a file. DELETE ... WHERE CURRENT deletes a single record identified by a cursor.

The FETCH statement is the main way to retrieve data into a program. Its syntax is slightly more complex than that of previous statements because it says where to put the data, column by column.

FETCH Statements

Example 5-13: FETCH statement

```
fetch_statement:
            FETCH cursor INTO target_commalist
        ;

target_commalist:
            target
        |   target_commalist ',' target
        ;

target:
            parameter_ref
        ;

parameter_ref:
            parameter
        |   parameter parameter
        |   parameter INDICATOR parameter
        ;

parameter:
        |   ':' NAME    /* embedded parameter */
        ;
```

Example 5-13 shows the rules for FETCH. FETCH is complicated because of all the possible targets. Each target is one or two parameters, with the optional second parameter being an indicator variable that says whether the data stored was valid or null. A parameter is a host language variable name preceded by a colon in embedded SQL. In a procedure in the module language, a parameter can also be a name declared as a parameter in the module header, but in that case the lexer must distinguish parameter names from column and range names or yacc gets dozens of shift/reduce conflicts because it can't tell which names are which. To keep our syntax checker relatively simple, we'll leave out the module language names. In a worked out example, the lexer would look up each name in the symbol table and return a different token, e.g., **MODPARAM** for module parameter names, and we'd add a rule:

```
parameter: MODPARAM ;
```

INSERT Statements

Example 5-14: INSERT statement

```
insert_statement:
            INSERT INTO table opt_column_commalist values_or_query_spec
        ;

values_or_query_spec:
            VALUES '(' insert_atom_commalist ')'
        |   query_spec
        ;

insert_atom_commalist:
            insert_atom
        |   insert_atom_commalist ',' insert_atom
        ;

insert_atom:
            atom
        |   NULLX
        ;

atom:
            parameter_ref
        |   literal
        |   USER
        ;
```

The INSERT statement (Example 5-14), which inserts new rows into a table, has two variants. In both cases it takes a table name and an optional list of column names. (We can reuse **opt_column_commalist** which we already used in CREATE VIEW.) Then comes either a list of values or a query specification. The list of values is "VALUE" and a comma-separated list of **insert_atoms**. Each insert atom is either NULL, a parameter, a literal string or number, or "USER" meaning the current user's ID. The query specification **query_spec**, defined, selects existing data in the data base to copy into the current table.

DELETE Statements

Example 5-15: DELETE statement

```
delete_statement_positioned:
        DELETE FROM table WHERE CURRENT OF cursor
    ;


delete_statement_searched:
        DELETE FROM table opt_where_clause
    ;


opt_where_clause:
        /* empty */
    |   where_clause
    ;


where_clause:
        WHERE search_condition
    ;
```

The DELETE statement deletes one or more rows from a table. Its rules are listed in Example 5-15. The positioned version deletes the row at the cursor. The searched version deletes the rows identified by an optional WHERE clause, or in the absence of the WHERE clause, deletes all rows from the table. The WHERE clause uses a search condition (defined below) to identify the rows to delete.

UPDATE Statements

Example 5-16: UPDATE statement

```
update_statement_positioned:
        UPDATE table SET assignment_commalist
        WHERE CURRENT OF cursor
    ;


assignment_commalist:
    |   assignment
    |   assignment_commalist ',' assignment
    ;


assignment:
        column COMPARISON scalar_exp
    |   column COMPARISON NULLX
    ;


update_statement_searched:
        UPDATE table SET assignment_commalist opt_where_clause
    ;
```

The UPDATE statement (Example 5-16) rewrites one or more rows. There are two versions, positioned and searched, like the two kinds of DELETE. In both cases, a comma-separated list of assignments sets columns of the appropriate rows to new values, which can be NULL or a scalar expression.

Scalar Expressions

Example 5-17: Scalar expressions

```
scalar_exp:
            scalar_exp '+' scalar_exp
     |      scalar_exp '-' scalar_exp
     |      scalar_exp '*' scalar_exp
     |      scalar_exp '/' scalar_exp
     |      '+' scalar_exp %prec UMINUS
     |      '-' scalar_exp %prec UMINUS
     |      atom
     |      column_ref
     |      function_ref
     |      '(' scalar_exp ')'
     ;

scalar_exp_commalist:
            scalar_exp
     |      scalar_exp_commalist ',' scalar_exp
     ;

function_ref:
            AMMSC '(' '*' ')' /* COUNT(*) */
     |      AMMSC '(' DISTINCT column_ref ')'
     |      AMMSC '(' ALL scalar_exp ')'
     |      AMMSC '(' scalar_exp ')'
     ;

scalar_exp_commalist:
            scalar_exp
     |      scalar_exp_commalist ',' scalar_exp
     ;
```

Scalar expressions (Example 5-17) resemble arithmetic expressions in conventional programming languages. They allow the usual arithmetic operations with the usual precedences. Recall that we used **%left** to set precedences at the beginning of the grammar, and a **%prec** gives unary "+" and "−" the highest precedence. SQL also has a few built-in functions. The token AMMSC is a shorthand for any of AVG, MIN, MAX, SUM, or COUNT. The syntax here is actually somewhat looser than SQL allows. "COUNT(*)" counts the number of rows in a selected set, and is the only place where a "*" argument is allowed. (Action code has to check the token value of the AMMSC and complain if it's not a COUNT.) DISTINCT means to remove duplicate values before performing the function; it only permits a column reference. Otherwise functions can take any scalar reference.

We could have made the syntax rules more complex to better match the allowable syntax, but this way has two advantages: the parser is slightly smaller and faster; action routines can issue much more informative messages (for example, "MIN does not allow a * argument" rather than just "syntax error").

The definition of scalar functions is quite recursive, so these rules let you write extremely complex expressions, e.g.:

```
SUM( (p.age*p.age) / COUNT( p.age ) )  -  AVG( p.age ) * AVG(p.age )
```

which computes the mathematical variance of the **age** column in table **p**, probably very slowly.

We also define **scalar_exp_commalist**, a comma separated list of scalar expressions, for use later.

SELECT Statements

Example 5-18: SELECT statement, query specifications and expressions

```
select_statement:
            SELECT opt_all_distinct selection
            INTO target_commalist
            table_exp
      ;

opt_all_distinct:
            /* empty */
      |     ALL
      |     DISTINCT
      ;

selection:
            scalar_exp_commalist
      |     '*'
      ;

query_exp:
            query_term
      |     query_exp UNION query_term
      |     query_exp UNION ALL query_term
      ;

query_term:
            query_spec
      |     '(' query_exp ')'
      ;
```

Example 5-18: SELECT statement, query specifications and expressions (continued)

```
query_spec:
            SELECT opt_all_distinct selection table_exp
        ;
```

The SELECT statement (Example 5-18) selects one row (possibly derived from a lot of different rows in different tables) from the data base and fetches it into a set of local variables, using a **table_exp** (defined in the next section), which is a table-valued expression that selects a table or subtable from the data base. The optional ALL or DISTINCT keeps or discards duplicate rows.

A query expression, **query_exp**, and query specification, **query_spec** (also in Example 5-18), are similar table-valued forms. A query specification has almost the same form as a SELECT statement, but without the INTO clause, since the query specification will be part of a larger statement. A query expression can be a UNION of several query specifications; the results of the queries are merged together. (The specifications must all have the same number and types of columns.)

Table Expressions

Example 5-19: Table expressions

```
table_exp:
            from_clause
            opt_where_clause
            opt_group_by_clause
            opt_having_clause
        ;

from_clause:
            FROM table_ref_commalist
        ;

table_ref_commalist:
            table_ref
        |   table_ref_commalist ',' table_ref
        ;

table_ref:
            table
        |   table range_variable
        ;

range_variable:
            NAME
        ;
```

Example 5-19: Table expressions (continued)

```
where_clause:
        WHERE search_condition
    ;

opt_group_by_clause:
        /* empty */
    |   GROUP BY column_ref_commalist
    ;

column_ref_commalist:
        column_ref
    |   column_ref_commalist ',' column_ref
    ;

opt_having_clause:
        /* empty */
    |   HAVING search_condition
    ;
```

Table expressions (Figure 5-19) are what gives SQL its power, since they let you define arbitrarily elaborate expressions that retrieve exactly the data you want. A table expression starts with a mandatory FROM clause, followed by optional WHERE, GROUP BY, and HAVING clauses. The FROM clause names the tables from which the expression is constructed. The optional range variables let you use the same table more than once in separate contexts in an expression, which is occasionally useful, e.g., managers and employees both in a personnel table. The WHERE clause specifies a search condition that controls which rows from a table to include. The GROUP BY clause groups rows by a common column value, particularly useful if your selection includes functions like SUM or AVG, since then they sum or average by group. The HAVING clause applies a search condition group by group; e.g., in a table of suppliers, part names, and prices, you could ask for all the parts supplied by suppliers who sell at least three parts:

```
SELECT supplier
FROM p
GROUP BY supplier
HAVING COUNT(*) >= 3
```

Search Conditions

Example 5-20: Search conditions

```
search_condition:
      |     search_condition OR search_condition
      |     search_condition AND search_condition
      |     NOT search_condition
      |     '(' search_condition ')'
      |     predicate
      ;

predicate:
            comparison_predicate
      |     between_predicate
      |     like_predicate
      |     test_for_null
      |     in_predicate
    . |     all_or_any_predicate
      |     existence_test
      ;

comparison_predicate:
            scalar_exp COMPARISON scalar_exp
      |     scalar_exp COMPARISON subquery
      ;

between_predicate:
            scalar_exp NOT BETWEEN scalar_exp AND scalar_exp
      |     scalar_exp BETWEEN scalar_exp AND scalar_exp
      ;

like_predicate:
            scalar_exp NOT LIKE atom opt_escape
      |     scalar_exp LIKE atom opt_escape
      ;

opt_escape:
            /* empty */
      |     ESCAPE atom
      ;

test_for_null:
            column_ref IS NOT NULLX
      |     column_ref IS NULLX
      ;

in_predicate:
            scalar_exp NOT IN '(' subquery ')'
      |     scalar_exp IN '(' subquery ')'
      |     scalar_exp NOT IN '(' atom_commalist ')'
      |     scalar_exp IN '(' atom_commalist ')'
      ;
```

Example 5-20: Search conditions (continued)

```
atom_commalist:
            atom
     |      atom_commalist ',' atom
     ;

all_or_any_predicate:
            scalar_exp COMPARISON any_all_some subquery
     ;

any_all_some:
            ANY
     |      ALL
     |      SOME
     ;

existence_test:
            EXISTS subquery
     ;

subquery:
            '(' SELECT opt_all_distinct selection table_exp ')'
     ;
```

Search conditions specify which rows from a group you want to use. A search condition is a combination of predicates combined with AND, OR, and NOT. There are seven different kinds of predicates, a grab bag of operations that people like to do on data bases. Example 5-20 defines their syntax.

A *COMPARISON* predicate compares two scalar expressions, or a scalar expression and a subquery. Recall that a COMPARISON token is any of the usual comparison operators such as "=" and "<>". A *subquery* is a recursive SELECT expression that is restricted (semantically, not in the syntax) to return a single column.

A *BETWEEN* predicate is merely a shorthand for a pair of comparisons. These two predicates are equivalent, for example:

```
p.age BETWEEN 21 and 65

p.age >= 21 AND p.age <= 65
```

A *LIKE* predicate does some string pattern matching, comparing a scalar expression to an atom, the latter being a literal string or a string parameter reference. The atom to which an expression is compared is treated as a simple pattern, similar to UNIX shell filename patterns. The optional ESCAPE clause lets you specify a quoting character analogous to "\" in filename patterns.

The left operand of a LIKE predicate has to be a column reference, not a general expression. We've used a scalar expression here to get around a yacc limitation. A more natural syntax for LIKE predicates would be this:

```
like_predicate:
          column_ref NOT LIKE atom opt_escape
    |     column_ref LIKE atom opt_escape
    ;
```

Yacc might see something like this in the context of a predicate:

```
Foods.flavor NOT ...
```

At the time it sees the NOT, it can't tell if it is in the middle of a NOT BETWEEN or a NOT LIKE, so it can't tell whether "Foods.flavor" is a **column_ref** for a LIKE predicate or a **scalar_exp** for a BETWEEN predicate. Yacc reacts to this with a shift/reduce conflict since it can't tell whether or not to reduce the rule that turns the **column_ref** into a **scalar_exp**. There are a couple of ways around this problem. We've adjusted the grammar to take the reduce side of the shift/reduce conflict, allowing a **scalar_exp** either way, since action code can easily check the left operand of a NOT LIKE to ensure it's a column reference. (This also gives an opportunity for a better error message.) Another possibility would be a lexical hack. We could define a token NOTLIKE which matches two words in the lexer:

```
NOT[ \t]+LIKE    { return NOTLIKE; }
```

and use that in the LIKE predicate:

```
like_predicate:
          column_ref NOTLIKE atom opt_escape
    |     column_ref LIKE atom opt_escape
    ;
```

This solves the problem because yacc can now tell as soon as it sees the NOTLIKE token that it's parsing a LIKE predicate. But the lexical hack is ugly. (This version fails if NOT and LIKE are on separate lines. If we added a "\n" to the whitespace between them, we'd need to check in the lexical action to see if there are any newlines and, if so, update **lineno**, adding more mess.)

A test for null is just what it sounds like, testing whether the contents of a particular column are or are not null. We use the token name NULLX to avoid colliding with the *stdio* NULL symbol in the lexer.

An IN predicate checks to see whether a value is one of a set specified either explicitly or via a subquery. The explicit version is equivalent to a group of comparisons:

```
q.Name IN ( 'Tom', 'Dick', 'Harry' )

q.Name = 'Tom' OR q.Name = 'Dick' OR q.Name = 'Harry'
```

An ANY or ALL predicate lets you test whether any or all values of an expression satisfy a comparison with a subquery. These are sometimes useful but always confusing; it's hard to write ANY and ALL predicates correctly. This example checks that all of the names in the **Name** column of table **p** match names in the **name** column of table **q**:

```
p.Name =ALL (SELECT q.Name from q)
```

Finally, an existence test lets you test whether there are any data that satisfy some subquery.

Using all of the predicates and subqueries, you can create queries and table expressions of truly awesome complexity which will take equally awesome amounts of time to execute. In practice, most SQL SELECT expressions are simple, but the ability to perform complex operations is there for people who need it.

Odds and Ends

Example 5-21: Conditions for embedded SQL

```
        /* embedded condition things */
sql:        WHENEVER NOT FOUND when_action
    |       WHENEVER SQLERROR when_action
    ;

when_action:    GOTO NAME
    |       CONTINUE
    ;
```

Example 5-21 defines some statements of use only in embedded SQL programs. They say that whenever a selection doesn't retrieve any data (NOT FOUND) or some other error (SQLERROR) the program should either jump to a specific label in the host program or else ignore the condition.

Using the Syntax Checker

Example 5-22: Makefile for SQL syntax checker

```
LEX = flex -I
YACC = byacc -dv
CFLAGS = -DYYDEBUG=1

all:  sql1

sql1: sql1.o scn1.o
      ${CC} -o $@ sql1.o scn1.o

sql1.c sql1.h:    sql1.y
        ${YACC} sql1.y
      mv y.tab.h sql1.h
      mv y.tab.c sql1.c
      mv y.output sql1.out

scn1.o:     sql1.h
```

To compile the syntax checker, we just run the lexer and scanner through lex and yacc and compile the resulting C programs together. Example 5-22 shows the *Makefile*. In this case we've used *make* rules to rename the outputs of lex and yacc to match the input files. Also, we use Berkeley yacc and flex* and define our own **main( )** and **yyerror( )** so we don't need to use either the lex or yacc library. To test the syntax checker we can either check files full of SQL or else type in directly:

```
% sql1 sqlmod
SQL parse worked
% sql1
FETCH foo INTO
:a ,
b c, -- two names are legal
d e f-- but three aren't
4: syntax error at f
SQL parse failed
```

---

*Bugs in AT&T lex make it unable to handle the SQL lexer, but all of the other versions of lex accept it without trouble. All versions of yacc accept the parser.

Embedded SQL

We finish this chapter by turning our SQL syntax checker into a very simple embedded SQL preprocessor. Let's assume we have a SQL implementation that can interpret SQL statements passed as text strings. The embedded SQL preprocessor need only turn the SQL statements into C procedure calls that pass the SQL statements to an interpreter routine.

This is a little more complex than it looks. The lexer must run in two different states: normal state in which it just passes text through, and SQL mode in which it buffers up a SQL statement to pass to the interpreter. We also need to handle parameter references, since in the compiled program there is no way for the interpreter to associate the string ":foo" with the variable **foo**. We'll extract the parameters in the lexer, substituting "#*N*" for the Nth variable mentioned, and then pass all of the mentioned variables by reference in the argument list to the interpreter. For example, this embedded SQL:

```
EXEC SQL FETCH flav INTO :name, :type ;
```

should turn into this C:

```
exec_sql(" FETCH flav INTO  #1,  #2 ",   &name, &type);
```

Here we highlight the changes to the lexer and the parser. The full code is in Appendix J.

Changes to the Lexer

Example 5-23: Definitions in embedded lexer

```
%{
#include "sql2.h"
#include <string.h>

int lineno = 1;
void yyerror(char *s);

        /* macro to save the text of a SQL token */
#define SV save_str(yytext)

        /* macro to save the text and return a token */
#define TOK(name) { SV;return name; }
%}

%s SQL
```

The lexer actually has the largest set of changes. Example 5-23 shows the modified definitions. We have defined two C macros, **SV** that calls **save_str()** to save the text of the current token, and **TOK()** which saves the token text and returns a token to the parser. We've also added a new start state called **SQL**, using the standard **INITIAL** state as the normal non-SQL state.

Example 5-24: Embedded lexer rules

```
EXEC[ \t]+SQL      { BEGIN SQL; start_save(); }

        /* literal keyword tokens */

<SQL>ALL           TOK(ALL)
<SQL>AND           TOK(AND)
<SQL>AVG           TOK(AMMSC)
```

... all the other reserved words and tokens ...

```
        /* names */
<SQL>[A-Za-z][A-Za-z0-9_]*    TOK(NAME)

        /* parameters */
<SQL>":"[A-Za-z][A-Za-z0-9_]*{
                    save_param(yytext+1);
                    return PARAMETER;
            }

        /* numbers */

<SQL>[0-9]+ |
<SQL>[0-9]+"."[0-9]* |
<SQL>"."[0-9]*          TOK(INTNUM)

<SQL>[0-9]+[eE][+-]?[0-9]+    |
<SQL>[0-9]+"."[0-9]*[eE][+-]?[0-9]+ |
<SQL>"."[0-9]*[eE][+-]?[0-9]+TOK(APPROXNUM)

        /* strings */

<SQL>'[^'\n]*'    {
            int c = input();

            unput(c);   /* just peeking */
            if(c != '\") {
                SV;return STRING;
            } else
                yymore();
        }

<SQL>'[^'\n]*$    {    yyerror("Unterminated string"); }
```

Example 5-24: Embedded lexer rules (continued)

```
<SQL>\n            { save_str(" ");lineno++; }
\n         { lineno++; ECHO; }

<SQL>[ \t\r]+    save_str(" ");    /* whitespace */

<SQL>"--".* ;      /* comment */

.              ECHO; /* random non-SQL text */
%%
```

Example 5-24 shows the revised lexer rules. The first new rule matches the "EXEC SQL" keyword and puts the scanner into SQL state. It also calls **start_save()** to initialize the buffer where we'll save the SQL command. Then we prefix all of the existing token rules with "<SQL>" so they only match in SQL mode, and change the actions to use **SV** or **TOK()** to save each token. Since we need to treat parameters a little differently from other tokens, we've added a new lex rule for parameters which matches a colon followed by a name, and call **save_param()** to save the parameter reference. Our SQL rules that match a newline and whitespace each save a single space; since all whitespace is equivalent in SQL this makes the saved string shorter. Finally, we add two rules without the <SQL> prefix that match and echo all characters when we're not in SQL mode. In the user subroutines section, we add a tiny routine **un_sql()** which switches the lexer from SQL mode to INITIAL mode; this routine has to be in the lexer since that's the only place the BEGIN macro is defined.

```
/* leave SQL lexing mode */
un_sql()
{
     BEGIN INITIAL;
} /* un_sql */
```

Changes to the Parser

The changes to the parser are much smaller than the changes to the lexer. We add a %token definition of PARAMETER. We add actions to the start rules:

```
sql_list:
          sql ';'     { end_sql(); }
     |    sql_list sql ';' { end_sql(); }
     ;
```

These call the routine **end_sql()** each time a complete SQL statement has been parsed to switch the lexer out of SQL mode.

Since we now have a special token for parameters, we change our **parameter** rule to refer to the new token:

```
parameter:
            PARAMETER    /* :name handled in parser */
        ;
```

Since embedded SQL doesn't use the module language, we ripped out the rules for the module language, leaving only the rules for cursor definitions, and made a cursor definition a top-level SQL statement:

```
sql:
            cursor_def
        ;
```

That's it—the parser is otherwise unchanged.

Auxiliary Routines

Example 5-25: Highlights of embedded SQL text support routines

```
char save_buf[2000];     /* buffer for SQL command */
char *savebp;            /* current buffer pointer */

#define NPARAM   20      /* max params per function */
char *varnames[NPARAM]; /* parameter names */

/* start an embedded command after EXEC SQL */
start_save(void);

/* save a SQL token */
save_str(char *s);

/* save a parameter reference */
save_param(char *n);

/* end of SQL command, now write it out */
end_sql(void);
```

We wrote some string processing routines to buffer up and write out the SQL commands as they are parsed. The data structures and entry points are in Example 5-25, and the full text is in Appendix J. We save the commands in a large fixed character buffer, **save_buf[]** and use the character pointer **savebp** to track the current position in the buffer. Each variable name used as a parameter is saved in **varnames[]**. If a variable is used twice in the same command, we will only save it once.

Routine **start_save()** initializes the buffer pointer when the lexer sees "EXEC SQL". Each token is saved with **save_str()**, which appends its argument to **save_buf**. Parameter references are handled by **save_param()** which looks up its argument, the variable name, in **varnames[]**, entering the name if not already present, and then saves a reference of the form "#*N*".

When the parser has seen an entire SQL command, it calls **end_sql()**, which writes out a call to the run-time interpreter routine **exec_sql()**. It passes the saved buffer as a quoted string, breaking it into lines as necessary, and also passes the address of each variable in the parameter table. Finally, it calls our lexer routine **un_sql()** to take the lexer out of the SQL state. All of the output goes to **yyout**, the default lex output stream, just as the ECHO statements in the lexer pass through non-SQL code.

Using the Preprocessor

We changed the Makefile to link in our auxiliary routines with the lexer and parser. Since we haven't changed the **main** routine, other than its messages (a purely cosmetic change) we run the preprocessor the same way we ran the syntax checker.

Example 5-26 shows the result of running the preprocessor on the embedded SQL in Example 5-2.

Example 5-26: Output from embedded SQL preprocessor

```
char flavor[6], name[8], type[5];
int SQLCODE;      /* global status variable */
exec_sql(" DECLARE flav CURSOR FOR  SELECT Foods.name, Foods.\
type  FROM Foods  WHERE Foods.flavor =  #1 ",
      &flavor);

main()
{
      scanf("%s", flavor);
      exec_sql(" OPEN flav ");

      for(;;) {
            exec_sql(" FETCH flav INTO  #1,  #2 ",
      &name,
      &type);
            if(SQLCODE != 0)
                  break;
            printf("%8.8s %5.5s\n", name, type);
      }
      exec_sql(" CLOSE flav ");

}
```

Exercises

1. In several places, the SQL parser accepts more general syntax than SQL itself permits. For example the parser accepts the invalid scalar expression "MIN(*)" and it accepts any expression as the left operand of a LIKE predicate, although that operand has to be a column reference. Fix the syntax checker to diagnose these erroneous inputs. You can either change the syntax or add action code to check the expressions. Try both and see which is easier, and which gives better diagnostics.

2. Turn the parser into a SQL cross-referencer, which reads a set of SQL statements and produces a report showing for each name where it is defined and where it is referenced.

3. (Term project) Modify the embedded SQL translator to interface to a real data base on your system.

In this chapter:
- Structure of a Lex Specification
- Topics Organized Alphabetically

6

A Reference for Lex Specifications

In this chapter, we discuss the format of the lex specification and describe the features and options available. This chapter summarizes the capabilities demonstrated in previous chapters and covers features that have not been discussed.

After the section on the structure of a lex program, the sections in this chapter are in alphabetical order by feature.

Structure of a Lex Specification

A lex program consists of three parts: the definition section, the rules section, and the user subroutines.

```
... definition section ...
%%
... rules section ...
%%
... user subroutines ...
```

The parts are separated by lines consisting of two percent signs. The first two parts are required, although a part may be empty. The third part and the preceding %% line may be omitted. (This structure is the same as that used by yacc, from which it was copied.)

Definition Section

The definition section can include the *literal block, definitions, internal table declarations, start conditions,* and *translations.* (There is a section on each in this reference.) Lines that start with whitespace are copied verbatim to the C file. Typically this is used to include comments enclosed in "/*" and "*/", preceded by whitespace.

Rules Section

The rules section contains pattern lines and C code. A line that starts with whitespace, or material enclosed in "%{" and "%}" is C code. A line that starts with anything else is a pattern line.

C code lines are copied verbatim to the generated C file. Lines at the beginning of the rules section are placed near the beginning of the generated **yylex()** function, and should be declarations of variables used by code associated with the patterns and initialization code for the scanner. C code lines anywhere else are copied to an unspecified place in the generated C file, and should contain only comments. (This is how you put comments in the rules section outside of actions.)

Pattern lines contain a pattern followed by some whitespace and C code to execute when the input matches the pattern. If the C code is more than one statement or spans multiple lines, it must be enclosed in braces { }.*

When a lex scanner runs, it matches the input against the patterns in the rules section. Every time it finds a match (the matched input is called a *token*) it executes the C code associated with that pattern. If a pattern is followed by a single vertical bar, instead of C code, the pattern uses the same C code as the next pattern in the file. When an input character matches no pattern, the lexer acts as though it matched a pattern whose code is "ECHO;" which writes a copy of the token to the output.

User Subroutines

The contents of the user subroutines section is copied verbatim by lex to the C file. This section typically includes routines called from the rules. If you redefine **input()**, **unput()**, **output()**, or **yywrap()**, the new versions or supporting subroutines might be here.

In a large program, it is sometimes more convenient to put the supporting code in a separate source file to minimize the amount of material recompiled when you change the lex file.

---

*In the absence of braces, some versions of lex take the entire rest of the line, others just take up to a semicolon. For maximum clarity and portability, use braces for all but the most trivial C code.

BEGIN

The BEGIN macro switches among start states. You invoke it, usually in the action code for a pattern, as:

```
BEGIN statename;
```

The scanner starts in state 0 (zero), also known as INITIAL. All other states must be named in %s or %x lines in the definition section. (See the section "Start States" later in this chapter.)

Notice that even though BEGIN is a macro, the macro itself doesn't take any arguments, and the *statename* need not be enclosed in parentheses, although it is good style to do so.

Bugs

Like any other computer programs, versions of lex have their share of bugs. There are also a few common pattern matching peculiarities that are worth mentioning.

Ambiguous Lookahead

Patterns that use the trailing context operator, where the end of the token can match the same text as the beginning of the trailing context, don't work reliably. For example:

```
(a|ab)/ba
zx*/xy*
```

This is a problem with the pattern matching algorithm usually used, so it is unlikely to be fixed soon. *flex* will issue a warning when this problem makes it impossible to generate a correct scanner.

AT&T Lex

No two ways about it, AT&T lex is buggy. This is partly because it was the first implementation, and partly because it was written by an undergraduate summer intern. There is a bug with counted repetitions of character ranges, so patterns like this don't work:

```
[0-9]+-[0-9]{2}-[0-9]
```

We've also had trouble with comments in the rules section. For example, this example from Chapter 1 gets a spurious error message from lex unless you remove the two comment lines:

```
%%
\n    { state = LOOKUP; }    /* end of line, return to default state */

      /* whenever a line starts with a reserved part of speech name */
      /* start defining words of that type */

^verb { state = VERB; }
^adj  { state = ADJ; }
^adv  { state = ADV; }
  . . .
```

There is also an unfortunate tendency for complicated scanners generated by AT&T lex to fail in hard-to-pinpoint ways.

Flex

flex is much more reliable than AT&T lex. As of version 2.3.7, the only bug of which we are aware is an obscure one related to the "|" action. This script looks for *troff* macros that make the word "lex" italic and de-italicizes them.

```
%%

^\.I\ +lex$          |
^\.I\ *\"lex\"$            { fputs("lex", yyout); }

%%
```

The input:

```
.I lex
```

produces `lexx` rather than the correct `lex`. If you write out the action twice, the bug goes away.*

Character Translations

Most versions of lex have character translations introduced by %T. Unfortunately, what they do in different versions varies wildly.

---

*We've told the maintainer of *flex* about this, so by the time you read this it may already be fixed.

In AT&T lex and MKS lex, a lexer normally uses the native character code that the C compiler uses, e.g., the code for the character "A" is the C value "A". Now and then it is convenient to use some other character code, either because the input stream uses a different code, such as baudot or EBCDIC, or because lex is looking for patterns in an input stream not consisting of text at all. Lex character translations let you define an explicit mapping between bytes that are read by **input( )** and the characters used in lex patterns. The translations are preceded and followed by lines consisting of %T. Each translation line contains a number, some whitespace, and then one or more characters. For example:

```
%T
1       aA
2       bB
3       cC
%T
```

In this example, an input byte with value 1 will match anywhere there is an "A" or "a" in a pattern, an input byte with value 2 will match anywhere there is a "B" or "b", and an input byte with value 3 will match anywhere there is a "C" or "c".

You may need to modify the **input( )** and **unput( )** macros in AT&T lex or **yygetc( )** in MKS lex to produce appropriate values if they do not come directly from a file.

If you use translations, every literal character used in a lex pattern must appear on the right side of a translation line.

flex has a different, nearly useless, version of translations which we do not document here. It is scheduled to be removed from future versions of *flex*. The simplest application of *flex*'s translations, folding upper and lowercase letters together, is available much more easily by using the *−i* flag with *flex*.

Context Sensitivity

Lex provides several ways to make your patterns sensitive to left and right context, that is, to the text that precedes or follows the token.

Left Context

There are three ways to handle left context: the special beginning of line pattern character, start states, and explicit code.

The character "^" at the beginning of a pattern tells lex to match the pattern only at the beginning of the line. The "^" doesn't match any characters, it just specifies the context.

Start states can be used to require that one token precede another:

```
%s MYSTATE
%%
first { BEGIN MYSTATE; }
. . .
<MYSTATE>second    { BEGIN 0; }
```

In this lexer, the token **second** is only recognized after the token **first**. There may be intervening tokens between **first** and **second**.

In some cases you can fake left context sensitivity by setting flags to pass context information from one token's routine to another:

```
%{
int flag = 0;
%}
%%
a      { flag = 1; }
b      { flag = 2; }
zzz    {
             switch(flag) {
       case 1:    a_zzz_token(); break;
       case 2:    b_zzz_token(); break;
       default: plain_zzz_token(); break;
             }
             flag = 0;
       }
```

Right Context

There are three ways to make token recognition depend on the text to the right of the token: the special end of line pattern character, the slash operator, and **yyless()**.

The "$" character at the end of a pattern makes the token only match at the end of a line, i.e., immediately before a \n character. Like the "^" character, "$" doesn't match any characters, it just specifies context. It is exactly equivalent to "/\n", and therefore, can't be used with trailing context.

The "'/'" characters in a pattern let you include explicit trailing context. For instance, the pattern "abc/de" matches the token "abc", but only if it is immediately followed by "de". The "/" itself matches no characters. Lex counts trailing context characters when deciding which of several patterns has the longest match, but the characters do not appear in **yytext[ ]**, nor are they counted in **yyleng**.

The **yyless( )** function tells lex to "push back" part of the token that was just read. The argument to **yyless( )** is the number of token characters to keep. For example:

```
abcde { yyless(3); }
```

has nearly the same effect as "abc/de" does because the call to **yyless( )** keeps three characters of the token and puts back the other two. The only differences are that in this case the token in **yytext[ ]** contains all five characters and **yyleng** contains five instead of three.

Definitions (Substitutions)

Definitions (or substitutions) allow you to give a name to all or part of a regular expression, and refer to it by name in the rules section. This can be useful to break up complex expressions and to document what your expressions are supposed to be doing. A definition takes this form:

```
NAME  expression
```

The name can contain letters, digits, and underscores, and must not start with a digit. Some implementations also allow hyphens.

In the rules section, patterns may include references to substitutions with the name in braces, for example, "{NAME}". The expression corresponding to the name is substituted literally into pattern. For example:

```
DIG   [0-9]
. . .
%%
{DIG}+          process_integer();
{DIG}+\.{DIG}*    |
\.{DIG}+   process_real();
```

There is one small way that the treatment of substitutions varies among versions of lex. In most versions, when the pattern corresponding to the name is substituted in, it is treated as though it were surrounded by parentheses. In a few versions, though, it is not. This makes a difference in some cases such as:

```
PAT    abc
%%
{PAT}+
```

If the pattern is treated as "(abc)+", it matches any number of copies of "abc", while if it is "abc+", it matches "abc" followed by any number of c's. To maximize portability, enclose the patterns in definitions in parentheses, as shown here:

```
PAT    (abc)
```

ECHO

In the C code associated with a pattern, the macro **ECHO** writes the token to the current output file *yyout*. It is equivalent to:

```
fprintf(yyout, "%s", yytext);
```

The default action in lex for input text that doesn't match any pattern is to write the text to the output, equivalent to **ECHO**. In flex, the command-line flag *–s* makes the default action abort, useful in the common case that the scanner is supposed to include patterns to handle all possible input.

In some versions of lex, you can redefine **ECHO** to do something else with the characters. If you redefine **ECHO**, you will also probably want to redefine **output()**, which normally sends a single character to *yyout*.

Include Operations (Logical Nesting of Files)

Many input languages have some sort of include statement that logically inserts another file in place of the include statement. At the beginning of your program, you can assign any open *stdio* file to **yyin** to have the scanner read from that file. Unfortunately, there is no portable way in lex to handle nested input files, but here are some hints for major implementations.

File Chaining with yywrap()

When a lexer reaches the end of the input file, it calls **yywrap()**. You can write your own **yywrap()** that switches to a new input file by changing or reopening **yyin**, and continue scanning. See the section "yywrap()" for more details.

File Nesting

You handle nested files differently in different versions of lex. We briefly describe the facilities provided by the major implementations.

AT&T Lex

In AT&T lex, you can redefine the standard **input()** and **unput()** macros to handle multiple input files. You'll need to keep a stack or linked list of structures containing the FILE pointer, the pushback buffer and indices, and line number in the file, and have **input()** and **unput()** use the top structure on the stack. At the end of a file, close the file, remove the top structure from the stack, and continue from the next file on the stack.

Flex

In flex you cannot redefine **input()** or **unput()**. (The lexer doesn't even use them itself, but takes characters from the underlying data structures for speed.) But you can redefine YY_INPUT, which is the macro that flex calls to read text from the input file. (See "Input from Strings.") Even more useful are flex buffers, defined as type *YY_BUFFER_STATE*. The routine **yy_create_buffer(***FILE*, sizez0***)**, makes a new flex buffer of the given size, usually YY_BUF_SIZE,* reading from the stdio FILE. A call to **yy_switch_to_buffer(***flexbuf***)** tells the scanner to read from the corresponding file, and **yy_delete_buffer(***flexbuf***)** gets rid of a flex buffer. The current buffer is YY_CURRENT_BUFFER. Also helpful is the special token pattern "<<EOF>>" which matches at the end of a file after the call to **yywrap()**.

MKS Lex

MKS lex defines routines **yySaveScan()** and **yyRestoreScan()** to save and restore the current state of the scanner. They use an object of type YY_SAVED that contains the state. To save the state, call **yySaveScan(***file***)**. It returns a YY_SAVED object, and arranging to read from the stdio stream *file*. To restore a previously saved state, call **yyRestoreScan(***saved***)** which restores a previously saved state.

---

* See "yytext" for the implications of changing the flex buffer size.

Abraxas Pclex

Although pclex is based on flex, pclex does not include the buffer-switching routines available in flex. Saving and restoring buffer states is so difficult as to be impractical.

One approach is to include multiple copies of the scanner and to switch scanners when you need to handle an included file. For more information, see "Multiple Lexers in One Program."

POSIX Lex

The POSIX.2 standard takes a simple approach to file inclusion: it doesn't support it at all. There is no standard way in POSIX lex to handle multiple input files other than **yywrap()**. Most implementations will provide some sort of support as an extension, but you'll have to consult the documentation for your specific version.

Input from Strings

Normally lex reads from a file, but sometimes you want it to read from some other source, such as a string in memory. All versions of lex make this possible, but the details vary considerably.

AT&T Lex

AT&T lex reads all of its input with the **input()** macro. To change the input source, redefine the **input()** and **unput()** macros. For example:

```
%{
extern char *mystring;

#undef input
#undef unput
#define input()   (*mystring++)
#define unput(c)  (*--mystring = c)
%}
```

At the end of the input data, **input()** should return 0.

Flex

Although flex provides an **input()** function, it gets characters using optimized in-line code. You can redefine YY_INPUT, the macro it uses to read blocks of data. It is called as:

```
YY_INPUT(buffer, result, max_size)
```

where **buffer** is a character buffer, **result** is a variable in which to store the number of characters actually read, and **max_size** is the size of the buffer. To read from a string, have your version of YY_INPUT copy data from your string buffer (Example 6-1).

Example 6-1: Taking flex input from a string

```
%{
#undef YY_INPUT
#define YY_INPUT(b, r, ms) (r = my_yyinput(b, ms))
%}
. . .
extern char myinput[];
extern char *myinputptr;/* current position in myinput */
extern int *myinputlim; /* end of data */

int
my_yyinput(char *buf, int max_size)
{
        int n = min(max_size, myinputlim - myinputptr);

        if(n > 0) {
                memcpy(buf, myinputptr, n);
                myinputptr += n;
        }
        return n;
}
```

Abraxas Pclex

Since pclex is derived from flex, it uses the same input mechanism. Redefine YY_INPUT() as described above to change the input source.

MKS Lex

MKS lex uses the macro **yygetc()** to read all input characters. To change the input source, redefine **yygetc()**. MKS lexers handle pushback automatically, so you need not worry about it. At the end of input, **yygetc()** returns

EOF. Here is a possible definition, slightly convoluted to return EOF when the character in the string is a null:

```
%{
extern char *mystring;
#undef yygetc
#define yygetc() (*mystring? *mystring++ : EOF)
%}
```

POSIX Lex

The POSIX standard doesn't define any way to change the input source, so programs that read from some other place than **yyin** are not portable from one implementation to another.

input()

The **input()** routine provides characters to the lexer. In some versions of lex, e.g., AT&T lex, it is a macro, while others, e.g., flex, define it as a function.

When the lexer matches characters it conceptually calls **input()** to fetch each character. Some implementations bypass **input()** for performance reasons, but the effect is the same.

The most likely place to call **input()** is in an action routine to do something special with the text that follows a particular token. For example, here is a way to handle C comments:

```
"/*" {      int c1 = 0, c2 = input();

            for(;;) {
                if(c2 == EOF)
                    break;
                if(c1 == '*' && c2 == '/')
                    break;
                c1 = c2;
                c2 = input();
            }
      }
```

The calls to **input()** process the characters until either end-of-file or the characters "*/" occur. This approach is the easiest way to handle C style comments in the absence of exclusive start states (see "Start States"), and is always the best way to handle long quoted strings and other tokens that might be too long for lex to buffer itself.

In some versions of lex it is possible to redefine **input( )** to take input from something other than a stdio file. Other versions of lex don't let you redefine **input( )**, but have other ways to change the input source. See "Input from Strings" for details. Remember that a redefined **input( )** has to be able to handle characters pushed back by **unput( )**.

Internal Tables (%N Declarations)

AT&T and MKS lex use internal tables of a fixed size which may not be big enough for large scanners, although they do allow the programmer to increase the size of the tables explicitly. You increase the sizes of the tables with "%a", "%e", "%k", "%n", "%o", and "%p" lines in the definition section, for example:

```
%p 6000
%e 3000
```

To find out what the current statistics are, run lex with the *–v* flag. For example, the MGL lexer in Example 4-7 produces this report:

```
151/2000 nodes(%e), 551/5000 positions(%p), 86/2500 (%n),
6182 transitions, 27/1000 packed char classes(%k),
234/5000 packed transitions(%a), 241/5000 output slots(%o)
```

Clearly, it normally takes a significantly larger grammar than this to fill the default size of the tables.

It is possible to construct regular expressions that will lead to very large state machines which need larger than normal tables. In general, it is better to simplify these expressions by either writing them in a simpler form, splitting them into multiple expressions, or writing C code to handle more of the work.

Except for very large projects, it should not be necessary to increase the table sizes. Unless lex complains that one of the tables has overflowed, you need not worry about them at all. To figure out optimal sizes for the tables, significantly increase the sizes of the tables that overflow, run lex with the *–v* flag, and adjust the values closer to the actual needs of the lexer.

Some very old versions of lex also accept "%r" to make lex generate a lexer in Ratfor and "%c" for a lexer in C.

lex Library

Most lex implementations come with a library of helpful routines. You can link in the library by giving the *−ll* flag at the end of the *cc* command line on UNIX systems, or the equivalent on other systems. The contents of the library vary among implementations, but it always contains **main( )**.

main( )

All versions of lex come with a minimal **main** program which can be useful for quickie programs and for testing. It's so simple we reproduce it here:

```
main(int ac, char **av)
{
        return yylex();
}
```

As with any library routine, you can provide your own **main( )**.

Other Library Routines

Many of the routines that you can call from lex scanners, e.g., **yymore( )**, **yyless( )**, and **yywrap( )** may also be in the library, along with routines that support other lex features such as **REJECT**.

Any lex program can redefine **yywrap( )** to change what happens at end of file. Many implementations also let you redefine **input( )**, **unput( )**, and **output( )**. See the sections on those routines for details.

Line Numbers and yylineno

If you keep track of the line number in the input file, you can report it in error messages. Some versions of lex define **yylineno** to contain this line number and automatically update it, but most do not.

Keeping track of the line number is easy. Initialize your line number variable to 1, and increment it in any lex rule that matches a newline character, as shown here:

```
%{
        int lineno = 1;
%}
%%
    . . .
\n      { lineno++; }
```

Lexers that handle nested include files have to save and restore the line number associated with each file.

Literal Block

The literal block in the definition section is C code bracketed by the lines "%{" and "%}".

```
%{
    ... C code and declarations ...
%}
```

The contents of the literal block are copied verbatim to the generated C source file near the beginning, before the beginning of **yylex( )**. The literal block usually contains declarations of variables and functions used by code in the rules section, as well as **#include** lines for header files.

Multiple Lexers in One Program

You may want to have lexers for two partially or entirely different token syntaxes in the same program. For example, an interactive debugging interpreter might have one lexer for the programming language and use another for the debugger commands.

There are two basic approaches to handling two lexers in one program: combine them into a single lexer, or put two complete lexers into the program.

Combined Lexers

You can combine two lexers into one by using start states. All of the patterns for each lexer are prefixed by a unique set of start states. When the lexer starts, you need a little code to put the lexer into the appropriate initial state for the particular lexer in use, e.g., the following code (which will be copied at the front of **yylex( )**):

```
%s INITA INITB INITC
%%
%{
        extern first_tok, first_lex;

        if(first_lex) {
                BEGIN first_lex;
                first_lex = 0;
        }
        if(first_tok) {
                int holdtok = first_tok;
```

```
                first_tok = 0;
                return holdtok;
        }
%}
```

In this case, before you call the lexer, you set **first_lex** to the initial state for the lexer. You will usually use a combined lexer in conjunction with a combined yacc parser, so you'll also usually have code to force an initial token to tell the parser which grammar to use. See "Variant and Multiple Grammars" in Chapter 8.

The advantage of this approach is that the object code is somewhat smaller, since there is only one copy of the lexer code, and the different rule sets can share rules. Disadvantages are that you have to be careful to use the correct start states everywhere, you cannot have both lexers active at once (i.e., you can't call **yylex( )** recursively), and it is difficult to use different input sources for the different lexers.

Multiple Lexers

The other approach is to include two complete lexers in your program. Lex doesn't make this easy, because every lexer it generates has the same entry point: **yylex( )**. Furthermore, most versions of lex put the scanning tables and scanner buffers in global variables with names like **yycrank** and **yysvec**. If you just translated two scanners and compiled and linked all the two resulting files (renaming at least one of them to something other than *lex.yy.c*), you would still get a long list of multiply defined symbols. The trick is to change the names that lex uses for its functions and variables.

Using the p Flag

Some versions of lex, notably MKS lex, provide a command-line switch –*p* to change the prefix used on the names in the scanner generated by lex. For example, the command:

```
lex -p pdq myscan.y
```

produces a scanner with the entry point **pdqlex( )**, which reads from file **pdqin** and so forth. The names affected are **yylex( )**, **yyin**, **yyout**, **yytext**, **yylineno**, **yyleng**, **yymore( )**, **yyless( )**, **yywrap( )**, as well as all of the implementation-specific variables. The other variables used in the lexer are renamed and are also made static. There is also a **-o** flag to specify the name of the generated lexer, e.g.:

```
lex -p pdq -o pdqtab.c mygram.y
```

produces *pdqtab.c*.

Faking It

Lex has no automatic way to change the names in the generated C routine, so you have to fake it. On UNIX systems, the easiest way to fake it is with the stream editor *sed*. Assuming you are using AT&T lex, create the file *yy-lsed* containing these *sed* commands. (Here we use the new prefix "pdq".)

```
s/yyback/pdqback/g
s/yybgin/pdqbgin/g
s/yycrank/pdqcrank/g
s/yyerror/pdqerror/g
s/yyestate/pdqestate/g
s/yyextra/pdqextra/g
s/yyfnd/pdqfnd/g
s/yyin/pdqin/g
s/yyinput/pdqinput/g
s/yyleng/pdqleng/g
s/yylex/pdqlex/g
s/yylineno/pdqlineno/g
s/yylook/pdqlook/g
s/yylsp/pdqlsp/g
s/yylstate/pdqlstate/g
s/yylval/pdqlval/g
s/yymatch/pdqmatch/g
s/yymorfg/pdqmorfg/g
s/yyolsp/pdqolsp/g
s/yyout/pdqout/g
s/yyoutput/pdqoutput/g
s/yyprevious/pdqprevious/g
s/yysbuf/pdqsbuf/g
s/yysptr/pdqsptr/g
s/yysvec/pdqsvec/g
s/yytchar/pdqtchar/g
s/yytext/pdqtext/g
s/yytop/pdqtop/g
s/yyunput/pdqunput/g
s/yyvstop/pdqvstop/g
s/yywrap/pdqwrap/g
```

Then, after you run lex, this command edits the generated scanner:

```
sed -f yy-lsed lex.yy.c > lex.pdq.c
```

You would probably want to put these rules in a *Makefile*:

```
lex.pdq.c: myscan.l
        lex -t myscan.l | sed -f yy-lsed > $@
```

If you are using MS-DOS and don't have access to *sed*, in the worst case you can go through the generated C file by hand, changing the names.

Another approach that may be easier in some cases is to use C preprocessor **#define s** at the beginning of the grammar to rename the variables:

```
%{
#define yyback pdqback
#define yybgin pdqbgin
#define yycrank pdqcrank
#define yyerror pdqerror
#define yyestate pdqestate
#define yyextra pdqextra
#define yyfnd pdqfnd
#define yyin pdqin
#define yyinput pdqinput
#define yyleng pdqleng
#define yylex pdqlex
#define yylineno pdqlineno
#define yylook pdqlook
#define yylsp pdqlsp
#define yylstate pdqlstate
#define yylval pdqlval
#define yymatch pdqmatch
#define yymorfg pdqmorfg
#define yyolsp pdqolsp
#define yyout pdqout
#define yyoutput pdqoutput
#define yyprevious pdqprevious
#define yysbuf pdqsbuf
#define yysptr pdqsptr
#define yysvec pdqsvec
#define yytchar pdqtchar
#define yytext pdqtext
#define yytop pdqtop
#define yyunput pdqunput
#define yyvstop pdqvstop
#define yywrap pdqwrap
%}
```

This avoids using *sed*. In practice you will probably want to rename both lex and yacc names, so put all of the definitions for both in a file, say *pdqdefs.h*. Wherever you use the names, include *pdqdefs.h* first, for instance, in the lex source file:

```
%{
#include "pdqdefs.h"
#include "pdq.tab.h"
%}
```

In this case *pdq.tab.h* is the yacc-generated header that includes the token name definitions. Since it usually defines **yylval**, it needs to follow *pdqdefs.h*.

For flex lexers, the variables that need to be renamed are:

```
yy_create_buffer
yy_delete_buffer
yy_init_buffer
yy_load_buffer_state
yy_switch_to_buffer
yyin
yyleng
yylex
yyout
yyrestart
yytext
```

You can use either of the two techniques above to rename them.

output()

Some versions of lex define a function or macro **output(***c***)** that writes its argument to the output file *yyout*. This is always equivalent to:

```
putc(c, yyout)
```

If it exists, you can use it in your actions, and the scanner may use it to implement the default action that sends unmatched characters to the output.

If **output()** is a macro, you may want to define it to do something different with unmatched input characters.

A well-designed lexer usually has cases that match all possible input, in which case **output()** should never be called automatically from inside the lexer.

If you redefine **output()**, also redefine the macro ECHO which copies the current contents of **yytext** to the output.

Portability of Lex Lexers

Lex lexers are fairly portable among C implementations. There are two levels at which you can port a lexer: the original lex specification or the C source file generated by lex.

Porting Lex Specifications

As long as you can avoid using the implementation-specific features of one implementation, you can usually write portable lex specifications. Particular issues are:

- Don't use exclusive start states if you want to port to AT&T lex.
- Maximum table sizes vary, so a lexer that fits in one implementation may be too big for another.
- The size of the token buffer **yytext** varies from as little as 100 bytes up to 8K bytes.
- Take input only from the usual input file **yyin**, since there is no standardization of taking input from anywhere else. See the sections "Input from Strings" and "Include Operations" for details.

Porting Generated C Lexers

Most versions of lex generate portable C code, and you can usually move the code to any C compiler without trouble.

Libraries

The lex library is usually provided only in object form. For the two standard library routines, **main()** and **yywrap()**, this is rarely a problem since you can easily write your own versions. See "lex Library." Some versions, notably AT&T lex, put other routines such as **yyreject()** and **yyless()** into the library. If you use them, you can't port lexers unless you have the library source. Flex uses no library, so its code is usually the most portable.

Buffer Sizes

You may want to adjust the size of some buffers. Flex uses two input buffers, each by default 8K, which may be too big for some microcomputer implementations. See "yytext" for details on adjusting buffer sizes.

Character Sets

The knottiest portability problem involves character sets. The C code generated by every lex implementation uses character codes as indexes into tables in the lexer. If both the original and target machine use the same character code, such as ASCII, the ported lexer will work. You may have to deal with different line end conventions: UNIX systems end a line with a plain "\n" while MS-DOS and other systems use "\r\n". You often can have lexers ignore "\r" and treat "\n" as the line end in either case.

When the original and target machine use different character sets, e.g., ASCII and EBCDIC, the lexer won't work at all, since all of the character codes used as indexes will be wrong. Sophisticated users have sometimes been able to post-process the tables to rebuild them for other character sets, but in general the only reasonable approach is to find a version of lex that runs on the target machine, or else to redefine the lexer's input routine to translate the input characters into the original character set. See "Input from Strings" for how to change the input routine.

The translation tables in AT&T lex and MKS lex provide a way to specify character codes explicitly, so if you are willing to use fixed numeric codes for all your characters, you can write very portable lexers. See "Character Translations."

Regular Expression Syntax

Lex patterns are an extended version of the regular expressions used by editors and utilities such as *grep*. *Regular expressions* are composed of normal characters, which represent themselves, and metacharacters which have special meaning in a *pattern*. All characters other than these listed below are regular characters. Whitespace (spaces and tabs) separate the pattern from the action and so must be quoted to include them in a pattern.

Metacharacters

.   Matches any single character except the newline character "\n".

[]   Match any one of the characters within the brackets. A range of characters is indicated with the "–" (dash), e.g., "[0–9]" for any of the 10 digits. If the first character after the open bracket is a dash or close bracket, it is not interpreted as a metacharacter. If the first character is a circumflex "^" it changes the meaning to match any character except those within the brackets. (Such a character class *will* match a newline unless you explicitly exclude it.) Other metacharacters have no special meaning within square brackets except that C escape sequences starting with "\" are recognized. POSIX lex adds more special square bracket patterns for internationalization. See below for details.

*   Matches zero or more of the preceding expression. For example, the pattern:

```
a.*z
```

matches any string that starts with "a" and ends with "z", such as "az" "abz" or "alcatraz".

\+   Matches one or more occurence of the preceding regular expression. For example:

```
x+
```

matches "x", "xxx", or "xxxxxx", but not an empty string, and

```
(ab)+
```

matches "ab", "abab", "ababab", and so forth.

?   Matches zero or one occurrence of the preceding regular expression. For example:

```
-?[0-9]+
```

indicates a number with an optional leading unary minus.

{}   Mean different things depending on what is inside. A single number "{n}" means n repetitions of the preceding pattern, e.g.,

```
[A-Z]{3}
```

matches any three uppercase letters. If the braces contain two numbers separated by a comma, "{n,m}", they are a minimum and maximum number of repetitions of the preceding pattern. For example:

```
A{1,3}
```

matches one to three occurrences of the letter "A". If the second number is missing, it is taken to be infinite, so "{1,}" means the same as "+" and "{0,}" the same as "*".

If the braces contain a name, it refers to the substitution by that name.

\   If the following character is a lowercase letter, then it is a C escape sequence such as "\t" for tab. Some implementations also allow octal and hex characters in the form "\123" and

"\x3f". Otherwise "\" quotes the following character, so "*" matches an asterisk.

( )   Group a series of regular expressions together. Each of "*", "+", and "[]" effects only the expression immediately to its left, and " | " normally affects everything to its left and right. Parentheses can change this, for example:

```
(ab|cd)?ef
```

matches "abef", "cdef", or just "ef".

| Match either the preceding regular expression or the subsequent regular expression. For example:

```
twelve|12
```

matches either "twelve" or "12".

"..."   Match everything within the quotation marks literally. Metacharacters other than "\" lose their meaning. For example:

```
"/*"
```

matches the two characters "/*".

/   Matches the preceding regular expression but only if followed by the following regular expression. For example:

```
0/1
```

matches "0" in the string "01" but does not match anything in the strings "0" or "02". Only one slash is permitted per pattern, and a pattern cannot contain both a slash and a trailing "$".

^   As the first character of a regular expression, it matches the beginning of a line; it is also used for negation within square brackets. Otherwise not special.

$ As the last character of a regular expression, it matches the end of a line—otherwise not special. Same meaning as "/\n" when at the end of an expression.

< >   A name or list of names in angle brackets at the beginning of a pattern makes that pattern apply only in the given start states.

<<EOF>>   (flex only) In flex the special pattern <<EOF>> matches the end of file.

POSIX Extensions

POSIX defines new regular expression syntax to handle character sets other than ASCII and languages other than English in a portable and language-independent way. These are supposed to be accepted by all utilities which handle regular expressions such as *sed* and *grep*, as well as in lex. The three new expressions are collating symbols, equivalence classes, and character classes.

A *collating symbol* is a multicharacter sequence which is treated as a single character, such as Spanish "ch" and "ll" or Dutch "ij". A collating symbol is written inside square brackets and dots, e.g., "[.ch.]". Collating symbols are only recognized within character class expressions, such as "[abc[.ch.]d]".

An *equivalence class* is a set of characters that sort together, typically accented versions of the same letter such as "a", "á", and "â". The characters in the class are enclosed inside square brackets and equal signs; for instance, "[=a=]" stands for any one of the characters in the class, in this example the same as "[aáâ]".

A *character class* expression stands for any character of a named type handled by the *ctype* macros, with the types being **alnum**, **alpha**, **blank**, **cntrl**, **digit**, **graph**, **lower**, **print**, **punct**, **space**, **upper**, and **xdigit**. The class name is enclosed in square brackets and colons. For example, "[:digit:]" would be equivalent to "[0123456789]".

As of this writing no versions of lex handle any of the POSIX extensions, but flex will handle them in the near future.

REJECT

Usually lex separates the input into non-overlapping tokens. But sometimes you want all occurrences of a token even if it overlaps with other tokens. The special action **REJECT** lets you do this. If an action executes **REJECT**, lex conceptually puts back the text matched by the pattern and finds the next best match for it. The example finds all occurrences of the words "pink", "pin", and "ink" in a file, even when they overlap:

```
   . . .
%%
pink  { npink++; REJECT; }
ink   { nink++; REJECT; }
pin   { npin++; REJECT; }
.    |
\n    ;      /* discard other characters */
```

If the input contains the word "pink," all three patterns will match. Without the **REJECT** statements, only "pink" would match.

Scanners that use **REJECT** may be much larger and slower than those that don't, since they need considerable extra information to allow backtracking and re-lexing.

Returning Values from yylex()

The C code executed when a pattern matches a token can contain a **return** statement which returns a value from **yylex()** to its caller, typically a parser generated by yacc. The next time **yylex()** is called, the scanner picks up where it left off.

When a scanner matches a token of interest to the parser (e.g., a keyword, variable name, or operator) it uses **return** to pass the token back to the parser. When it matches a token not of interest to the parser (e.g., whitespace or a comment) it does not return, and the scanner immediately proceeds to match another token.

This means that you cannot restart a lexer just by calling **yylex()**. You have to reset it into the default state using **BEGIN INITIAL**, discard any input text buffered up by **unput()**, and otherwise arrange so that the next call to **input()** will start reading the new input.

Flex makes restarting considerably easier. A call to **yyrestart(***file***)**, where *file* is a standard I/O file pointer, arranges to start reading from that file.

In pclex you can reset the scanner's state with the macro **YY_INIT**. You'll probably want to rewind **yyin** or assign it to a new file.

In MKS lex you can use **YY_INIT**, a macro that only works within the scanner file, or call **yy_reset()** which is a routine that you can call from anywhere.

Start States

You can declare *start states*, also called *start conditions* or *start rules*, in the definition section. Start states are used to limit the scope of certain rules, or to change the way the lexer treats part of the file. For example, suppose we have the following C preprocessor directive:

```
#include <somefile.h>
```

Normally, the angle brackets and the filename would be scanned as the five tokens "<", "somefile", ".", "h", and ">", but after "#include" they are a single filename token. You can use a start state to apply a set of rules only at certain times. Be warned that those rules that do not have start states can apply in *any* state!* The BEGIN statement (q.v.) in an action sets the current start state. For example:

```
^"#include" { BEGIN INCLMODE; }
<INCLMODE>"<"[^>\n]+">"   {  ... do something with the name ...  }
<INCLMODE>\n      { BEGIN INITIAL; /* return to normal */ }
```

You declare a start state with %s lines. For example:

```
%s PREPROC
```

creates the start state PREPROC. In the rules section, then, a rule that has <PREPROC> prepended to it will *only* apply in state PREPROC. The standard state in which lex starts is state zero, also known as INITIAL.

Flex and most versions other than AT&T lex also have exclusive start states declared with %x. The difference between regular and exclusive start states is that a rule with no start state is *not* matched when an exclusive state is active. In practice, exclusive states are a lot more useful than regular states, and you will probably want to use them if your version of lex supports them.

Exclusive start states make it easy to do things like recognize C language comments:

```
%x CMNT
%%
"/*" BEGIN CMNT;            /* switch to comment mode */
<CMNT>.                |
<CMNT>\n ;                  /* throw away comment text */
<CMNT>"*/"BEGIN INITIAL;    /* return to regular mode */
```

This wouldn't work using regular start states since all of the regular token patterns would still be active in CMNT state.

---

*Indeed, this is a singularly common lex programming mistake. This problem is fixed by exclusive start states, as described in this section.

In versions of lex that lack exclusive start states, you can get the same effect more painfully by giving an explicit state to your normal state and by putting a start state on each expression. Assuming that the normal state is called **NORMAL**, the example above becomes:

```
%s NORMAL CMNT
%%
%{
      BEGIN NORMAL;     /* start in NORMAL state */
%}
<NORMAL>"/*"              BEGIN CMNT; /* switch to comment mode */
<CMNT>.           |
<CMNT>\n     ;      /* throw away comment text */
<CMNT>"*/"  BEGIN NORMAL;      /* return to regular mode */
```

This isn't quite equivalent to the scanner above, because the **BEGIN NORMAL** is executed each time the routine **yylex()** is called, which it will be after any token that returns a value to the parser. If that causes a problem, you can have a "first time" flag, e.g.:

```
%s NORMAL CMNT
%{
      static int first_time = 1;
%}
. . .
%%
%{
      if(first_time) {
            BEGIN NORMAL;
            first_time = 0;
      }
%}
. . .
```

unput()

The routine **unput(**c**)** returns the character c to the input stream. Unlike the analogous stdio routine **unputc()**, you can call **unput()** several times in a row to put several characters back in the input. The limit of data "pushed back" by **unput()** varies, but it is always at least as great as the longest token the lexer recognizes.

Some implementations let you redefine **input()** and **unput()** to change the source of the scanner's input. If you redefine **unput()**, you have to be prepared to handle multiple pushed back characters. If the scanner itself calls **unput()**, it will always put back the same characters it just got from **input()**, but there is no requirement that calls to **unput()** from user code to do so.

When expanding macros such as C's **#define**, you need to insert the text of the macro in place of the macro call. One way to do this is to call **unput()** to push back the text, e.g.:

```
... in lexer action code ...
char *p = macro_contents();
char *q = p + strlen(p);

while(q > p)
      unput(*--q);        /* push back right-to-left */
```

yyinput(), yyoutput(), yyunput()

Some versions of lex, notably AT&T lex, provide the functions **yyinput()**, **yyoutput()**, and **yyunput()** as wrappers for the macros **input()**, **output()**, and **unput()**, respectively. These exist so that they can be called from other source modules, in particular the lex library. If you need them, and your version of lex doesn't define them, define them yourself in the user subroutines section:

```
int yyinput(void) { return input(); }
int yyoutput(int c) { output(c); }
int yyunput(int c) { unput(c); }
```

yyleng

Whenever a scanner matches a token, the text of the token is stored in the null terminated string **yytext** and its length is in **yyleng**. The length in **yyleng** is the same as the value that would be returned by **strlen(yytext)**.

yyless()

You can call **yyless(*n*)** from the code associated with a rule to "push back" all but the first *n* characters of the token. This can be useful when the rule to determine the boundary between tokens is inconvenient to express as a regular expression. For example, consider a pattern to match quoted strings, but where a quotation mark within a string can be escaped with a backslash:

```
\"[^"]*\"   { /* is the char before close quote a \ ? */
          if(yytext[yyleng-2] == '\\') {
                yyless(yyleng-1); /* return last quote */
                yymore();         /* append next string */
```

```
        }
   }
```

If the quoted string ends with a backslash before the closing quotation mark, it uses **yyless()** to push back the closing quote, and **yymore ()** (q.v.) to tell lex to append the next token to this one. The next token will be the rest of the quoted string starting with the pushed back quote, so the entire string will end up in **yytext**.

A call to **yyless()** has the same effect as calling **unput()** with the characters to be pushed back, but **yyless()** is often much faster because it can take advantage of the fact that the characters pushed back are the same ones just fetched from the input.

Another use of **yyless()** is to reprocess a token using rules for a different start state:

```
sometoken   { BEGIN OTHER_STATE; yyless(0); }
```

BEGIN tells lex to use another start state, and the call to **yyless()** pushes back all of the token's characters so they can be reread using the new start state. If the new start state doesn't enable different patterns that take precedence over the current one, **yyless(0)** will cause an infinite loop in the scanner as the same token is repeatedly recognized and pushed back.

yylex()

The scanner created by lex has the entry point **yylex()**. You call **yylex()** to start or resume scanning. If a lex action does a **return** to pass a value to the calling program, the next call to **yylex()** will continue from the point where it left off. (See "Returning Values from yylex()" for how to begin scanning a new file.)

User Code in yylex()

All code in the rules section is copied into **yylex()**. Lines starting with whitespace are presumed to be user code. Lines of code immediately after the "%%" line are placed near the beginning of the scanner, before the first executable statement. This is a good place to declare local variables used in code for specific rules. Keep in mind that although the contents of these variables are preserved from one rule to the next, if the scanner returns and is called again, automatic variables will not keep the same values.

Code on a pattern line is executed when that pattern is matched. The code should either be one statement on one line, ending with a semicolon, or else a block of code enclosed in braces. When code is not enclosed in braces, some implementations copy the entire line, while others only copy one statement. For example, in the following case:

```
[0-9]+          yylval.ival = atoi(yytext); return NUMBER;
```

some versions will throw away the **return** statement. (Yes, this is poor design.) As a rule, use braces if there is more than one statement:

```
[0-9]+          { yylval.ival = atoi(yytext); return NUMBER; }
```

If the code on a line is a single vertical bar, the pattern uses the same code as the next pattern does:

```
%%
colour      |
color { printf("Color seen\n");
```

Code lines starting with whitespace that occur after the first pattern line are also copied into the scanner, but there is no agreement among implementations where they end up. These lines should contain only comments:

```
rule1 { some statement; }

        /* this comment describes the following rules */

rule2 { other statement; }
```

yymore()

You can call **yymore()** from the code associated with a rule to tell lex to append the next token to this one. For example:

```
%%
hyper yymore();
text  printf("Token is %s\n", yytext);
```

If the input string is "hypertext," the output will be "Token is hypertext."

Using **yymore()** is most often useful where it is inconvenient or impractical to define token boundaries with regular expressions. See "yyless()" for an example.

yytext

Whenever a lexer matches a token, the text of the token is stored in the null terminated string **yytext**. In some implementations of lex, **yytext** is a character array declared by:

```
extern char yytext[];
```

In others it is a character pointer declared by:

```
extern char *yytext;
```

Since the C language treats arrays and pointers in almost the same way, it is almost always possible to write lex programs that work either way. If you reference **yytext** in other source files, you must ensure that they reference it correctly. POSIX lex includes the new definition lines **%array** and **%pointer** which you can use to force **yytext** to be defined one way or the other, for compatibility with code in other source files.

The contents of **yytext** are replaced each time a new token is matched. If the contents of **yytext** are going to be used later, e.g., by an action in a yacc parser which calls the lex scanner, save a copy of the string by using **strdup()**, which makes a copy of the string in freshly allocated storage, or a similar routine.

If **yytext** is an array, any token which is longer than **yytext** will overflow the end of the array and cause the lexer to fail in some hard to predict way. In AT&T lex, the standard size for **yytext[]** is 200 characters, and in MKS lex it is 100 characters. Even if **yytext** is a pointer, the pointer points into an I/O buffer which is also of limited size, and similar problems can arise from very long tokens. In flex the default I/O buffer is 16K, which means it can handle tokens up to 8K, almost certainly large enough. In pclex the buffer is only 256 bytes. This is why it is a bad idea to try to recognize multi-line comments as single tokens, since comments can be very long and will often overflow a buffer no matter how large.

Enlarging yytext

You can usually write lexers so that no single token is larger than the default token buffer of your version of lex, but sometimes the default buffer is just too small. For example, you may be handling a language that allows 128 character names with a lexer whose default size is 100 characters. The technique for increasing the buffer size varies among versions.

AT&T and MKS Lex

Both of these versions make **yytext** a static character array whose size is set by the compile-time symbol YYLMAX. In both cases, you can redefine YYL-MAX in the definitions section of a scanner:

```
%{
#undef YYLMAX          /* remove default definition */
#define YYLMAX 500     /* new size */
%}
```

Flex

Since the default flex token size is 8K bytes, it's hard to imagine a situation where you need it to be bigger, but if memory is particularly tight you might want to make the buffer smaller. Flex buffers are created on the fly by a routine called **yy_create_buffer()**, and the current buffer is pointed to by **yy_current_buffer**. You can create a buffer of any size by putting in the user subroutines section a routine to create a smaller buffer, and calling it before you start scanning. (The routine has to be in the scanner file because some of the variables it refers to are declared to be static.)

```
%%
setupbuf(size)
int size;
{
        yy_current_buffer = yy_create_buffer( yyin, size );
}
```

Pclex

Abraxas pclex is based on flex so it uses a similar buffering scheme to flex, but with much smaller statically declared buffers. The buffer size is YY_BUF_SIZE which is defined to be twice F_BUFSIZ, which is by default 128. You can change the buffer size by changing either. The maximum input line length YY_MAX_LINE is also by default defined to be F_BUFSIZ so it is probably easier to increase F_BUFSIZ which automatically increases the others:

```
%{
#undef F_BUFSIZ        /* remove default definition */
#define F_BUFSIZ 256   /* new size */
%}
```

For both of the MS-DOS versions of lex, keep in mind that most MS-DOS C compilers have a 64K limit on the total amount of static data and stack, and that a very large token buffer can eat up a lot of that 64K.

yywrap()

When a lexer encounters an end of file, it calls the routine **yywrap()** to find out what to do next. If **yywrap()** returns 0, the scanner continues scanning, while if it returns 1 the scanner returns a zero token to report the end of file.

The standard version of **yywrap()** in the lex library always returns 1, but you can replace it with one of your own. If **yywrap()** returns 0 to indicate that there is more input, it needs first to adjust **yyin** to point to a new file, probably using **fopen()**.

As of version 2.3.7, flex defines **yywrap()** as a macro which makes it slightly harder to define your own version since you have to undefine the macro before you can define your routine or macro. To do so, put this at the beginning of the rules section:

```
%{
#undef yywrap
%}
```

Future versions of flex will conform to the POSIX lex standard which declares that **yywrap()** is a routine in the library, in which case a version that you define automatically takes priority.

7

A Reference for Yacc Grammars

In this chapter, we discuss the format of the yacc grammar and describe the various features and options available. This chapter summarizes the capabilities demonstrated in the examples in previous chapters and covers features not yet mentioned.

After the section on the structure of a yacc grammar, the sections in this chapter are in alphabetical order by feature.

Structure of a Yacc Grammar

A yacc grammar consists of three sections: the definition section, the rules section, and the user subroutines section.

```
... definition section ...
%%
... rules section ...
%%
... user subroutines section ...
```

The sections are separated by lines consisting of two percent signs. The first two sections are required, although a section may be empty. The third section and the preceding "%%" line may be omitted. (Lex uses the same structure.)

Symbols

A yacc grammar is constructed from *symbols*, the "words" of the grammar. Symbols are strings of letters, digits, periods, and underscores that do not start with a digit. The symbol **error** is reserved for error recovery, otherwise yacc attaches no *a priori* meaning to any symbol.

Symbols produced by the lexer are called *terminal symbols* or *tokens*. Those that are defined on the left-hand side of rules are called *non-terminal symbols* or *non-terminals*. Tokens may also be literal quoted characters. (See "Literal Tokens.") A widely-followed convention makes token names all uppercase and non-terminals lowercase. We follow that convention throughout the book.

Definition Section

The definition section can include a *literal block*, C code copied verbatim to the beginning of the generated C file, usually containing declaration and #include lines. There may be **%union**, **%start**, **%token**, **%type**, **%left**, **%right**, and **%nonassoc** declarations. (See "%union Declaration," "Start Declaration," "Tokens," "%type Declarations," and "Precedence and Operator Declarations.") It can also contain comments in the usual C format, surrounded by "/*" and "*/". All of these are optional, so in a very simple parser the definition section may be completely empty.

Rules Section

The rules section contains grammar rules and actions containing C code. See "Actions" and "Rules" for details.

User Subroutines Section

Yacc copies the contents of the user subroutines section verbatim to the C file. This section typically includes routines called from the actions.

In a large program, it is sometimes more convenient to put the supporting code in a separate source file to minimize the amount of material recompiled when you change the yacc file.

Actions

An *action* is C code executed when yacc matches a rule in the grammar. The action must be a C compound statement, e.g.:

```
date: month '/' day '/' year { printf("date found"); } ;
```

The action can refer to the values associated with the symbols in the rule by using a dollar sign followed by a number, with the first symbol after the colon being number 1, e.g.:

```
date: month '/' day '/' year
            { printf("date %d-%d-%d found", $1, $3, $5); }
        ;
```

The name "$$" refers to the value for the symbol to the left of the colon. Symbol values can have different C types. See "Tokens," "%type Declaration," and "%union Declaration" for details.

For rules with no action, yacc uses a default of:

```
    { $$ = $1; }
```

Embedded Actions

Even though yacc's parsing technique only allows actions at the end of a rule, yacc automatically simulates actions embedded within a rule. If you write an action within a rule, yacc invents a rule with an empty right hand side and a made-up name on the left, makes the embedded action into the action for that rule, and replaces the action in the original rule with the made-up name. For example, these are equivalent:

```
thing:          A { printf("seen an A"); } B ;

thing:          A fakename B ;
fakename:   /* empty */ { printf("seen an A"); } ;
```

Although this feature is quite useful, it has some peculiarities. The embedded action turns into a symbol in the rule, so its value (whatever it assigns to "$$") is available to an end-of-rule action like any other symbol:

```
thing:          A { $$ = 17; } B C
                { printf("%d", $2); }
        ;
```

This example prints "17". Either action can refer to the value of **A** as **$1**, and the end-of-rule action can refer to the value of the embedded action as **$2**, and the values of **B** and **C** as **$3** and **$4**.

Embedded actions can cause shift/reduce conflicts in otherwise acceptable grammars. For example, this grammar causes no problem:

```
%%
thing:      abcd | abcz ;

abcd: 'A' 'B' 'C' 'D' ;
abcz: 'A' 'B' 'C' 'Z' ;
```

But if you add an embedded action it has a shift/reduce conflict:

```
%%
thing:       abcd | abcz ;

abcd: 'A' 'B' { somefunc(); } 'C' 'D' ;
abcz: 'A' 'B' 'C' 'Z' ;
```

In the first case the parser doesn't need to decide whether it's parsing an abcd or an abcz until it's seen all four tokens, when it can tell which it's found. In the second case, it needs to decide after it parses the 'B', but at that point it hasn't seen enough of the input to decide which rule it is parsing. If the embedded action came after the 'C' there would be no problem, since yacc could use its one-token lookahead to see whether a 'D' or a 'Z' is next.

Symbol Types for Embedded Actions

Since embedded actions aren't associated with grammar symbols, there is no way to declare the type of the value returned by an embedded action. If you are using %union and typed symbol values, you have to put the value in angle brackets when referring to the action's value, e.g., $<*type*>$ when you set it in the embedded action and $<*type*>3 (using the appropriate number) when you refer to it in the action at the end of the rule. See "Symbol Values." If you have a simple parser that uses all *int* values, as in the example above, you don't need to give a type.

Obsolescent Feature

Early versions of yacc required an equal sign before an action. Old grammars may still contain them, but they are no longer required nor considered good style.

Ambiguity and Conflicts

Yacc may fail to translate a grammar specification because the grammar is ambiguous or contains conflicts. In some cases the grammar is truly ambiguous, that is, there are two possible parses for a single input string, and yacc cannot handle that. In others, the grammar is unambiguous, but the parsing technique that yacc uses is not powerful enough to parse the grammar. The problem in an unambiguous grammar with conflicts is that the parser would need to look more than one token ahead to decide which of two possible parses to use.

See "Precedence, Associativity, and Operator Declarations" and Chapter 8, *Yacc Ambiguities and Conflicts*, for more details and suggestions on how to fix these problems.

Types of Conflicts

There are two kinds of conflicts that can occur when yacc tries to create a parser: "shift/reduce" and "reduce/reduce."

Shift/Reduce Conflicts

A *shift/reduce* conflict occurs when there are two possible parses for an input string, and one of the parses completes a rule (the reduce option) and one doesn't (the shift option). For example, this grammar has one shift/reduce conflict:

```
%%
e:        'X'
    |     e '+' e
    ;
```

For the input string "X+X+X" there are two possible parses,"(X+X)+X" or "X+(X+X)". (See Figure 3-3 for an illustration of a similar conflict.) Taking the reduce option makes the parser use the first parse, the shift option the second. Yacc always chooses the shift unless the user puts in operator declarations. See the "Precedence and Operator Declarations" section for more information.

Reduce/Reduce Conflicts

A *reduce/reduce* conflict occurs when the same token could complete two different rules. For example:

```
%%
prog: proga | progb ;

proga:    'X' ;
progb:    'X' ;
```

An "X" could either be a **proga** or a **progb**. Most reduce/reduce conflicts are less obvious than this, but in nearly every case they represent mistakes in the grammar. See Chapter 8, *Yacc Ambiguities and Conflicts*, for details on handling conflicts.

Bugs in Yacc

Although yacc is a fairly mature program (the source code for AT&T yacc has been essentially unchanged for over ten years) one bug is commonly in distributed versions and quite a few quirks are often misinterpreted as bugs.

Real Bugs

There are a few real yacc bugs, particularly in AT&T yacc. (Thanks to Dave Jones of Megatest Corp. for these examples.)

Error Handling

Some older versions of AT&T yacc mishandle this grammar:

```
%token a
%%
s      : oseq
       ;
oseq:  /* empty */
       | oseq a
       | oseq error
       ;
```

The buggy version does a default reduction in the error state. In particular, in the **y.output** listing file in state 2 there is a default reduction:

```
.   reduce 1
```

The correct default behavior is to detect an error:

```
.   error
```

The mistake is an off-by-one coding error in the yacc source. Any vendor with AT&T source can easily fix it.

Even with the fix, there is an unfortunate interaction between error recovery and yacc's default reductions. Yacc doesn't take the error token into account when it computes its shift and reduce tables, and sometimes reduces rules even when it has a lookahead token from which it could tell that there is a syntax error and it shouldn't reduce the rule. Look at the *y.output* file if you plan on doing error recovery to see what rules will be reduced before entering the error state. You may have to do more work to recover than you had planned.

Declaring Literal Tokens

AT&T yacc fails to diagnose attempts to change the token number of a literal token:

```
%token '9' 17
```

This generates invalid C code in the output file.

Infinite Recursion

A common error in yacc grammars is to create a recursive rule with no way to terminate the recursion. Berkeley yacc, at least through version 1.8, doesn't diagnose this grammar:

```
%%
xlist:    xlist 'X' ;
```

Other versions do produce diagnostics.

Unreal Bugs

There are a few places where yacc seems to misbehave but actually is doing what it should.

Interchanging Precedences

People occasionally try to use **%prec** to swap the precedence of two tokens:

```
%token  NUMBER
%left PLUS
%left MUL
%%
expr :    expr PLUS expr %prec MUL
     |    expr MUL expr %prec PLUS
     |    NUMBER
     ;
```

This example seems to give PLUS higher precedence than MUL, but in fact it makes them the same. The precedence mechanism resolves shift/reduce conflicts by comparing the precedence of the token to be shifted to the precedence of the rule. In this case, there are several conflicts. A typical conflict arises when the parser has seen "expr PLUS expr" and the next token is a MUL. In the absence of a **%prec**, the rule would have the precedence of PLUS which is lower than that of MUL, and yacc takes the shift. But with **%prec**, both the rule and the token have the precedence of MUL, so it reduces because MUL is left associative.

One possibility would be to introduce pseudo-tokens, e.g., **XPLUS** and **XMUL**, with their own precedence levels to use with **%prec**. A far better solution is to rewrite the grammar to say what it means, in this case exchanging the **%left** lines (see "Precedence, Associativity, and Operator Declarations.")

Embedded Actions

When you write an action in the middle of a rule rather than at the end, yacc has to invent an anonymous rule to trigger the embedded action. Occasionally the anonymous rule causes unexpected shift/reduce conflicts. See "Actions" for more details.

End Marker

Each yacc grammar includes a pseudo-token called the end marker which marks the end of input. In yacc listings, the end marker is usually indicated as **$end**.

The lexer must return a zero token to indicate end of input.

Error Token and Error Recovery

When yacc detects a syntax error, i.e., when it receives an input token that it cannot parse, it attempts to recover from the error using this procedure:

1. It calls **yyerror** ("syntax error"). This usually reports the error to the user.
2. It discards any partially parsed rules until it returns to a state in which it could shift the special **error** symbol.
3. It resumes parsing, starting by shifting an **error**.
4. If another error occurs before three tokens have been shifted successfully, yacc does not report another error but returns to step 2.

See Chapter 9, *Error Reporting and Recovery,* for more details on error recovery. Also, see the sections about "YYERROR," "YYRECOVERING( )," "yyclearin," and "yyerrok" for details on features that help control error recovery.

Some versions of AT&T yacc contain a bug that makes error recovery fail. See "Bugs in Yacc" for more information.

%ident Declaration

Berkeley yacc allows an **%ident** in the definitions section to introduce an identification string into the module:

```
%ident "identification string"
```

It produces an **#ident** in the generated C code. C compilers typically place these identification strings in the object module in a place where the UNIX *what* command can find them.

No other versions of yacc currently support **%ident**. A more portable way to get the same effect is:

```
%{
#ident "identification string"
%}
```

Inherited Attributes ($0)

Yacc symbol values usually act as *inherited attributes* or *synthesized attributes*. (What yacc calls values are usually referred to in compiler literature as attributes.) Attributes start as token values, the leaves of the parse tree. Information conceptually moves up the parse tree each time a rule is reduced and its action synthesizes the value of its resulting symbol ($$) from the values of the symbols on the right-hand side of the rule.

Sometimes you need to pass information the other way, from the root of the parse tree toward the leaves. Consider this example:

```
declaration:    class type namelist ;

class:          GLOBAL          { $$ = 1; }
        |       LOCAL     { $$ = 2; }
        ;

type:           REAL      { $$ = 1; }
        |       INTEGER         { $$ = 2; }
        ;

namelist:       NAME          { mksymbol($0, $-1, $1); }
        |       namelist NAME    { mksymbol($0, $-1, $2); }
        ;
```

It would be useful to have the class and type available in the actions for **namelist**, both for error checking and to enter into the symbol table. Yacc makes this possible by allowing access to symbols on its internal stack to the left of the current rule, via **$0**, **$-1**, etc. In the example, the $0 in the call to **mksymbol()** refers to the value of the **type** which is stacked just before the symbol(s) for the namelist production, and will have the value 1 or 2 depending on whether the type was **REAL** or **INTEGER**, and **$-1** refers to the class which will have the value 1 or 2 if the class was **GLOBAL** or **LOCAL**.

Although inherited attributes can be very useful, they can also be a source of hard-to-find bugs. An action that uses inherited attributes has to take into account every place in the grammar where its rule is used. In this example, if you changed the grammar to use a namelist somewhere else, you'd have to make sure that in the new place where the namelist occurs appropriate symbols precede it so that **$0** and **$-1** will get the right values:

```
declaration:     STRING namelist ; /* won't work! */
```

Inherited attributes can occasionally be very useful, particularly for syntactically complex constructs like C language variable declarations. But in many cases it is safer and nearly as easy to use synthesized attributes. In the example above, the namelist rules could create a linked list of references to the names to be declared and return a pointer to that list as its value. The action for declaration could take the class, type, and namelist values and at that point assign the class and type to the names in the namelist.

Symbol Types for Inherited Attributes

When you use the value of an inherited attribute, the usual value declaration techniques (e.g., **%type**) don't work. Since the symbol corresponding to the value doesn't appear in the rule, yacc cannot tell what the correct type is. You have to supply type names in the action code using an explicit type. In the previous example, if the types of **class** and **type** were **cval** and **tval**, the last two lines would actually read like this:

```
namelist:   NAME        { mksymbol($<tval>0, $<cval>-1, $1); }
        |   namelist NAME    { mksymbol($<tval>0, $<cval>-1, $2); }
```

See "Symbol Values" for additional information.

Lexical Feedback

Parsers can sometimes feed information back to the lexer to handle other-wise difficult situations. For example, consider an input syntax like this:

```
message (any characters)
```

where in this particular context the parentheses are acting as string quotes. (This isn't great language design, but you are often stuck with what you've got.) You can't just decide to parse a string any time you see an open parenthesis, because they might be used differently elsewhere in the gram-mar.

A straightforward way to handle this situation is to feed context information from the parser back to the lexer, e.g., set a flag in the parser when a con-text-dependent construct is expected:

```
/* parser */
%{
int parenstring = 0;
}%
. . .
%%
statement: MESSAGE { parenstring = 1; } '(' STRING ')' ;
```

and look for it in the lexer:

```
%{
extern int parenstring;
%}
%s PSTRING
%%
. . .
"message"   return MESSAGE;
"("   {     if(parenstring)
                  BEGIN PSTRING;
            return '(';
      }
<PSTRING>[^)]*   {
            yylval.svalue = strdup(yytext);   /* pass string to parser */
            BEGIN INITIAL;
            return STRING;
            }
```

This code is not bullet-proof, because if there is some other rule that starts with **MESSAGE**, yacc might have to use a lookahead token in which case the in-line action wouldn't be executed until after the open parenthesis had been scanned. In most real cases that isn't a problem because the syntax tends to be simple.

In this example, you could also handle the special case in the lexer by setting **parenstring** in the lexer, e.g.:

```
"message"    { parenstring = 1; return MESSAGE; }
```

This could cause problems, however, if the token **MESSAGE** is used elsewhere in the grammar and is not always followed by a parenthesized string. You usually have the choice of doing lexical feedback entirely in the lexer or doing it partly in the parser, with the best solution depending on how complex the grammar is. If the grammar is simple and tokens do not appear in multiple contexts, you can do all of your lexical hackery in the lexer, while if the grammar is more complex it is easier to identify the special situations in the parser.

This approach can be taken to extremes—one of the authors wrote a complete Fortran 77 parser in yacc (but not lex, since tokenizing Fortran is just too strange) and the parser needed to feed a dozen special context states back to the lexer. It was messy, but it was far easier than writing the whole parser and lexer in C.

Literal Block

The literal block in the definition section is bracketed by the lines %{ and %}.

```
%{
... C code and declarations ...
%}
```

The contents of the literal block are copied verbatim to the generated C source file near the beginning, before the beginning of **yyparse()**. The literal block usually contains declarations of variables and functions used by code in the rules section, as well as **#include** lines for any necessary header files.

Literal Tokens

Yacc treats a character in single quotes as a token. In this example,

```
expr: '(' expr ')' ;
```

the open and close parentheses are literal tokens. The token number of a literal token is the numeric value in the local character set, usually ASCII, and is the same as the C value of the quoted character.

The lexer usually generates these tokens from the corresponding single characters in the input, but as with any other token, the correspondence between the input characters and the generated tokens is entirely up to the lexer. A common technique is to have the lexer treat all otherwise unrecognized characters as literal tokens. For example, in a lex scanner:

```
.       return yytext[0];
```

this covers all of the single-character operators in a language, and lets yacc catch all unrecognized characters in the input.

Some versions of yacc allow multiple character literal tokens, e.g., "<=", but it is a bad idea to use them, as different versions of yacc treat them in different, incompatible, ways. If a token's input representation is more than one character, it is better style to give it a name:

```
%token LE
```

and in the scanner:

```
"<="    return LE;
```

Portability of Yacc Parsers

Yacc parsers are in general very portable among C implementations. There are two levels at which you can port a parser: the original yacc grammar, or the generated C source file.

Porting Yacc Grammars

Different versions of yacc are for the most part very compatible. Each has a few unique features, but it's usually possible to write a grammar that uses only common features. (For example, a parser that uses *bison 's* reentrant parser feature will only work with *bison.*)

Different yacc versions handle errors slightly differently. In particular, when a parser receives a token that is in error, the parser may or may not reduce rules that ended with the previous token, depending on the way the version of yacc produced the parser. The exact behavior of **YYERROR( )** varies. Again, some versions complete the reduction of the current rule and remove the RHS tokens from the parse stack before starting error recovery, and some don't.

Different versions of yacc have different translation limits: one that most often is a problem is the maximum number of symbolic tokens, which can be as low as 127 in AT&T yacc. You can usually evade this limit by using literal characters as tokens; see "Character Sets."

Porting Generated C Parsers

Most versions of yacc generate very portable C code, and you can usually move the code to any C compiler without trouble.

Libraries

The only routines in the yacc library are usually **main( )** and **yyerror( )**. Most parsers use their own versions of those two routines, so the library usually isn't necessary.

Character Codes

Moving a generated parser between machines that use different character codes can be tricky. In particular, you must avoid literal tokens like "0" since the parser uses the character code as an index into internal tables, so a parser generated on an ASCII machine where the code for "0" is 48 will fail on an EBCDIC machine where the code is 240.

Yacc assigns its own numeric values to symbolic tokens, so a parser that uses only symbolic tokens should port sucessfully.

Precedence, Associativity, and Operator Declarations

Normally, all yacc grammars have to be unambiguous. That is, there is only one possible way to parse any legal input using the rules in the grammar.

Sometimes, an ambiguous grammar is easier to use. Ambiguous grammars cause *conflicts*, situations where there are two possible parses and hence two different ways that yacc can process a token. When yacc processes an ambiguous grammar, it uses default rules to decide which way to parse an ambiguous sequence. Often these rules do not produce the desired result, so yacc includes operator declarations that let you change the way it handles shift/reduce conflicts that result from ambiguous grammars. (See also "Ambiguity and Conflicts.")

Precedence and Associativity

Most programming languages have complicated rules that control the interpretation of arithmetic expressions. For example, the C expression:

```
a = b = c + d / e / f
```

is treated as:

```
a = (b = (c + ((d / e) / f))))
```

The rules for determining what operands group with which operators are known as precedence and associativity.

Precedence

Precedence assigns each operator a precedence "level." Operators at higher levels bind more tightly, e.g., if "*" has higher precedence than "+", "A+B*C" is treated as "A+(B*C)", while "D*E+F" is "(D*E)+F".

Associativity

Associativity controls how the grammar groups expressions using the same operator or different operators with the same precedence, whether they group from the left, from the right, or not at all. If "–" were left associative, the expression "A–B–C" would mean "(A–B)–C", while if it were right associative it would mean "A–(B–C)".

Some operators such as Fortran **.GE.** are not associative either way, i.e., "A .GE. B .GE. C" is not a valid expression.

Operator Declarations

Operator declarations appear in the definitions section. The possible declarations are **%left**, **%right**, and **%nonassoc**. (In very old grammars you may find the obsolete equivalents **%<**, **%>**, and **%2** or **%binary**.) The **%left** and **%right** declarations make an operator left or right associative, respectively. You declare non-associative operators with **%nonassoc**.

Operators are declared in increasing order of precedence. All operators declared on the same line are at the same precedence level. For example, a Fortran grammar might include:

```
%left '+' '-'
%left '*' '/'
%right POW
```

The lowest precedence operators here are "+" and "−", the middle predecence are "*" and "/", and the highest is POW which represents the "**" power operator.

Using Precedence and Associativity to Resolve Conflicts

Every token in a grammar can have a precedence and an associativity assigned by an operator declaration. Every rule can also have a precedence and an associativity, which is taken from a **%prec** clause in the rule or, failing that, the rightmost token in the rule that has a precedence assigned.

Whenever there is a shift/reduce conflict, yacc compares the precedence of the token that might be shifted to that of the rule that might be reduced. It shifts if the token's precedence is higher or reduces if the rule's precedence is higher. If both have the same precedence, yacc checks the associativity. If they are left associative it reduces, if they are right associative it shifts, and if they are non-associative yacc generates an error.

Typical Uses of Precedence

Although you can in theory use precedence to resolve any kind of shift/reduce conflict, precedence rarely resolves the conflict more cleanly than rewriting the grammar. Precedence declarations were designed to handle expression grammars, with large numbers of rules like:

```
expr OP expr
```

Expression grammars are almost always written using precedence.

The only other common use is if-then-else, where you can resolve the "dangling else" problem more easily with precedence than by rewriting the grammar.

See Chapter 8, *Yacc Ambiguities and Conflicts*, for details. Also see "Bugs in Yacc" for a common pitfall using **%prec**.

Recursive Rules

To parse a list of items of indefinite length, you write a *recursive* rule, one that is defined in terms of itself. For example, this parses a possibly empty list of numbers:

```
numberlist: /* empty */
      | numberlist NUMBER
      ;
```

The details of the recursive rule vary depending on the exact syntax to be parsed. The next example parses a non-empty list of expressions separated by commas, with the symbol **expr** being defined elsewhere in the grammar:

```
exprlist:   expr
      |     exprlist ',' expr
      ;
```

Any recursive rule must have at least one non-recursive alternative (one that does not refer to itself). Otherwise there is no way to terminate the string that it matches, which is an error. (Berkeley yacc fails to diagnose this problem.)

Left and Right Recursion

When you write a recursive rule, you can put the recursive reference at the left end or the right end of the right-hand side of the rule, e.g.:

```
exprlist:   exprlist ',' expr ;    /* left recursion */

exprlist:   expr ',' exprlist ;    /* right recursion */
```

In most cases you can write the grammar either way. Yacc handles left recursion much more efficiently than right recursion. This is because its internal stack keeps track of all symbols seen so far for all partially parsed rules. If you use the right recursive version of **exprlist** and have an expression with ten expressions in it, by the time the tenth expression is read there will be 20 entries on the stack, an **expr** and a comma for each of the ten expressions. When the list ends, all of the nested **exprlist** s will be reduced, starting from right to left. On the other hand, if you use the left recursive version, the **exprlist** rule is reduced after each **expr**, so the list will never have more than three entries on the internal stack.

A ten-element expression list poses no problems in a parser, but grammars often parse lists hundreds of items long, particularly when a program is defined as a list of statements:

```
%start program
%%
program:    statementlist ;

statementlist:    statement
            | statementlist statement
            ;
statement:  . . .
```

In this case, a 400 statement program is parsed as a 400 element list of statements, and a right recursive list of 400 elements is too large for most yacc parsers.

Right recursive grammars can be useful for a list of items which you know will be short and which you want to make into a linked list of values:

```
thinglist:  THING { $$ = $1; }
        |      THING thinglist { $1->next = $2; $$ = $1; }
        ;
```

With a left recursive grammar, either you end up with the list linked in reverse order, or you need extra code to search for the end of the list at each stage in order to add the next thing to the end. A compromise is to create the list in the "wrong" order, then when the entire list has been created, run down it and reverse it.

Rules

A yacc grammar consists of a set of *rules*. Each rule starts with a non-terminal symbol and a colon, and is followed by a possibly empty list of symbols, literal tokens, and actions. Rules by convention end with a semi-colon, although in most versions of yacc the semicolon is optional. For example,

```
date: month '/' day '/' year ;
```

says that a date is a month, a slash, a day, another slash, and a year. (The symbols month, day, and year must be defined elsewhere in the grammar.) The initial symbol and colon are called the *left-hand side* of the rule, and the rest of the rule is the *right-hand side*. The right-hand side may be empty.

If several consecutive rules in a grammar have the same left-hand side, the second and subsequent rules may start with a vertical bar rather than the name and the colon. These two fragments are equivalent:

```
declaration:    EXTERNAL name ;
declaration:    ARRAY name '(' size ')' ;

declaration:    EXTERNAL name
      |    ARRAY name '(' size ')' ;
```

The form with the vertical bar is better style. The semicolon must be omitted before a vertical bar.

An *action* is a C compound statement that is executed whenever the parser reaches the point in the grammar where the action occurs:

```
date: month '/' day '/' year
                   { printf("Date recognized.\n"); }
      ;
```

The C code in actions may have some special constructs starting with "$" that are specially treated by yacc. (See "Actions" for details.) Actions that occur anywhere except at the end of a rule are treated specially. (See "Embedded Actions," page 183, for details.)

An explicit precedence at the end of a rule:

```
expr: expr '*' expr
    | expr '-' expr
    | '-' expr %prec UMINUS ;
```

The precedence is only used to resolve otherwise ambiguous parses. See "Precedence, Associativity, and Operator Declarations" for details.

Special Characters

Since yacc deals with symbolic tokens rather than literal text, its input character set is considerably simpler than lex's. Here is a list of the special characters that it uses:

%   A line with two percent signs separates the parts of a yacc grammar. (see "Structure of a Yacc Grammar.") All of the declarations in the definition section start with %, including %{ %}, **%start**, **%token**, **%type**, **%left**, **%right**, **%nonassoc**, and **%union**. See "Literal Block," "Start Declaration," "%type Declaration," "Precedence, Associativity, and Operator Declarations," and "%union Declaration."

\   The backslash is an obsolete synonym for a percent sign. It also has its usual effect in C language strings in actions.

$ In actions, a dollar sign introduces a value reference, e.g., **$3** for the value of the third symbol in the rule's right-hand side. See "Symbol Values."

' Literal tokens are enclosed in single quotes, e.g., '**Z**'. See "Literal Tokens."

" Some versions of yacc treat double quotes the same as single quotes in literal tokens. Such use is not at all portable.

< > In a value reference in an action, you can override the value's default type by enclosing the type name in angle brackets, e.g., **$<xtype>3**. See "Symbol Types." Also, **$<** and **$>** are obsolete equivalents for **%left** and **%right**. See "Precedence, Associativity and Operator Declarations."

{ } The C code in actions is enclosed in curly braces. (See "Actions.") C code in the literal block declarations section is enclosed in "%{" and "%}". See "Literal Block."

; Each rule in the rules section should end with a semicolon, except those that are immediately followed by a rule that starts with a vertical bar. In most versions of yacc the semicolons are optional, but they are always a good idea. See "Rules."

| When two consecutive rules have the same left-hand side, the second rule may replace the symbol and colon with a vertical bar. See "Rules."

: In each rule, a colon follows the symbol on the rule's left-hand side. See "Rules."

_ Symbols may include underscores along with letters, digits, and periods.

. Symbols may include periods along with letters, digits, and underscores. This can cause trouble because C identifiers cannot include periods. In particular, do not use tokens whose names contain periods, since the token names are all **#define** 'd as C preprocessor symbols.

= Early versions of yacc required an equal sign before an action, and most versions still accept them. They are now neither required nor recommended. See "Actions."

Start Declaration

Normally, the start rule, the one that the parser starts trying to parse, is the one named in the first rule. If you want to start with some other rule, in the declaration section you can write:

```
%start somename
```

to start with rule *somename*.

In most cases the clearest way to present the grammar is top-down, with the start rule first, so no **%start** is needed.

Symbol Values

Every symbol in a yacc parser, both tokens and non-terminals, can have a value associated with it. If the token were NUMBER, the value might be the particular number, if it were STRING, the value might be a pointer to a copy of the string, and if it were SYMBOL, the value might be a pointer to an entry in the symbol table that describes the symbol. Each of these kinds of value corresponds to a different C type, **int** or **double** for the number, **char** * for the string, and a pointer to a structure for the symbol. Yacc makes it easy to assign types to symbols so that it automatically uses the correct type for each symbol.

Declaring Symbol Types

Internally, yacc declares each value as a C union that includes all of the types. You list all of the types in a **%union** declaration, q.v. Yacc turns this into a typedef for a union type called YYSTYPE. Then for each symbol whose value is set or used in action code, you have to declare its type. Use **%type** for non-terminals. Use **%token**, **%left**, **%right**, or **%nonassoc** for tokens, to give the name of the union field corresponding to its type.

Then, whenever you refer to a value using **$$**, **$1**, etc., yacc automatically uses the appropriate field of the union.

Calculator Example

Here is a simple although not particularly realistic calculator. It can add numbers and compare strings. All results are numbers.

```
%union {
        double dval;
        char *sval;
}
. . .
%token <dval> REAL
%token <sval> STRING
%type <dval> expr
%%
calc: expr { printf("%g\n", $1); }

expr: expr '+' expr { $$ = $1 + $3; }
        | REAL { $$ = $1; }
        | STRING '=' STRING { $$ = strcmp($1, $3) ? 0.0: 1.0; }
```

There are two value types: **dval**, which is a *double*, and **sval**, which is a character pointer. The token **REAL** and the non-terminal **expr** automatically use the union member **dval**, and the token **STRING** uses the union member **sval**.

Yacc doesn't understand any C, so any symbol typing mistakes you make, such as using a type name that isn't in the union or using a field in a way that C doesn't allow, will cause errors in the generated C program.

Explicit Symbol Types

Yacc allows you to declare an explicit type for a symbol value reference by putting the type name in angle brackets between the dollar sign and the symbol number, or between the two dollar signs, e.g., **$<xxx>3** or **$<zzz>$**.

The feature is rarely used, since in nearly all cases it is easier and more readable to declare the symbols. The most plausible uses are when referring to inherited attributes and when setting and referring to the value returned by an embedded action. See "Inherited Attributes" and "Actions" for details.

Tokens

Tokens or *terminal symbols* are symbols that the lexer passes to the parser. Whenever a yacc parser needs another token it calls **yylex()** which returns the next token from the input. At the end of input **yylex()** returns zero.

Tokens may either be symbols defined by **%token** or individual characters in single quotes. (See "Literal Tokens.") All symbols used as tokens must be defined explicitly in the definitions section, e.g.:

```
%token UP DOWN LEFT RIGHT
```

Tokens can also be declared by **%left**, **%right**, or **%nonassoc** declarations, each of which has exactly the same syntax options as has **%token**. See "Precedence, Associativity, and Operator Declarations."

Token Numbers

Within the lexer and parser, tokens are identified by small integers. The token number of a literal token is the numeric value in the local character set, usually ASCII, and is the same as the C value of the quoted character.

Symbolic tokens usually have values assigned by yacc, which gives them numbers higher than any possbile character's code, so they will not conflict with any literal tokens. You can assign token numbers yourself by following the token name by its number in **%token**:

```
%token UP 50 DOWN 60 LEFT 17 RIGHT 25
```

It is a serious error to assign two tokens the same number, but most versions of yacc don't even notice—they just generate bad parsers. In most cases it is easier and more reliable to let yacc choose its own token numbers.

The lexer needs to know the token numbers in order to return the appropriate values to the parser. For literal tokens, it uses the corresponding C character constant. For symbolic tokens, you can tell yacc with the $-d$ command-line flag to create a C header file with definitions of all of the token numbers. If you **#include** that header file in your lexer you can use the symbols, e.g., UP, DOWN, LEFT, and RIGHT, in its C code. The header file is normally called *y.tab.h*. On MS-DOS systems, MKS yacc calls it *ytab.h* and pcyacc calls it *yytab.h*. Bison, POSIX yacc, and both MS-DOS versions have command-line options to change the name of the generated header file.

Token Values

Each symbol in a yacc parser can have an associated value. (See "Symbol Values.") Since tokens can have values, you need to set the values as the lexer returns tokens to the parser. The token value is always stored in the variable **yylval**. In the simplest parsers, **yylval** is a plain *int* variable, and you might set it like this in a lex scanner:

```
[0-9]+      { yylval = atoi(yytext); return NUMBER; }
```

In most cases, though, different symbols have different value types. See "%union Declaration," "Symbol Values," and "%type Declaration."

In the parser you must declare the value types of all tokens that have values. Put the name of the appropriate union tag in angle brackets in the **%token** or precedence declaration. You might define your values types like this:

```
%union {
        enum optype opval;
        double dval;
        char *sval;
}
 . . .
%token <dval> REAL
%token <sval> STRING
%nonassoc <opval> RELOP
```

(In this case **RELOP** might be a relational operator such as "==" or ">", and the token value says which operator it is.)

You set the appropriate field of **yylval** when you return the token. In this case, you'd do something like this in lex:

```
%{
#include "y.tab.h"
%}
 . . .
[0-9]+\.[0-9]*   { yylval.dval = atof(yytext); return REAL; }
\"[^"]*\"   { yylval.sval = strdup(yytext); return STRING; }
"=="         { yyval.opval = OPEQUAL; return RELOP; }
```

The value for **REAL** is a *double* so it goes into **yylval.dval**, while the value for **STRING** is a *char* *so it goes into **yylval.sval**.

%type Declaration

You declare the types of non-terminals using **%type**. Each declaration has the form:

```
%type <type> name,name,...
```

The *type* name must have been defined by a **%union**. (See "%union Declaration.") Each *name* is the name of a non-terminal symbol. See "Symbol Types" for details and an example.

Use **%type** to declare non-terminals. To declare tokens, you can also use **%token, %left, %right,** or **%nonassoc.** See "Tokens" and "Precedence, Associativity, and Operator Declarations" for details.

%union Declaration

The **%union** declaration identifies all of the possible C types that a symbol value can have. (See "Symbol Values.") The declaration takes this form:

```
%union {
  ... field declarations ...
}
```

The field declarations are copied verbatim into a C **union** declaration of the type YYSTYPE in the output file. Yacc does not check to see if the contents of the **%union** are valid C.

In the absence of a **%union** declaration, yacc defines YYSTYPE to be **int** so all of the symbol values are integers.

You associate the types declared in **%union** with particular symbols using the **%type** declaration.

Yacc puts the generated C union declaration both in the generated C file and in the optional generated header file (usually called *y.tab.h*) so you can use YYSTYPE in other source files by including the generated header file. Conversely, you can put your own declaration of YYSTYPE in an include file that you reference with **#include** in the definition section. In this case, there must be at least one **%type** to warn yacc that you are using explicit symbol types.

Variant and Multiple Grammars

You may want to have parsers for two partially or entirely different grammars in the same program. For example, an interactive debugging interpreter might have one parser for the programming language and another for debugger commands. A one-pass C compiler might need one parser for the preprocessor syntax and another for the C language itself.

There are two ways to handle two grammars in one program: combine them into a single parser, or put two complete parsers into the program.

Combined Parsers

You can combine several grammars into one by adding a new start rule that depends on the first token read. For example:

```
%token CSTART PPSTART
%%
combined:   CSTART cgrammar
        |   PPSTART ppgrammar
        ;

cgrammar:   . . .

ppgrammar:  . . .
```

In this case if the first token is **CSTART** it parses the grammar whose start rule is **cgrammar**, while if the first token is **PPSTART** it parses the grammar whose start rule is **ppgrammar**.

You also need to put code in the lexer that returns the appropriate special token the first time that the parser asks the lexer for a token:

```
%%
%{
        extern first_tok;

        if(first_tok) {
                int holdtok = first_tok;

                first_tok = 0;
                return holdtok;
        }
%}
    . . . <the rest of the lexer>
```

In this case you set **first_tok** to the appropriate token before calling **yyparse( )**.

One advantage of this approach is that the program is smaller than it would be with multiple parsers, since there is only one copy of the parsing code. Another is that if you are parsing related grammars, e.g., C preprocessor expressions and C itself, you may be able to share some parts of the grammar. The disadvantages are that you cannot usually call one parser while the other is active (but see "Recursive Parsing," later in this chapter) and that you have to use different symbols in the two grammars except where they deliberately share rules.

In practice, this approach is useful when you want to parse slightly different versions of a single language, e.g., a full language that is compiled and an interactive subset that you interpret in a debugger.

Multiple Parsers

The other approach is to include two complete parsers in a single program. Yacc doesn't make this easy, because every parser it generates has the same entry point, **yyparse()**, and calls the same lexer, **yylex()**, which uses the same token value variable **yylval**. Furthermore, most versions of yacc put the parse tables and parser stack in global variables with names like **yyact** and **yyv**. If you just translate two grammars and compile and link the two resulting files (renaming at least one of them to something other than *y.tab.c*) you get a long list of multiply defined symbols. The trick is to change the names that yacc uses for its functions and variables.

Using the -p Flag

Modern versions of yacc (including bison, MKS yacc, and any POSIX-compliant implementation) provide a command-line switch *-p* to change the prefix used on the names in the parser generated by yacc. For example, the command:

```
yacc -p pdq mygram.y
```

produces a parser with the entry point **pdqparse()**, which calls the lexer **pdqlex()** and so forth. Specifically, the names affected are **yyparse()**, **yylex()**, **yyerror()**, **yylval**, **yychar**, and **yydebug**. (The variable **yychar** holds the most recently read token, which is sometimes useful when printing error messages.) The other variables used in the parser may be renamed or may be made *static* or *auto*; in any event they are guaranteed not to collide. There is also a *-b* flag to specify the prefix of the generated C file; e.g.,

```
yacc -p pdq -b pref mygram.y
```

would produce *pref.tab.c* assuming the standard name was *y.tab.c*.

You have to provide properly named versions of **yyerror()** and **yylex()**.,

Faking It

Older versions of yacc have no automatic way to change the names in the generated C routine, so you have to fake it. On UNIX systems, the easiest way to fake it is with the stream editor *sed*. Assuming you are using AT&T yacc, create the file *yy-sed* containing these 26 *sed* commands. (In this case the new prefix is "pdq".)

```
s/yyact/pdqact/g
s/yychar/pdqchar/g
s/yychk/pdqchk/g
s/yydebug/pdqdebug/g
s/yydef/pdqdef/g
s/yyerrflag/pdqerrflag/g
s/yyerror/pdqerror/g
s/yyexca/pdqexca/g
s/yylex/pdqlex/g
s/yylval/pdqlval/g
s/yynerrs/pdqnerrs/g
s/yypact/pdqpact/g
s/yyparse/pdqparse/g
s/yypgo/pdqpgo/g
s/yyps/pdqps/g
s/yypv/pdqpv/g
s/yyr1/pdqr1/g
s/yyr2/pdqr2/g
s/yyreds/pdqreds/g
s/yys/pdqs/g
s/yystate/pdqstate/g
s/yytmp/pdqtmp/g
s/yytoks/pdqtoks/g
s/yyv/pdqv/g
s/yyval/pdqval/g
```

After you run yacc, these commands edit the generated parser:

```
sed -f yy-sed y.tab.c > pdq.tab.c
sed -f yy-sed y.tab.h > pdq.tab.h
```

You would probably want to put these rules in a *Makefile*:

```
pdq.tab.h pdq.tab.c: yvexamp.y
        yacc -vd yvexamp.y
        sed -f yy-sed y.tab.c > pdq.tab.c
        sed -f yy-sed y.tab.h > pdq.tab.h
```

Another approach is to use C preprocessor **#define s** at the beginning of the grammar to rename the variables:

```
%{
#define yyact pdqact
#define yychar pdqchar
#define yychk pdqchk
#define yydebug pdqdebug
#define yydef pdqdef
#define yyerrflag pdqerrflag
#define yyerror pdqerror
#define yyexca pdqexca
#define yylex pdqlex
#define yylval pdqlval
#define yynerrs pdqnerrs
#define yypact pdqpact
#define yyparse pdqparse
```

```
#define yypgo pdqpgo
#define yyps pdqps
#define yypv pdqpv
#define yyr1 pdqr1
#define yyr2 pdqr2
#define yyreds pdqreds
#define yys pdqs
#define yystate pdqstate
#define yytmp pdqtmp
#define yytoks pdqtoks
#define yyv pdqv
#define yyval pdqval
%}
```

This avoids using *sed*, but has the disadvantage that the definitions do not appear in the generated header file, but only the generated C file. To deal with that problem, put all the definitions in a file, call it *pdqdefs.h*, and in the parser put the following:

```
%{
#include "pdqdefs.h"
%}
```

In the files where you use the header file, include *pdqdefs.h* first, e.g., in the lexer:

```
%{
#include "pdqdefs.h"
#include "y.tab.h"
%}
```

Recursive Parsing

A slightly different problem is that of recursive parsing, calling **yyparse()** a second time while the original call to **yyparse()** is still active. This can be an issue when you have combined parsers. If you have a combined C language and C preprocessor parser, you'll want to call **yyparse()** in C language mode once to parse the whole program, and call it recursively whenever you see a **#if** to parse a preprocessor expression.

Unfortunately, most versions of yacc provide no easy way to handle recursive calls to the parser. If you really need recursive parsing, you will have to do some non-trivial editing of the generated C file. In an AT&T yacc parser, for example, you need to make the variables **yyv**, **yypv**, **yys**, and **yyps** automatic variables local to the parser, and save and restore the values of **ystate**, **yytmp**, **yynerrs**, **yyerrflag**, and **yychar** around the recursive call to **yyparse()**.

The one version that does support recursive parsing is bison, when you give it the **%pure_parser** declaration. This declaration makes the parser reenterable and also changes the calling sequence to **yylex( )**, passing as arguments pointers to the current copies of **yylval** and **yylloc**. (The latter is a part of an optional bison-specific feature that tracks the exact source position of each token to allow more precise error reports.)

Lexers for Multiple Parsers

If you use a lex lexer with your multiple parsers, you need to make adjustments to the lexer to correspond to the changes to the parser. (See "Multiple Lexers" in Chapter 6.) You will usually want to use a combined lexer with a combined parser, and multiple lexers with multiple parsers.

If you use multiple parsers and lexers and your versions of yacc and lex don't provide automatic renaming, you will probably want to combine the *sed* or include files that rename yacc variables with those that rename lex variables since the techniques are the same and some of the same names, e.g., **yylex( )** and **yylval**, need to be changed in both places.

y.output Files

Every version of yacc has the ability to create a log file, named *y.output* under UNIX and *y.out* or *yy.lrt* on MS-DOS, that shows all of the states in the parser and the transitions from one state to another. Use the *−v* flag to generate a log file.

The precise format of the file is specific to each version of yacc, but the following excerpt from an expression grammar is typical:

```
state 1
      e : ID .   (2)

      .   reduce 2


state 2
      e : '(' . e ')'   (3)

      ID  shift 1
      '('  shift 2
      .  error

      e  goto 5
```

The dot in each state shows how far the parser has gotten parsing a rule when it gets to that state. When the parser is in state 2, for example, if the parser sees an **ID**, it shifts the **ID** onto the stack and switches to to state 1. If it sees an open parenthesis it shifts the paren onto the stack and switches back to state 2, and any other token is an error. In state 1, it always reduces rule number 2. (Rules are numbered in the order they appear in the input file.) After the reduction the **ID** is replaced on the parse stack by an **e** and the parser pops back to state 2, at which point the **e** makes it go to state 5.

When there are conflicts, the states with conflicts show the conflicting shift and reduce actions.

```
9: shift/reduce conflict (shift 7, reduce 4) on '+'
state 9
        e : e . '+' e   (4)
        e : e '+' e .   (4)

        '+'   shift 7
        ';'   reduce 4
        ')'   reduce 4
```

In this case there is a shift/reduce conflict when yacc sees a plus sign. You could fix it either by rewriting the grammar or by adding an operator declaration for the plus sign. See "Precedence, Associativity, and Operator Declarations."

Yacc Library

Every implementation comes with a library of helpful routines. You can include the library by giving the *−ly* flag at the end of the *cc* command line on UNIX systems, or the equivalent on other systems. The contents of the library vary among implementations, but it always contains **main()** and **yyerror()**.

main()

All versions of yacc come with a minimal main program which is sometimes useful for quickie programs and for testing. It's so simple we can reproduce it here:

```
main(ac, av)
{
     yyparse();
     return 0;
}
```

As with any library routine, you can provide your own **main()**. In nearly any useful application you will want to provide a **main()** that accepts command-line arguments and flags, opens files, and checks for errors.

yyerror()

All versions of yacc also provide a simple error reporting routine. It's also simple enough to list in its entirety:

```
yyerror(char *errmsg)
{
        fprintf(stderr, "%s\n", errmsg);
}
```

This sometimes suffices, but a better error routine that reports at least the line number and the most recent token (available in **yytext** if your lexer is written with lex) will make your parser much more usable.

YYABORT

The special statement

```
YYABORT;
```

in an action makes the parser routine **yyparse()** return immediately with a non-zero value, indicating failure.

It can be useful when an action routine detects an error so severe that there is no point in continuing the parse.

Since the parser may have a one-token lookahead, the rule action containing the YYABORT may not be reduced until the parser has read another token.

YYACCEPT

The special statement

```
YYACCEPT;
```

in an action makes the parser routine **yyparse()** return immediately with a value 0, indicating success.

It can be useful in a situation where the lexer cannot tell when the input data ends, but the parser can.

Since the parser may have a one-token lookahead, the rule action containing the YYACCEPT may not be reduced until the parser has read another token.

YYBACKUP

Some versions of yacc, including the original AT&T yacc, have a poorly documented macro YYBACKUP that lets you unshift the current token and replace it with something else. The syntax is:

> sym: TOKEN { YYBACKUP(*newtok, newval*); }

It discards the symbol **sym** that would have been substituted by the reduction and pretends that the lexer just read the token **newtok** with the value **newval**. If there is a look-ahead token or the rule has more than one symbol on the right side, the rule fails with a call to **yyerror()**.

It is extremely difficult to use YYBACKUP() correctly and it is not at all portable, so we suggest you not use it. (We document it here in case you come across an existing grammar that does use it.)

yyclearin

The macro **yyclearin** in an action discards a lookahead token if one has been read. It is most often useful in error recovery in an interactive parser to put the parser into a known state after an error:

```
stmtlist: stmt | stmtlist stmt ;

stmt: error  { reset_input(); yyclearin; } ;
```

After an error this calls the user routine **reset_input()** which presumably puts the input into a known state, then uses **yyclearin** to prepare to start reading tokens anew.

See the sections "YYRECOVERING()" and "yyerrok" for more information.

yydebug and YYDEBUG

Most versions of yacc can optionally compile in trace code that reports everything that the parser does. These reports are extremely verbose but are often the only way to figure out what a recalcitrant parser is doing.

YYDEBUG

Since the trace code is large and slow, it is not automatically compiled into the object program. To include the trace code, either use the *−t* flag on the yacc command line, or else define the C preprocessor symbol **YYDEBUG** to be non-zero either on the C compiler command line or by including something like this in the definition section:

```
%{
#define YYDEBUG 1
%}
```

yydebug

The integer variable **yydebug** in the running parser controls whether the parser actually produces debug output. If it is non-zero, the parser produces debugging reports, while if it is zero it doesn't. You can set **yydebug** non-zero in any way you want, for instance, in response to a flag on the program's command line, or by patching it at run-time with a debugger.

yyerrok

After yacc detects a syntax error, it normally refrains from reporting another error until it has shifted three consecutive tokens without another error. This somewhat alleviates the problem of multiple error messages resulting from a single mistake as the parser gets resynchronized.

If you know when the parser is back in sync, you can return to the normal state in which all errors are reported. The macro **yyerrok** tells the parser to return to the normal state.

For example, assume you have a command interpreter in which all commands are on separate lines. No matter how badly the user botches a command, you know the next line is a new command.

```
cmdlist: cmd | cmdlist cmd ;

cmd:  error '\n' { yyerrok; } ;
```

The rule with **error** skips input after an error up to a newline, and the **yyerrok** tells the parser that error recovery is complete.

See also "YYRECOVERING( )" and "yyclearin."

YYERROR

Sometimes your action code can detect context-sensitive syntax errors that the parser itself cannot. If your code detects a syntax error, you can call the macro **YYERROR** to produce exactly the same effect as if the parser had read a token forbidden by the grammar. As soon as you invoke **YYERROR** the parser calls **yyerror( )** and goes into error recovery mode looking for a state where it can shift an **error** token. See "Error Token" and "Error Recovery" for details.

yyerror( )

Whenever a yacc parser detects a syntax error, it calls **yyerror( )** to report the error to the user, passing it a single argument, a string describing the error. (Usually the only error you ever get is "syntax error.") The default version of **yyerror** in the yacc library merely prints its argument on the standard output. Here is a slightly more informative version:

```
yyerror(const char *msg)
{
        printf("%d: %s at '%s'\n", yylineno, msg, yytext);
}
```

We assume **yylineno** is the current line number. (See "Line Numbers and yylineno" in Chapter 6.) and **yytext** is the lex token buffer that contains the current token. Since different versions of lex declare **yytext** differently, some as an array and some as a pointer, for maximum portability the best place to put this routine is in the user subroutines section of the lexer file, since that is the only place where **yytext** is automatically defined for you.

Since yacc doggedly tries to recover from errors and parse its entire input, no matter how badly garbled, you may want to have **yyerror( )** count the number of times it's called and exit after ten errors, on the theory that the parser is probably hopelessly confused by the errors that have already been reported.

You can and probably should call **yyerror( )** yourself when your action routines detect other sorts of errors.

yyparse()

The entry point to a yacc-generated parser is **yyparse()**. When your program calls **yyparse()**, the parser attempts to parse an input stream. The parser returns a value of zero if the parse succeeds and non-zero if not.

Every time you call **yyparse()** the parser starts parsing anew, forgetting whatever state it might have been in the last time it returned. This is quite unlike the scanner **yylex()** generated by lex, which picks up where it left off each time you call it.

See also "YYACCEPT" and "YYABORT."

YYRECOVERING()

After yacc detects a syntax error, it normally enters a recovery mode in which it refrains from reporting another error until it has shifted three consecutive tokens without another error. This somewhat alleviates the problem of multiple error messages resulting from a single mistake as the parser gets resynchronized.

The macro **YYRECOVERING()** returns non-zero if the parser is currently in the error recovery mode and zero if it is not. It is sometimes convenient to test **YYRECOVERING()** to decide whether to report errors discovered in an action routine.

See also "yyclearin" and "yyerrok."

In this chapter:
- *The Pointer Model and Conflicts*
- *Common Examples of Conflicts*
- *How Do I Fix the Conflict?*
- *Summary*
- *Exercises*

8

Yacc Ambiguities and Conflicts

This chapter focuses on finding and correcting *conflicts* within a yacc grammar. Conflicts occur when yacc reports shift/reduce and reduce/reduce errors. Finding them can be challenging because yacc points to them in *y.output,** which we will describe in this chapter, rather than in your yacc grammar file. Before reading this chapter, you should understand the general way that yacc parsers work, described in in Chapter 3, *Using Yacc.*

The Pointer Model and Conflicts

To describe what a conflict is in terms of the yacc grammar, we introduce a model of yacc's operation. In this model, a *pointer* moves through the yacc grammar as each individual token is read. When you start, there is one pointer (represented here as an up-arrow, ↑) at the beginning of the start rule:

```
%token A B C
%%
start:      ↑ A B C;
```

As the yacc parser reads tokens, the pointer moves. Say it reads **A** and **B**:

```
%token A B C
%%
start:      A B ↑ C;
```

---

*MS-DOS versions of yacc call the listing file *y.out* or *yy.lrt*, and the format of the information in them is different. All versions of yacc use the same parsing strategy and get the same conflicts, so the listing files contain the same information.

At times, there may be more than one pointer because of the alternatives in your yacc grammar. For example, suppose with the following grammar it reads **A** and **B**:

```
%token A B C D E F
%%
start:     x
     |     y;
x:     A B ↑ C D;
y:     A B ↑ E F;
```

(For the rest of the examples in this chapter, we will leave out the **%token** and the **%%**.) There are two ways for pointers to disappear. One is for a token to eliminate one or more pointers because only one still matches the input. If the next token that yacc reads is **C**, the second pointer will disappear, and the first pointer advances:

```
start:     x
     |     y;
x:     A B C ↑ D;
y:     A B E F;
```

The other way for pointers to disappear is for them to merge in a common subrule. In this example, **z** appears in both **x** and **y**:

```
start:     x
     |     y;
x:     A B z R;
y:     A B z S;
z:C D
```

After reading **A**, there are two pointers:

```
start:     x
     |     y;
x:     A ↑ B z R;
y:     A ↑ B z S;
z:     C D
```

After **A B C**, there is only one pointer:

```
start:     x
     |     y;
x:     A B z R;
y:     A B z S;
z:     C ↑ D;
```

And after **A B C D**, there again are two:

```
start:      x
       |    y;
x:     A B z ↑ R;
y:     A B z ↑ S;
z:     C D;
```

When a pointer reaches the end of a rule, the rule is *reduced.* Rule z was reduced when the pointer got to the end of it after yacc read **D**. Then the pointer returns to the rule from which the reduced rule was called, or as in the case above, the pointer splits up into the rules from which the reduced rule was called.

There is a *conflict* if a rule is reduced when there is more than one pointer. Here is an example of reductions with only one pointer:

```
start:      x
       |    y;
x:     A ↑ ;
y:     B ;
```

After A, there is only one pointer—in rule x—and rule x is reduced. Similarly, after B, there is only one pointer—in rule y—and rule y is reduced.

Here is an example of a conflict:

```
start:      x
       |    y;
x:     A ↑ ;
y:     A ↑ ;
```

After **A**, there are two pointers, at the ends of rules **x** and **y**. They both want to reduce, so it is a **reduce/reduce** conflict.

There is no conflict if there is only one pointer, even if it is the result of merging pointers into a common subrule and even if the reduction will result in more than one pointer:

```
start:      x
       |    y;
x:     z R ;
y:     z S ;
z:     A B ↑ ;
```

After **A B**, there is one pointer, at the end of rule **z**, and that rule is reduced, resulting in two pointers:

```
start:      x
       |      y;
x:      z ↑ R;
y:      z ↑ S;
z:      A B;
```

But at the time of the reduction, there is only one pointer, so it is *not* a conflict.

Types of Conflicts

There are two kinds of conflicts, reduce/reduce and shift/reduce. Conflicts are categorized based upon what is happening with the other pointer when one pointer is reducing. If the other rule is also reducing, it is a reduce/reduce conflict. The following example has a *reduce/reduce* conflict in rules **x** and **y**:

```
start:      x
       |      y;
x:      A ↑ ;
y:      A ↑ ;
```

If the other pointer is not reducing, then it is shifting, and the conflict is a *shift/reduce* conflict. The following example has a shift/reduce conflict in rules **x** and **y**:

```
start:      x
       |      y R;
x:      A ↑ R;
y:      A ↑ ;
```

After yacc reads **A**, rule **y** needs to reduce to rule **start**, where **R** can then be accepted, while rule **x** can accept **R** immediately.

If there are more than two pointers at the time of a reduce, yacc lists the conflicts in pairs. The following example has a reduce/reduce conflict in rules **x** and **y** and another reduce/reduce conflict in rules **x** and **z**:

```
start:      x
       |      y
       |      z;
x:      A ↑ ;
y:      A ↑ ;
z:      A ↑ ;
```

Let's define exactly when the reduction takes place with respect to token *lookahead* and pointers disappearing so we can keep our simple definition of conflicts correct. Here is a reduce/reduce conflict:

```
start:      x B
     |      y B;
x:   A ↑ ;
y:   A ↑ ;
```

But there is no conflict here:

```
start:      x B
     |      y C;
x:   A ↑ ;
y:   A ↑ ;
```

The reason the second example is not a conflict is because yacc can look ahead one token beyond the **A**. If it sees a **B**, the pointer in rule y disappears before rule **x** is reduced. Similarly, if it sees a **C**, the pointer in rule **x** disappears before rule **y** reduces.

Yacc can only look ahead one token. The following is not a conflict in a compiler that can look ahead two tokens, but in yacc, it is a reduce/reduce conflict:

```
start:      x B C
     |      y B D;
x:   A ↑ ;
y:   A ↑ ;
```

Parser States

Rather than telling where your conflicts lie in your yacc grammar, yacc tells where they are in *y.output*, which is a description of the state machine it is generating. We will discuss what the states are, describe the contents of *y.output*, then discuss how to find the problem in your yacc grammar given a conflict described in *y.output*. You can generate *y.output* by running yacc with the *−v* (verbose) option.

Each state corresponds to a unique combination of possible pointers in your yacc grammar. Every nonempty yacc grammar has at least two unique possible states: one at the beginning, when no input has been accepted, and one at the end, when a complete valid input has been accepted. The following simple example has two more states:

```
start:     A <one here> B <another here> C;
```

For future examples, we will number the states as a clear means of identification. Although yacc numbers the states, the order of the numbers is not significant:

```
start:     A <state 1> B <state 2> C;
```

When a given stream of input tokens can correspond to more than one possible pointer position, then all the pointers for a given token stream correspond to one state:

```
start:     a
     |     b;
a:   X <state 1> Y <state 2> Z;
b:   X <state 1> Y <state 2> Q;
```

Different input streams can correspond to the same state when they correspond to the same pointer:

```
start:       threeAs;
threeAs: /* empty */
     | threeAs A <state 1> A <state2>
                     A <state 3>;
```

The grammar above accepts some multiple of three A's. State 1 corresponds to 1, 4, 7, ... A's; state 2 corresponds to 2, 5, 8, ... A's; and state 3 corresponds to 3, 6, 9, ... A's. Although not as good design, we rewrite this with right recursion in order to illustrate the next point.

```
start:       threeAs;
threeAs: /* empty */
     | A A A threeAs;
```

(The next example would have a conflict if we used left recursion.) A position in a rule does not necessarily correspond to only one state. A given pointer in one rule can correspond to different pointers in another rule, making several states:

```
start:       threeAs X
     |       twoAs Y;
threeAs: /* empty */
     | A A A threeAs;
twoAs: /* empty */
     | A A twoAs;
```

The grammar above accepts multiples of 2 or 3 A's, followed by an X for multiples of 3, or a Y for multiples of 2. (Without the X or Y, the grammar would have a conflict, not knowing whether a multiple of 6 **A**'s satisfied **threeAs** or **twoAs**.) If we number the states as follows:

```
state 1: 1, 7, ... A's accepted
state 2: 2, 8, ... A's accepted
...
state 6: 6, 12, ... A's accepted
```

then the corresponding pointer positions are as follows:

```
start:      threeAs X
   |        twoAs Y;
threeAs: /* empty */
       | A <1,4> A <2,5> A <3,6> threeAs;
twoAs: /* empty */
     | A <1,3,5> A <2,4,6> twoAs;
```

That is, after the first **A** in **threeAs**, yacc could have accepted 6i+1 or 6i+4 **A**s, where i is 0, 1, etc. Similarly, after the first **A** in **twoAs**, yacc could have accepted 6i+1, 6i+3, or 6i+5 **A**'s.

Contents of y.output

Now that we have defined states, we can look at the conflicts described in *y.output*. The format of the file varies among versions of yacc, but it always includes a listing of all of the parser states. For each states, it lists the rules and positions that correspond to the state, the shifts and reductions the parser will do when it reads various tokens in that state, and what state it will switch to after a reduction produces a non-terminal in that state. The listings below come from various versions of yacc, so you can see that the differences are small. We'll show some ambiguous grammars and the *y.output* reports that identify the ambiguities.

Reduce/Reduce Conflicts

Consider the following ambiguous grammar:

```
start:      a Y
   |        b Y ;
a:   X ;
b:   X ;
```

When we run it through Berkeley yacc, a typical state description is:

```
state 3
      start : a . Y   (1)

      Y   shift 5
      .   error
```

In this state, the parser has already reduced an **a**. If it sees a **Y** it shifts the Y and moves to state 5. Anything else (represented by a dot) is an error. The ambiguity produces a reduce/reduce conflict in state 1:

```
1: reduce/reduce conflict (reduce 3, reduce 4) on Y
state 1
        a : X .   (3)
        b : X .   (4)

      .   reduce 3
```

The first line says that state 1 has a reduce/reduce conflict between rule 3 and rule 4 when token **Y** is read. In this state, it's read an **X** which may be an **a** or a **b**. The third and fourth lines show the two rules that might be reduced. The dot* shows where in the rule you are before receiving the next token. This corresponds to the pointer in the yacc grammar. For reduce conflicts, the pointer is always at the end of the rule. The last line shows that yacc chose to reduce rule 3, since it resolves reduce/reduce conflicts by reducing the rule that appears earlier in the grammar.

The rules may have tokens or rule names in them. The following ambiguous grammar:

```
start:     a Z
      |    b Z;
a:    X y;
b:    X y;
y:    Y;
```

produces a parser with this state:

```
6: reduce/reduce conflict (reduce 3, reduce 4) on Z
state 6
        a : X y .   (3)
        b : X y .   (4)

      .   reduce 3
```

In this state, the parser has already reduced a **Y** to a **y**, but the y could complete either a **a** or a **b**. Non-terminals can cause reduce/reduce conflicts just like tokens can. It's easy to tell the difference if you use uppercase token names, as we have.

---

*Yacc's use of dot to show where you are in the rule can get confusing if you have rules with dots in them. Some versions of yacc use an underscore rather than a dot, which can be equally confusing if you have rules with underscores in them.

The rules that conflict do not have to be identical. The grammar:

```
start:      A B x Z
     |        y Z;
x:    C;
y:    A B C;
```

when processed by AT&T yacc produces a grammar containing this state:

```
7: reduce/reduce conflict (red'ns 3 and 4 ) on Z
state 7
      x :  C_     (3)
      y :  A B C_     (4)

      .  reduce 3
```

In state 7, yacc has already accepted **A B C**. Rule **x** only has **C** in it, because in the **start** rule from which **x** is called, **A B** is accepted before calling **x**. The **C** could complete either an **x** or a **y**. Yacc again resolves the conflict by reducing the earlier rule in the grammar, in this case rule 3.

Shift/Reduce Conflicts

Identifying a shift/reduce conflict is a little harder. To identify the conflict, we will do the following:

- Find the shift/reduce error in *y.output*
- Pick out the reduce rule
- Pick out the relevant shift rules
- See where the reduce rule reduces to
- Deduce the token stream that will produce the conflict

This grammar contains a shift/reduce conflict:

```
start:      x
     |        y R;
x:    A R;
y:    A;
```

AT&T yacc produces this complaint:

```
4: shift/reduce conflict (shift 6, red'n 4) on R
state 4
      x :  A_R
      y :  A_     (4)

      R  shift 6
      .  error
```

State 4 has a shift/reduce conflict between shifting token **R**, and moving to state 6, and reducing rule 4 when it reads an **R**. Rule 4 is rule **y**, as shown in the line:

```
y : A_     (4)
```

You can find the reduce rule in a shift/reduce conflict the same way you find both rules in a reduce/reduce conflict. The reduction number is in parentheses on the right. In the case above, the rule with the shift conflict is the only rule left in the state:

```
x:     A_R;
```

Yacc is in rule **x**, having accepted **A** and about to accept **R**. The shift conflict rule was easy to find in this case, because it is the only rule left, and it shows that the next token is **R**. Yacc resolves shift/reduce conflicts in favor of the shift, so in this case if it receives an **R** it shifts to state 6.

The next thing showing may be a rule instead of a token:

```
start:     x1
     |     x2
     |     y R;
x1:   A R;
x2:   A z;
y:    A;
z:    R;
```

Berkeley yacc reports several conflicts, including this one:

```
1: shift/reduce conflict (shift 6, reduce 6) on R
state 1
      x1 : A . R   (4)
      x2 : A . z   (5)
      y : A .   (6)

      R   shift 6

      z   goto 7
```

In the example above, the reduction rule is:

```
y : A .   (6)
```

so that leaves two candidates for the shift conflict:

```
x1 : A . R   (4)
x2 : A . z   (5)
```

Rule **x1** uses the next token, **R**, so you know it is part of the shift conflict, but rule **x2** shows the next non-terminal (not token). You have to look at the rule for **z** to find out if it starts with an **R**. In this case it does, so there is a three-way conflict for an **A** followed by an **R**: it could be an **x1**, an **x2** which includes a **z**, or a **y** followed by an **R**.

There could be more rules in a conflicting state, and they may not all accept an R. Consider this extended version of the grammar:

```
start:     x1
   |       x2
   |       x3
   |       y R;
x1:    A R;
x2:    A z1;
x3:    A z2;
y:     A;
z1:    R;
z2:    S;
```

MKS yacc produces a listing with this state:

```
State 1
           x1:        A.R
           x2:        A.z1
           x3:        A.z2
     (8)   y:         A.   [ R ]

    Shift/reduce conflict (10,8) on R
        R       shift 10
        S       shift 7
        .       error

        z2        goto 8
        z1        goto 9
```

(The **R** in brackets means that in the grammar, a **y** in this context must be followed by an **R**.) The conflict is between shifting to state 10 and reducing rule 8. The reduce problem, rule 8, is the rule for **y**. The rule for **x1** is a shift problem, because it shows the next token after the dot to be **R**. It is not immediately obvious about **x2** or **x3**, because they show rules **z1** and **z2** following the dots. When you look at rules **z1** and **z2**, you find that **z1** contains an R next and **z2** contains an S next, so **x2** which uses **z1** is part of the shift conflict and **x3** is not.

In each of our last two shift/reduce conflict examples, can you also see a reduce/reduce conflict? Run yacc and look in *y.output* to check your answer.

Review of Conflicts in y.output

Let's review the relationship between our pointer model, conflicts, and *y.output*. First, here is a reduce/reduce conflict:

```
start:      A B x Z
     |       y Z;
x:    C;
y:    A B C;
```

The AT&T yacc listing contains:

```
7: reduce/reduce conflict (red'ns 3 and 4 ) on Z
state 7
x :  C_     (3)
y :  A B C_     (4)
```

There is a conflict because if the next token is Z, yacc wants to reduce both rules 3 and 4, the rules for both x and y. Or using our pointer model, there are two pointers and both are reducing:

```
start:      A B x Z
     |       y Z;
x:    C ↑ ;
y:    A B C ↑ ;
```

Here is a shift/reduce example:

```
start:      x
     |       y R;
x:    A R;
y:    A;
```

Berkeley yacc reports this conflict:

```
1: shift/reduce conflict (shift 5, reduce 4) on R
state 1
       x : A . R  (3)
       y : A .  (4)

       R   shift 5
```

There is a conflict, because if the next token is R, yacc wants to reduce the rule for y and shift an **R** in the rule for x. Or there are two pointers and one is reducing:

```
start:      x
     |       y R;
x:    A ↑ R;
y:    A ↑ ;
```

Common Examples of Conflicts

The three most common situations that produce shift/reduce conflicts are expression grammars, IF—THEN—ELSE, and nested lists of items. After we see how to identify these three situations, we look at ways to get rid of the conflicts.

Expression Grammars

Our first example is from the original UNIX yacc manual. We have added a terminal for completeness:

```
expr: TERMINAL
    | expr '-' expr ;
```

The state with a conflict is:

```
4: shift/reduce conflict (shift 3, red'n 2) on -
     state 4
     expr :  expr_- expr
     expr :  expr - expr_    (2)
```

Yacc tells us that there is a shift/reduce conflict when you get the minus token. Adding our pointers:

```
expr: expr ↑ - expr ;
expr: expr - expr ↑ ;
```

These are the same rule, not even different alternatives under the same name. This shows that you can have a state where your pointers can be in two different places in the same rule. This is because the grammar is recursive. (In fact, all of the examples in this section are recursive. We have found that most of the tricky yacc problems are recursive.)

After accepting two **expr**'s and "−", the pointer is at the end of rule **expr**, as shown in the second line of the pointer example above. But "expr − expr" is also an **expr**, so your pointer can also be just after the first **expr**, as shown in the first line of the example above. If the next token is not "−", then the pointer in the first line disappears because it wants "−" next, so you are back to one pointer. But if the next token is "−", then the second line wants to reduce, and the first line wants to shift.

To solve this conflict, look at *y.output*, shown above, to find the source of the conflict. Get rid of irrelevant rules in the state (there are not any here), and you get the two pointers we just discussed. It becomes clear that the problem is:

```
expr - expr - expr
```

The middle **expr** might be the second **expr** of an "expr – expr", in which case the input is interpreted as:

```
(expr - expr) - expr
```

which is left associative, or might be the first **expr** in which case the input is interpreted as:

```
expr - (expr - expr)
```

which is right associative. After reading "expr – expr", the parser could reduce if using left associativity or shift using right associativity. If not instructed to prefer one or the other, this ambiguity causes a shift/reduce conflict, which yacc resolves by choosing the shift. Figure 8-1 shows the two possible parses.

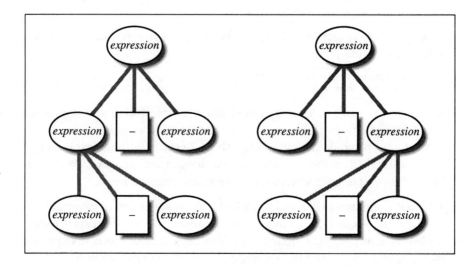

Figure 8-1: Ambiguous input expr – expr – expr

Later in this chapter, we discuss what to do about this kind of conflict.

IF—THEN—ELSE

Our next example is also from the UNIX yacc manual. Again we have added a terminal symbol for completeness:

```
stmt: IF '(' cond ')' stmt
    | IF '(' cond ')' stmt ELSE stmt
    | TERMINAL;
cond: TERMINAL;
```

AT&T yacc complains:

```
8: shift/reduce conflict (shift 9, red'n 1) on ELSE
state 8
        stmt :  IF ( cond ) stmt_     (1)
        stmt :  IF ( cond ) stmt_ELSE stmt
```

In terms of pointers this is:

```
stmt: IF ( cond ) stmt ↑ ;
stmt: IF ( cond ) stmt ↑ ELSE stmt ;
```

The first line is the reduce part of the conflict, and the second, the shift part. This time they are different rules with the same left-hand side. To figure out what is going wrong, we see where the first line reduces to. It has to be a call to **stmt**, followed by an **ELSE**. There is only one place where that can happen:

```
stmt: IF ( cond ) stmt <return to here> ELSE stmt ;
```

After the reduction, the pointer returns to the exact spot where it is for the shift part of the conflict. In fact, that is the same as what was happening with "expr – expr – expr" in the previous example. And using similar logic, in order to reduce "IF (cond) stmt" into "stmt" and end up here:

```
stmt: IF ( cond ) stmt <here> ELSE stmt ;
```

you have to have this token stream:

```
IF ( cond ) IF ( cond ) stmt ELSE
```

Again, do you want to group it like this:

```
IF ( cond ) { IF ( cond ) stmt } ELSE stmt
```

or like this:

```
IF ( cond ) { IF ( cond ) stmt ELSE stmt }
```

The next section explains what to do about this kind of conflict.

Nested List Grammars

Our final example is a simple version of a problem we have helped people track down a number of times. Novice yacc programmers often run into it:

```
start:           outerList Z ;
outerList:  /* empty */
       |      outerList outerListItem ;

outerListItem:    innerList ;

innerList:  /* empty */
       |      innerList innerListItem ;

innerListItem:    I ;
```

AT&T yacc reports this conflict:

```
2: shift/reduce conflict (shift 3, red'n 5) on Z
state 2
      start : outerList_Z
      outerList : outerList_outerListItem
      innerList : _     (5)
```

Let's go through the steps. The reduce rule is the empty alternative of innerList. That leaves two candidates for the shift problem. Rule **start** is one, because it explicitly takes **Z** as the next token. The nonempty alternative of **outerList** might be a candidate, if it takes **Z** next. We see that **outerList** includes an **outerListItem**, which is an **innerList**. The **innerList** can't include an **innerListItem**, because that includes an **I**, and this conflict only occurs when the next token is a **Z**. But an **innerList** can be empty, so the **outerListItem** involves no tokens, so we might actually be at the end of the **outerList** as well, since as the first line in the conflict report told us, an **outerList** can be followed by a **Z**.

This all boils down to this state: we have just finished an **innerList**, possibly empty, or an **outerList**, possibly empty. How can it not know which list it has just finished? Look at the two list expressions. They can both be empty, and the inner one sits in the outer one without any token to say it is starting or finishing the inner loop. Assume the input stream consists solely of a **Z**. Is it an empty **outerList**, or it might be an **outerList** with one item, an empty **innerList**? That's ambiguous.

The grammar is redundant. You have a loop within a loop, with nothing to separate them. Since this grammar actually accepts a possibly empty list of I's followed by a Z, you can write it using only one recursive rule:

```
start:          outerList Z ;
outerList: /* empty */
    |       outerList outerListItem ;
outerListItem:   I ;
```

Or perhaps you forgot some tokens in **outerListItem** to delimit the inner from the outer loop.

How Do I Fix the Conflict?

The rest of this chapter describes what to do with a conflict once you've figured out what it is. We'll discuss how to fix classes of conflicts that commonly cause trouble for yacc users. We welcome feedback from readers about specific problems they've had that can add to this section in future editions. Two examples in the second edition came from a reader in Minneapolis.

When trying to resolve conflicts, consider changing the language you're parsing. Sometimes you work with a language that's already defined, but if not, you can often simplify the yacc description a great deal by making minor adjustments to the language. In fact, the location of a keyword in your language could make the difference between the yacc description being practical, impractical, or even impossible. Languages that yacc has trouble parsing are often hard for people to parse in their heads; you'll end up with a better langauge design once you change your language to remove the conflicts.

IF—THEN—ELSE (Shift/Reduce)

This is one of the examples from earlier in this chapter. Here we describe what to do with the shift/reduce conflict once you've tracked it down. It turns out that the default way that yacc resolves this particular conflict is usually what you want it to do anyway. How do you know it's doing what you want it to do? Your choices are to (1) be good enough at reading yacc descriptions, (2) be masochistic enough to decode the y.output listing, or (3) test the generated code to death. Once you've verified that you're getting what you want, you ought to make yacc quit complaining. Conflict warnings may confuse or annoy anyone trying to maintain your code, and make it easier for you to miss an important warning.

You can rewrite the grammar this way to avoid the conflict:

```
stmt:      matched
      |    unmatched
      ;
matched:   other_stmt
      |    IF expr THEN matched ELSE matched
      ;
unmatched: IF expr THEN stmt
      |    IF expr THEN matched ELSE unmatched
      ;
other_stmt: /* rules for other kinds of statement */ ...
```

The non-terminal **other_stmt** represents all of the other possible statements in the language. Although this works, it adds ugly complication to the grammar.

You can set explicit precedences will stop yacc from issuing a warning.

```
%nonassoc LOWER_THAN_ELSE
%nonassoc ELSE

%%

stmt:      IF expr stmt            %prec LOWER_THAN_ELSE ;
      |    IF expr stmt ELSE stmt;
```

If your language uses a THEN keyword (like Pascal does) you can do this:

```
%nonassoc THEN
%nonassoc ELSE

%%

stmt:      IF expr THEN stmt
      |    IF expr stmt ELSE stmt
      ;
```

A shift/reduce conflict is a conflict between shifting a token (ELSE in the example above) and reducing a rule (**stmt**). You need to assign a precedence to the token (**%nonassoc ELSE** in our example) and to the rule (**%nonassoc THEN** or **%nonassoc LOWER_THAN_ELSE** and **%prec LOWER_THAN_ELSE**.) The precedence of the token to shift must be higher than the precedence of the rule to reduce, so the **%nonassoc ELSE** must come after the **%nonassoc THEN** or **%nonassoc LOWER_THAN_ELSE**. It makes no difference for this application if you use **%nonassoc**, **%left**, or **%right**.

The goal here is to hide a conflict you know about and understand, and *not* to hide any others. When you're trying to mute yacc's warnings about other shift/reduce conflicts, the further you get from the example above, the more careful you should be. Other shift/reduce conflicts may be amenable to a simple change in the yacc description. And, as we mentioned above, *any* conflict can be fixed by changing the language. For example, the IF-THEN-ELSE conflict can be eliminated by insisting on BEGIN-END or braces around the **stmt**.

What would happen if you swapped the precedences of the token to shift and the rule to reduce? The normal IF-ELSE handling makes the following two equivalent:

```
if expr if expr stmt else stmt
if expr { if expr stmt else stmt }
```

It seems only fair that swapping the precedences would make the following two equivalent, right?

```
if expr if expr stmt else stmt
if expr { if expr stmt } else stmt
```

Wrong! That's not what it does. Having higher precedence on the shift (normal IF-ELSE) makes it always shift the ELSE. Swapping the precedences makes it *never* shift the ELSE, so your IF-ELSE can no longer have an else.

Normal IF-ELSE processing associates the ELSE with the most recent IF. Suppose you want it some other way. One possibility is that you only allow one ELSE with a sequence of IFs, and the ELSE is associated with the first IF. This would require a two-level statement definition, as follows:

```
%nonassoc LOWER_THAN_ELSE
%nonassoc ELSE

%%

stmt:      IF expr stmt2 %prec LOWER_THAN_ELSE
    |      IF expr stmt2 ELSE stmt;

stmt2: IF expr stmt2;
```

We don't encourage this; such a language is extremely counterintuitive.

Loop Within a Loop (Shift/Reduce)

```
start:          outerList Z ;
outerList: /* empty */
    |       outerList outerListItem ;

outerListItem:  innerList ;
```

```
innerList:  /* empty */
         |    innerList innerListItem ;

innerListItem:    I ;
```

Resolution depends on whether you want repetitions to be treated as one outer loop and many inner loops, or many outer loops of one inner loop each. The difference is whether the code associated with **outerListItem** gets executed once for each repetition, or once for each set of repetitions. If it makes no difference, arbitrarily choose one or the other. If you want many outer loops, remove the inner loop:

```
start:           outerList Z ;

outerList:  /* empty */
         |    outerList innerListItem ;

innerListItem:    I ;
```

If you want many inner loops, remove the outer loop:

```
start:           innerList Z ;

innerList:  /* empty */
         |    innerList innerListItem ;

innerListItem: I ;
```

Expression Precedence (Shift/Reduce)

```
expr:        expr '+' expr
      |      expr '-' expr
      |      expr '*' expr
      |      ...
      ;
```

If you describe an expression syntax using the technique above, but forget to define the precedences with **%left** and **%right**, you get a truckload of shift/reduce conflicts. Assigning precedences to all of the operators should resolve the conflicts. Keep in mind that if you use any of the operators in other ways, e.g., using a "−" to indicate a range of values, the precedence can also mask conflicts in the other contexts.

Limited Lookahead (Shift/Reduce or Reduce/Reduce)

A class of shift/reduce conflicts are due to yacc's limited lookahead. That is, a parse that could look farther ahead would not have a conflict. For example:

```
rule: command optional_keyword '(' identifier_list ')'
    ;

optional_keyword: /* blank */
    |        '(' keyword ')'
    ;
```

The example describes a command line that starts with a required command, ends with a required identifier list in parentheses, and has in the middle an optional keyword in parentheses. Yacc gets a shift/reduce conflict with this when it gets to the first parenthesis in the input stream, it doesn't know if it goes with the optional keyword or the identifier list. In the first case yacc would shift the parenthesis within the optional_keyword rule, and in the second it would reduce an empty optional_keyword and move on to the identifier list. If yacc could look farther ahead it could tell the difference between the two. But it can't.

The default is for yacc to choose the shift, which means it always assumes the optional keyword is there. (You can't really call it optional in that case.) If you apply precedences you could get the conflict to resolve in favor of the reduction, which would mean you could never have the optional keyword.

Yacc cannot parse the command line with the example description above, no matter how you fiddle with precedences, because yacc lacks the lookahead depth required. Our only choice, if we can't change the syntax of the command language, is to flatten the description:

```
rule:       command '(' keyword ')' '(' identifier_list ')'
    |   command '(' identifier_list ')'
    ;
```

By flattening the list, we allow the parser to scan ahead with multiple possible pointers until it sees a keyword or identifier, at which point it can tell which rule to use.

Flattening is a practical solution in this example, but when more rules are involved it rapidly becomes impractical due to the exponential expansion of the yacc description. You may run into a shift/reduce conflict from limited look-ahead for which your only practical solutions are to change the language, or not to use yacc.

It's also possible to get a reduce/reduce conflict due to limited look-ahead. One way is to have an overlap of alternatives:

```
rule:       command_type_1 ':' '[' ...
    |       command_type_2 ':' '(' ...

command_type_1:  CMD_1 | CMD_2 | CMD_COMMON ;

command_type_2: CMD_A | CMD_B | CMD_COMMON ;
```

The solutions for this are flattening, as we did above. or making the alternatives disjoint, as described in the following section.

You can also get a reduce/reduce conflict from limited lookahead because actions in the middle of a rule are really anonymous rules that must be reduced:

```
rule:       command_list { <action for '[' form> } ':' '[' ...
    |       command_list { <action for '(' form> } ':' '(' ...
```

This is already flattened, so there's nothing you can do to get it to work in yacc. It simply needs a two token lookahead, and yacc doesn't have that. Unless you're doing some sort of exotic communication between the parser and lexer, you can just move the action over:

```
rule:       command_list ':' '[' { <action for '[' form> } ...
    |       command_list ':' '(' { <action for '(' form> } ...
```

Overlap of Alternatives (Reduce/Reduce)

In this case, you have two alternative rules with the same LHS, and the inputs accepted by them overlap partially. Your best bet is to make the two input sets disjoint. For example:

```
rule:       girls
    |       boys
    ;

girls:          ALICE
    |       BETTY
    |       CHRIS
    |       DARRYL
    ;

boys:       ALLEN
    |       BOB
    |       CHRIS
```

```
        |     DARRYL
        ;
```

You will get a reduce/reduce conflict on **CHRIS** and **DARRYL** because yacc can't tell whether they're intended to be **girls** or **boys**. There are several ways to resolve the conflict. One is:

```
rule:       girls | boys | either;

girls:              ALICE
        |    BETTY
        ;

boys:       ALLEN
        |    BOB
        ;

either:             CHRIS
        |    DARRYL
        ;
```

But what if these lists were really long, or were complex rules rather than just lists of keywords, so you wanted to minimize duplication, and **girls** and **boys** were referenced many other places in the yacc description? Here's one possibility:

```
rule:       just_girls
        |    just_boys
        |    either
        ;

girls:              just_girls
        |    either
        ;

boys:       just_boys
        |    either
        ;

just_girls: ALICE
        |    BETTY
        ;

just_boys:  ALLEN
        |    BOB
        ;

either:             CHRIS
        |    DARRYL
        ;
```

All references to "boys | girls" have to be fixed. There's no way to avoid either having to fix references to "boys | girls" or to fix the lists.

But what if it's impractical to make the alternatives disjoint? If you just can't figure out a clean way to break up the overlap, then you'll have to leave the reduce/reduce conflict. Yacc will use its default disambiguating rule for reduce/reduce, which is to choose the first definition in the yacc description. So in the first "girls | boys" example above, CHRIS and DARRYL would always be **girls**. Swap the positions of the **boys** and **girls** lists, and CHRIS and DARRYL are always **boys**. You'll still get the reduce/reduce warning, and yacc will make the alternatives disjoint for you, exactly what you were trying to avoid. You have to rewrite the grammar.

Summary

Ambiguities and conflicts within the yacc grammar are just one type of coding error, one that is problematical to find and correct. This chapter has presented some techniques for correcting these errors. In the chapter that follows, we will largely be looking at other sources of errors.

Our goal in this chapter has been for you understand the problem at a high enough level that you can fix it.

To review how to get to that point:

- Find the shift/reduce error in *y.output*
- Pick out the reduce rule
- Pick out the relevant shift rules
- See where the reduce rule will reduce back to
- With this much information, you ought to be able to deduce the token stream leading up to the conflict.

Seeing where the reduce rule reduces to is typically as easy as we have shown. Sometimes a grammar is so complicated that it is not practical to use our "hunt-around" method, and you will need to learn the detailed operation of the state machine to find the states to which you reduce.

Exercises

1. All reduce/reduce conflicts and many shift/reduce conflicts are caused by ambiguous grammars. Beyond the fact that yacc doesn't like them, why are ambiguous grammars usually a bad idea?

2. Find a grammar for a substantial programming language like C, C++, or Fortran and run it through yacc. Does the grammar have conflicts? (Nearly all of them do.) Go through the *y.output* listing and determine what causes the conflicts. How hard would they be to fix?

3. After doing the previous exercise, speculate about why languages are usually defined and implemented with ambiguous grammars.

9

Error Reporting
and Recovery

The previous two chapters discussed techniques for finding errors within yacc grammars. In this chapter, we turn our attention to the other side of error correction and detection—how the parser and lexical analyzer detect errors. This chapter presents some techniques to incorporate error detection and reporting into the grammar. To ground the discussion in a complete example, we will refer to the menu generation language defined in Chapter 4, *A Menu Generation Language*.

Yacc provides the **error** token and the **yyerror** routine, which are typically sufficient for early versions of a tool. However, as any program begins to mature, especially a programming tool, it becomes important to provide better error recovery, which allows for detection of errors in the later portions of the file, and better error reporting.

Error Reporting

Error reporting should give as much detail about the error as is possible. The default yacc error only declares that a syntax error exists and to stop parsing. In our examples, we typically added a mechanism for reporting the line number. This provides the location of the error but does not report any other errors within the file or where in the specified line the error occurs.

It is best to categorize the possible errors, perhaps building an array of error types and defining symbolic constants to identify the errors. For example, in the MGL a possible error is to fail to terminate a string. Another error might be using the wrong type of string (quoted string instead of an identifier or vice versa). At a minimum, the MGL should report:

• General syntactic errors (e.g., a line that makes no sense)

• A nonterminated string

- The wrong type of string (quoted instead of unquoted or vice versa)
- A premature end-of-file
- Duplicate names used

Our existing mechanism that reports a syntax error with the line number is a good one; if we cannot identify the error, we will use this as a fallback. We will place other more specific error reports where we recognize the possibility of such an error. In general, this should be enough to point out the offending line in the input file, which in turn is often enough to determine the nature of the error.

The duty for error correction does not lie with yacc alone, however. Many fundamental errors are better detected by lex. For instance, the normal quoted string matching pattern is:

```
\"[^\"\n]*\"
```

We would like to detect an unterminated quoted string. One potential solution is to add a new rule to catch unterminated strings as we did in the SQL parser in Chapter 5. If a quoted string runs all the way to the end of the line without a closing quote, we print an error:

```
\"[^\"\n]*\"      {
                yylval.string = yytext;
                return QSTRING;
        }

\"[^\"\n]*$ {
                warning("Unterminated string");
                yylval.string = yytext;
                return QSTRING;
        }
```

This technique of accepting illegal input and then reporting it with an error or warning is a powerful one that can be used to improve the error reporting of the compiler. If we had not added this rule, the compiler would have used the generic "syntax error" message; by reporting the specific error, we can tell the user precisely what to fix. Later in this chapter, we will describe ways to resynchronize and attempt continuing operation after such errors.

The yacc equivalent of accepting erroneous input is demonstrated by testing for the improper use of a quoted string for an identifier and vice versa.

For instance, the following MGL specification fragment should generate such an error:

```
screen "flavors"
```

instead of:

```
screen flavors
```

It is a lot more useful to tell the user that the string is the wrong type rather than just saying "syntax error"; this is the type of error a beginning user makes. To handle the wrong type of string, we modify the yacc grammar to recognize the error condition and report it. Thus, we can introduce a non-terminal to replace the currently used tokens **QSTRING** and **ID**. Currently, the MGL has the rules:

```
screen_name: SCREEN ID { start_screen($2); }
           | SCREEN    { start_screen(strdup("default")); }
           ;

screen_terminator: END ID { end_screen($2); }
                 | END { end_screen(strdup("default")); }
                 ;

screen_contents: titles lines
               ;

titles: /* empty */
      | titles title
      ;

title: TITLE qstring { add_title($2); }
     ;
```

Instead, use the following rules to replace the **QSTRING** and **ID** tokens:

```
id:             ID    { $$ = $1; }
     |          QSTRING { warning("String literal inappropriate", $1);
                         $$ = $1; /* use it anyway */
                }
     ;

qstring:        QSTRING { $$ = $1; }
     |          ID { warning("Non-string literal inappropriate", $1);
                     $$ = $1; /* use it anyway */
                }
     ;
```

Now when the yacc grammar detects an improper string literal or identifier, it can pinpoint the type of error. We use the improper literal anyway; the generated C code may be wrong but this lets the parser continue and look for more errors. Sometimes error recovery is impossible; often it is desirable to issue a warning but not to actually do any error recovery. For example, *pcc*, the portable C compiler, aborts when it sees an illegal character in the input stream. The compiler writers decided that there was a point when resynchronizing and continuing were not possible. However, *pcc* reports questionable assignments and then recovers, as in this C fragment:

```
int i = "oops";
```

In this case, it issues an error message but processing continues.

Our next example detects reused names. This illustrates a type of error detection that occurs within the compiler code, rather than within the lexical analyzer or the parser; indeed, it cannot be implemented inside the grammar or lexical analyzer because it requires *memory* of the tokens previously seen. The approach we took with the MGL was straightforward. In this instance, duplicate names are syntactically OK but cause duplicates in the C code the MGL generates, so whenever we see a new name, we "register" it in a list of used names. Prior to registration, we scan the list to see if the name is already registered; if it is, we report a duplicate name error. The full code is shown in Appendix I, *MGL Compiler Code*.

Better Lex Error Reports

Some simple lex hackery can let you produce better error reports than the rather dull defaults. A very simple technique that we used in the SQL parser reports the line number and current token. We track the line number on each \n character, and the current token is always available in **yytext**.

```
\n          lineno++;

%%

void yyerror(char *s)
{
    printf("%d: %s at %s\n", lineno, s, yytext);
}
```

A slightly more complex trick saves the input a line at a time:

```
%{
char linebuf[500];
%}
%%
\n.* { strcpy(linebuf, yytext+1); /* save the next line */
       lineno++;
       yyless(1);        /* give back all but the \n to rescan */
```

```
        }
%%

void yyerror(char *s)
{
        printf("%d: %s at %s in this line:\n%s\n",
               lineno, s, yytext, linebuf);
}
```

The pattern "\n.*" matches a newline character and the entire next line. The action code saves the line, then gives it back to the scanner with **yyless( )**.

To pinpoint the exact position of an erroneous token in the input line, keep a variable that records the current position in the line, setting it to zero on each "\n.*" token and incrementing it by **yyleng** on each token. Assuming the line position is in **tokenpos**, you can report the error position like this:

```
void yyerror(char *s)
{
        printf("%d: %s:\n%s\n",
               lineno, s, linebuf);
        printf("%*s\n", 1+tokenpos, "^");
}
```

The second **printf** prints a caret at position **tokenpos**, like this:

```
3: syntax error:
CREATE TABLE sample ( color CHAR(10) NOT DEFAULT 'plaid' )
                                       ^
```

Error Recovery

We concentrated on error reporting in the previous section; in this section, we discuss the problem of error recovery. When an error is detected, the yacc parser is left in an ambiguous position. It is unlikely that meaningful processing can continue without some adjustment to the existing parser stack.

There is no reason error recovery is necessary. Many programs do not attempt to continue once an error has been detected. For compilers, this is often undesirable, because running the compiler itself is expensive. For example, a C compiler typically consists of several stages: the preprocessor, the parser, the data flow analyzer, and the code generator. Reporting an error in the parser stage and ceasing operation will require that the single problem be repaired and the process started again—but the work by the preprocessor must be redone. Instead, it may be possible to recover from the error and continue examining the file for additional errors, stopping the compiler before invoking the next stage. This technique improves the productivity of the programmer by shortening the edit-compile-test cycle, since several errors can be repaired in each iteration of the cycle.

Typically, error recovery becomes increasingly valuable as the compiler becomes increasingly complex. However, the issues involved in error recovery can be illustrated with a simple compiler such as the MGL.

Yacc Error Recovery

Yacc has some provision for error recovery, by using the **error** token. Essentially, the error token is used to find a *synchronization point* in the grammar from which it is likely that processing can continue. Note that we said *likely*. Sometimes our attempts at recovery will not remove enough of the erroneous state to continue, and the error messages will cascade. Either the parser will reach a point from which processing *can* continue or the entire parser will abort.

After reporting a syntax error, a yacc parser discards any partially parsed rules until it finds one in which it can shift an **error** token. It then reads and discards input tokens until it finds one which can follow the **error** token in the grammar. This latter process is called *resynchronizing*.

In the MGL, we could use screens as synchronization points. For example, after seeing an erroneous token, it could discard the entire screen record and restart at the next screen. In Chapter 4, *A Menu Generation Language*, our rule for a screen was:

```
screens:    /* nothing */
          | preamble screens screen
          | screens screen
          ;


screen:    screen_name screen_contents screen_terminator
         | screen_name screen_terminator
         ;
```

We can augment this to synchronize in the **screen** rule:

```
screen:    screen_name screen_contents screen_terminator
         | screen_name screen_terminator
         | screen_name error screen_terminator
               { warning("Skipping to next screen",(char *)0); }
         ;
```

This is the basic "trick" to error recovery—attempting to move forward in the input stream far enough that the new input is not adversely affected by the older input.

Error recovery is enhanced with proper language design. Modern programming languages use statement terminators, which serve as convenient synchronization points. For instance, when parsing a C grammar, a logical synchronizing character is the semicolon. Error recovery can introduce other problems, such as missed declarations if the parser skips over a declaration looking for a semicolon, but these can also be included in the overall error recovery scheme.

The potential for cascading errors caused by lost state (discarded variable declarations, for example) discourages a strategy that throws away large portions of the input stream. One mechanism for counteracting the problem of cascading errors is to count the number of error messages reported and abort the compilation process when the count exceeds some arbitrary number. For example, many C compilers abort after reporting ten errors within a file.

Like any other yacc rule, one that contains **error** can be followed with action code. It would be typical at this type of point to clean up after the error, reinitialization of data state, or other necessary "housekeeping" activities, so when recovery is done, processing can continue. For example, the previous error recovery fragment from MGL might be expressed as:

```
screen:    screen_name screen_contents screen_terminator
      | screen_name screen_terminator
      | screen_name error
            { recover(); }
          screen_terminator
                { warning("Skipping to next screen",(char *)0); }
      ;
```

Unfortunately, this means the entire input must be parsed up to a **screen_terminator** before the state machine has recovered. This means that if the screen terminator were not found, the parser would throw away the rest of the input file looking for it, causing a fatal syntax error. (Recall that we have no error recovery at the level above the screen rule in this example). Normally, the parser refrains from generating any more error messages until it has successfully shifted three tokens without an intervening syntax error, at which point it decides that it has resynchronized and returns to its normal state. If we wish to force immediate resynchronization, we can use the special yacc action **yyerrok**. This informs the parser that recovery is complete and resets the parser to its normal mode. Our previous example then becomes:

```
screen:    screen_name screen_contents screen_terminator
      |  screen_name screen_terminator
      |  screen_name error
            { yyerrok; recover(); }
         screen_terminator
            { warning("Skipping to next screen",(char *)0); }
      ;
```

The **recover( )** routine should ensure that the next token read is an **END**, which is what **screen_terminator** needs, or you may immediately get another syntax error.

The most common place to use **yyerrok** is in interactive parsers. If you were reading commands from the user, each starting on a new line:

```
commands:   /* empty */
      |     commands command
      ;

command:    ...
      |     error {
                  yyclearin;  /* discard lookahead */
                  yyerrok;
                  printf("Enter another command\n");
            }
```

The macro **yyclearin** discards any lookahead token, and **yyerrok** tells the parser to resume normal parsing, so it will start anew with the next command the user types.

If your code reports its own errors, your error routines should use the yacc macro **YYRECOVERING( )** to test if the parser is trying to resynchronize, in which case you shouldn't print any more errors, e.g.:

```
warning(char *err1, char *err2)
{
      if(YYRECOVERING())
            return;     /* no report at this time */
      . . .
}
```

Where to Put Error Tokens

Proper placement of **error** tokens in a grammar is a black art with two conflicting goals. You want to be as sure as possible that the resynchronization will succeed, so you want error tokens in the highest level rules in the grammar, maybe even the start rule, so there will always be a rule to which the parser can recover. On the other hand, you want to discard as little input as possible before recovering, so you want the error tokens in the lowest level rules to minimize the number of partially matched rules the parser has to discard during recovery.

If your top level rule matches a list (e.g., the list of screens in the MGL) or a list of declarations and definitions in a C compiler, make one of the alternatives for a list entry contain **error**, as in the command and screen examples above. This applies equally for relatively high-level lists such as the list of statements in a C function.

If punctuation separates elements of a list, use that punctuation in error rules to help find synchronization points. For example, in a C compiler, you might write this:

```
stmt:       . . .
        |   RETURN expr ';'
        |   '{' opt_decls stmt_list '}'
        |   error ';'
        |   error '}'
        ;
```

Since each C statement ends with ";" if it's a simple statment or "}" if it's a compound statement, the two **error** rules tell the parser that it should start looking for the next statement after a ";" or "}".

You can also put error rules at lower levels, e.g., as a rule for an expression, but in our experience, unless the language provides punctuation or keywords that make it easy to tell where the expression ends, the parser can rarely recover at such a low level.

Compiler Error Recovery

In the previous section, we described the mechanisms that yacc provides for error recovery. In this section, we discuss external recovery mechanisms, provided by the programmer.

The inherent difficulty with error recovery is that it usually depends upon semantic knowledge of the grammar rather than just syntactic knowledge. This greatly complicates complex recovery within the grammar itself.

Previously we suggested that a user-provided mechanism for resetting internal data structures of the compiler might be in order; in addition, it may be desirable for the recovery routine to scan the input itself and, using a heuristic, perform appropriate error recovery. For instance, a C compiler writer might decide that errors encountered during the declarations section of a code block are best recovered from by skipping the entire block rather than continuing to report additional errors. She might also decide that an error encountered during the code section of the code block need only skip to the next semicolon. A truly ambitious writer of compilers or interpreters might wish to report the error and attempt to describe potential correct solutions.

Once the compiler has performed such error recovery, it should clear the yacc lookahead buffer which contains the erroneous token, using **yyclearin**, and probably also use **yyerrok** so the compiler immediately reports any other errors found. (You might not call **yyerrok** if you're not confident that you've recovered properly.)

Typically, sophisticated error correction uses both yacc error recovery for fundamental syntactic errors and user-provided routines for semantic errors and data structure recovery (e.g., discarding data for local variables, nested BEGIN blocks and loops if recovery skipped to the end of a routine.) Our final version of MGL, in Appendix I, *MGL Compiler Code*, includes some of these error recovery techniques.

Exercises

1. Add error recovery to the SQL grammar in Chapter 5 and Appendix J. At the very least, you should resynchronize at the ";" between SQL statements. Create some deliberately wrong SQL and give it to your parser. How well does it recover? Usually it takes several attempts to get error rules that recover effectively.

2. (Term project) Yacc's error recovery works by discarding input tokens until it comes up with something that is syntactically correct. Another approach inserts rather than discards tokens, because in many cases it is easy to predict what token must come next. For example, in a C program, every **break** and **continue** must be followed by a semicolon, and every **case** must be preceded by a semicolon or a close brace. How hard would it be to augment a yacc parser so that in case of an input error, it can suggest appropriate tokens to insert?

    You'll need to know more about the insides of yacc for this exercise. See the Bibliography for suggested readings.

A

AT&T Lex

AT&T lex is the most common version found on UNIX systems. If you're not sure which version of lex you have, try running a lexer through it with the *−v* flag. If the produces a terse two-line summary like this, it's AT&T lex:

```
5/2000 nodes(%e), 16/5000 positions(%p), 5/2500 (%n),
4 transitions, 0/1000 packed char classes(%k), 6/5000
packed transitions(%a), 113/5000 output slots(%o)
```

If produces a page of statistics with lex's version number on the first line, it's flex.

Lex processes a specification file and generates source code for a lexical analyzer. By convention, the specification file has a *.l* extension. The file that lex generates is named *lex.yy.c*.

The syntax of the AT&T lex command is:

> **lex** *[options] file*

where *options* are as follows:

−c Writes the lexer in C (default). The obsolescent flag is not present in many versions.

−n Don't print the summary line with the table sizes. This is the default unless the definition section changes the size of one of lex's internal tables.

−r Actions are written in RATFOR, a dialect of FORTRAN. This option no longer works in most versions of lex, and is not even present in many of them.

−t Source code is sent to standard output instead of to the default file *lex.yy.c*. This is useful in *Makefiles* and shell scripts that direct the output of lex to a named file.

−v Generates a one-line statistical summary of the finite state machine. This option is implied when any of the tables sizes are specified in the definitions section of the lex specification.

−*f*   Translate faster by not packing the generated tables. (Only practical for small lexers.) Present only in BSD-derived versions of lex.

You must specify options before the file on the command line. You can specify one or more files, but they are treated as a single specification file. Standard input is used if no file is specified.

The lex library *libl.a* contains **yyreject**, an internal routine required by any lexer that uses **REJECT**, and default versions of **main( )** and **yywrap( )**.

See Chapter 6, *A Reference for Lex Specifications*, for more information on lex specifications.

Error Messages

This section discusses correcting problems and errors reported by AT&T lex. The error messages are listed alphabetically and are intended for reference use.

Action does not terminate
> While processing an action, lex encountered the end of the file before the action terminated. This usually means the closing brace of the action is missing.
> Solution: Add the missing brace.

bad state %d %o
> This is an internal lex error.
> Solution: Report problem to system's software maintainer.

bad transition %d %d
> This is an internal lex error.
> Solution: Report problem to system's software maintainer.

Can't open %s
> Lex was unable to open the output file *lex.yy.c*. This is usually because you do not have write permission on the directory or the file exists and is not writable.
> Solution: Remove the file; change permission on the directory; change directories.

Can't read input file %s
> Lex was unable to open the file specified on the command line.
> Solution: Invoke lex with a valid filename.

ch table needs redeclaration

While reading a %T declaration from the lex file, the number of characters defined exceeded the amount of space lex has allocated for character tables.

Solution: Either remove characters from the translation table or, if you have the lex source code, rebuild lex to maintain a larger translation table.

Character '%c' used twice
Character %o used twice

While processing a new translation table, a character was redeclared.

Solution: Remove the extraneous declaration.

Character value %d out of range

While processing a new translation table, lex saw an invalid character value. Valid values are in the range 1 to 256.

Solution: Correct the invalid character value.

Definition %s not found

After seeing a {definition}, lex was unable to find it in the list of declared substitutions.

Solution: Replace substitution; define it in definition section.

Definitions too long

Lex has a limit on the size of a definition. The length of the definition is too large.

Solution: Make the definition shorter (perhaps by breaking into two); rebuild lex to allow longer definitions.

EOF inside comment

While processing a comment, lex encountered the end of the file. This is usually caused because there is an unterminated comment.

Solution: Add the missing "*/".

Executable statements should occur right after %

While processing the rules section, lex saw an action without an associated pattern. It is legal to place executable code immediately following the rules break (this code will then be executed on each call to **yylex()**). Such code can't appear anywhere else in the rules section. Solution: Either fix the pattern associated with the action or move the code to the beginning of the rules section.

Extra slash removed

An invalid "/" character was ignored. This probably means that a literal "/" in a pattern wasn't quoted.

Solution: Quote the "/", or fix the error.

Invalid request %s

While processing the definition section, a lex declaration (beginning with "%") was seen, but the declaration was not valid. Valid requests are either "%{" to start a literal block, or "%" followed by a letter. See "Internal Tables" and "Literal Block" in Chapter 6.

Iteration range must be positive

Can't have negative iteration

An iteration range (using {count,count}) was used with a negative value, or a zero value for the second count.

No space for char table reverse

Internal lex error.

Solution: Report problem to system's software maintainer.

No translation given – null string assumed

While processing the definition section, lex saw a substitution string that had no substitution text. Lex uses an empty string. This is a warning message only.

Non-portable character class

While scanning through a rule, a non-portable escape sequence was specified. This occurs whenever an octal constant is used in a character class.

Solution: Live with non-portability, or don't use an octal constant there.

Non-terminated string

Non-terminated string or character constant

EOF in string or character constant

While reading a rule or processing a string in action code, lex has encountered a string that does not terminate before the end of line.

Solution: If the string is supposed to continue to the next line, add a "\" continuation marker; if not, add the missing ".".

OOPS – calloc returns a 0

Internal error, or system out of virtual memory.

Solution: Report problem to system's software maintainer.

output table overflow

Internal error.

Solution: Report problem to system's software maintainer.

Parse tree too big %s

Lex has exhausted the parse tree space.

Solution: Simplify the lex specification; increase the parse tree space with the %e declaration in the definition section.

Premature eof

While processing the definition section, a "%{" was seen but no "%}".

Solution: Add the missing "%}".

Start conditions too long

The total length of the names of start states (also known as start conditions) exceeds the size of an internal table.

Solution: Shorten the name of the start condition.

String too long

While reading a rule, lex encountered a string that is too long to store inside its internal (static) buffer.

Solution: Shorten the string; rewrite the string expression to use a more compact form; rebuild lex to allow larger strings.

Substitution strings may not begin with digits

While processing the definition section, lex saw a substitution string name that began with a digit.

Solution: Replace the substitution string with one not beginning with a digit.

syntax error

Lex has seen a line that is syntactically incorrect.

Solution: Fix the error.

Too late for language specifier

While processing the definition section, lex saw a %c or %r (language choice of C or RATFOR) after it had already started to write the output file.

Solution: Declare the language earlier.

Too little core for final packing

Too little core for parse tree

Too little core for state generation

Too little core to begin
>   Internal error, or system out of virtual memory.
>   Solution: Report problem to system's software maintainer.

Too many characters pushed
>   Lex has exhausted the stack space available for an input token.
>   Solution: Shorten the size of the token; rebuild lex to accept larger-sized tokens.

Too many definitions
>   While parsing the input file, lex has exhausted its static space for storing definitions.
>   Solution: Remove some definitions; rebuild lex to use a larger definitions table.

Too many large character classes
>   Lex has exhausted internal storage for large character classes. A large character class is used to describe the ranges that occur inside brackets ([]).
>   Solution: Shorten the number of different large character classes; rebuild lex to allow more large character classes.

Too many packed character classes
>   Solution: Use the %k declaration.

Too many positions %s
>   Lex has exhausted the space for positions.
>   Solution: Use the %p declaration.

Too many positions for one state – acompute
>   Lex has used more than 300 positions for a single state, which is an internal lex limit. This error indicates an overly complex state.
>   Solution: Simplify the lex specification; rebuild lex to allow more positions per state.

Too many right contexts
>   Lex has exhausted the space for right contexts, the pattern text after the "/" pattern character.
>   Solution: Decrease the number of right contexts used; rebuild lex to allow more right contexts.

Too many start conditions

While processing the definition section, the number of *start conditions* exceeded the size of lex's static internal table.

Solution: Use fewer start conditions; recompile lex with a larger number of start conditions.

Too many start conditions used

Too many start conditions were specified for a particular rule for lex to handle.

Solution: Decrease the number of starting positions; rebuild lex to allow a larger number of start conditions per rule.

Too many states %s

Solution: Use the %n declaration.

Too many transitions %s

Solution: Use the %a declaration.

Undefined start condition %s

A <start state> was used in a pattern, but lex was unable to find it in the list of declared start state.

Solution: Declare the start state, or correct the name if it's misspelled.

Unknown option %c

Lex was invoked with an unknown switch. The valid switches are listed above.

yacc stack overflow

Lex was written using a yacc grammar. The yacc-generated grammar has exhausted its stack space. (We'll be impressed if you see this one!)

Solution: Shorten or reorder the expressions in the lex specification; rebuild lex with a larger yacc stack area.

B

AT&T Yacc

Options

AT&T yacc is distributed with most versions of UNIX, except for the most recent verions of Berkeley UNIX, which have Berkeley yacc. If you're not sure which version of yacc you have, try running it with no arguments. If it says:

```
fatal error: cannot open input file, line 1
```

it's AT&T yacc. If it gives you a summary of the command syntax, it's Berkeley yacc.

Yacc processes a file containing a grammar and generates source code for a parser. By convention, the grammar file has a *.y* extension. The file that yacc generates is named *y.tab.c*.

The syntax of the yacc command is:

> **yacc** *[options] file*

where *options* are as follows:

-*d*   Generates the header file *y.tab.h* that contains definitions of token names.

-*l*   Omits **#line** constructs in the generated code.

-*t*   Includes runtime debugging code when *y.tab.c* is compiled.

-*v*   Produces the file *y.output*, which contains a listing of all of the states in the generated parser and other useful information.

In order to compile the parser generated by yacc, you must supply a **main** routine and a supporting routine, **yyerror**. The UNIX library *liby.a* contains default versions of these routines.

See Chapter 7, *A Reference for Yacc Grammars*, for information on yacc specifications.

Error Messages

This section discusses correcting problems and errors reported by yacc, aside from the shift/reduce and reduce/reduce errors discussed in Chapter 8, *Yacc Ambiguities and Conflicts.* The error messages are organized alphabetically.

%d rules never reduced

Some rules in the grammar were never reduced, either because they were never mentioned on the right-hand side of other rules or because they were involved in reduce/reduce conflicts. Yacc reports the number of rules that did not reduce.

Solution: Resolve the conflicts, or look for spelling errors.

'000' is illegal

An octal escape specified the null character, which AT&T yacc reserves for its internal use.

Solution: Remove the offending escape.

action does not terminate

An action in the input runs off the end of the file, probably because of an extra '{' or a missing '}'.

Solution: Fix the erroneous action.

action table overflow

no space in action table

While parsing the input file (or processing the input), the yacc static action table overflowed.

Solution: Simplify actions; recompile yacc with a larger action table; use bison or Berkeley yacc.

bad %start construction

A %start directive didn't contain a non-terminal name.

Solution: Change the %start so it has an argument.

bad syntax in %type

The type argument to a **%type** directive was not valid. This occurs because the directive had no arguments.

Solution: Remove the **%type** or give it arguments.

bad syntax on $<ident> clause

While reading an action, an invalid value type appeared.

Solution: Correct the invalid type declaration either by removing the offending declaration or by fixing the type declaration.

bad syntax on first rule

The first rule was syntactically incorrect. For example, yacc never found the colon following the first rule.

Solution: Fix the first rule.

bad tempfile

Internal error, or system ran out of disk space.

Solution: Rerun yacc; report problem to system's software maintainer.

cannot open input file

Yacc could not open the input file specified on the command line, or no name appeared.

Solution: Correct the filename.

cannot open temp file

Yacc attempted to open the *yacc.tmp* temporary file but failed. This probably occurred because the current directory was not writable or because an unwritable *yacc.tmp* already exists.

Solution: Remove *yacc.tmp* or change the directory permissions.

cannot open y.output

cannot open y.tab.c

cannot open y.tab.h

Yacc attempted to open one of its output files but failed. This probably occurred because the current directory was not writable or because an unwritable version of the file already exists.

Solution: Remove the file or change the directory permissions.

cannot place goto %d

Internal error.

Solution: Report problem to system's software maintainer.

cannot reopen action tempfile

Yacc keeps all its actions in a temporary file called *yacc.acts*. This file has disappeared; it was probably deleted while yacc was running.

Solution: Do not delete yacc's temporary files while running yacc.

clobber of a array, pos'n %d, by %d

Internal error.

Solution: Report problem to system's software maintainer.

default action causes potential type clash

A rule has no action, so it uses the default "$$ = $1", but the type of $1 is different from that of $$. of the rule.

```
%union{
        int integer;
        char *string;
}

%TOKEN <integer> int
%type <string> s
%%
        ...
int:  s ;
```

Solution: Add an explicit action or correct the types. The last line might be corrected to:

```
int:  s { $$ = atoi($1); } ;
```

eof before %

While reading the input file, yacc failed to find the rules section, probably because the "%%" was omitted.

Solution: Add the "%%".

EOF encountered while processing %union

The file ended in the middle of a **%union** directive, probably because of a missing "}".

Solution: Add the missing brace.

EOF in string or character constant

EOF inside comment

The file ended inside a string, character constant, or comment.

Solution: Add the closing quotation mark or "*/".

Error; failure to place state %d

Internal error.

Solution: Report problem to system's software maintainer.

illegal %prec syntax

No symbol name follows a **%prec** directive.

Solution: Add one.

illegal comment

A "/", in the rules section outside an action is not followed by a "*".

Solution: Remove the slash or add an asterisk.

illegal \nnn construction

An octal character escape contains something other than octal digits, e.g.:

```
%left '\2z'
```

Solution: Correct the octal character escape.

illegal option: %c

Yacc was run with an option other than the valid ones listed above.

illegal or missing ' or "

While reading a string literal or character literal, yacc failed to find the closing single or double quote.
Solution: Supply the closing quotation mark or marks.

illegal rule: missing semicolon or | ?

Yacc saw in invalid character such as a "%" in a rule.
Solution: Revise the rule.

internal yacc error: pyield %d

Internal error.
Solution: Report problem to system's software maintainer.

invalid escape

The character after a "\" is not a valid escaped character.
Solution: Correct or remove the escape.

illegal reserved word: %s

The directive following a "%" is not one that yacc understands.
Solution: Fix the directive if possible. Also, check to see if the directive is a bison directive. See Appendix D, *GNU Bison*.

item too big

In the process of building the output strings, yacc has encountered an item that is too large to fit inside its internal buffer.
Solution: Use a shorter name (this error occurs when the name of the item was quite large; in the implementation we used, 370 characters was the limit).

more than %d rules

While reading rules in from the specified grammar, yacc has over-flowed the static space allocated for rules.

Solution: Simplify the grammar; recompile yacc with larger state tables; use bison or Berkeley yacc.

must return a value, since LHS has a type

A rule with a typed left-hand side does not set "$$".

Solution: Add a return value by assigning an appropriate value to "$$".

must specify type for %s

A %token directive, no type was specified for the directive.

Solution: Add a type.

must specify type of $%d

In an action, yacc has found a value reference usage which must be typed.

Solution: Declare the type of the symbol in the definition section.

newline in string or char. const.

A string or character constant runs past the end of the line.

Solution: Add the closing quotation mark or marks.

nonterminal %s illegal after %prec

A %prec directive was followed by a non-terminal.

Solution: Correct the erroneous %prec.

nonterminal %s never derives any token string

A recursive rule loops endlessly, because there is no non-recursive alternative for the left-hand side. Example:

```
x_list:'X' x_list
```

with no other rule for **x_list**.

Solution: Remove the rule or add a non-recursive alternative. This example could be rewritten:

```
x_list:'X' x_list | 'X' ;
```

nonterminal %s not defined!

A non-terminal symbol never appears in the left-hand side of the rule. Yacc reports the line where the undefined non-terminal was used.
Solution: Define the symbol or fix the spelling error.

optimizer cannot open tempfile

The temporary file yacc uses cannot be opened.
Solution: Do not delete yacc temporary files while yacc is running.

out of space

While running through the optimizer, yacc has exhausted its static internal working space.

out of space in optimizer a array

a array overflow

out of state space

One of yacc's internal tables ran out of space.
Solution: Simplify grammar; rebuild yacc with more space in the "a" array; use bison or Berkeley yacc.

Ratfor Yacc is dead: sorry.

The −*r* flag used to produce a RATFOR parser.
Solution: Stick with C.

redeclaration of precedence of %s

The specified token has its precedence declared in more than one **%left**, **%right**, or **%nonassoc** directive.

```
%left PLUS MINUS
%left TIMES DIVIDE
%left PLUS
```

Solution: Remove all the extra declaration.

Rule not reduced: %s

A rules was never reduced, either because it was never mentioned on the right-hand side of other rules or because they were involved in reduce/reduce conflicts. This error message is reported in *y.output*.
Solution: Examine the rule and rewrite so that it does reduce.

syntax error

Yacc did not understand the statement.
Solution: Fix the statement.

token illegal on LHS of grammar rule

A token was found on the left-hand side of the rule on the specified line. Tokens can appear only on the right-hand side.

```
%token FOO
%%
FOO: ;
```

Solution: Correct the rule.

too many characters in ids and literals

While processing the input file, yacc has exhausted the internal static storage for identifiers and literals.

Solution: Simplify grammar; rebuild yacc with larger static tables; use bison or Berkeley yacc.

too many lookahead sets

An internal buffer overflowed.

Solution: Simplify the grammar or rebuild yacc with more lookahead set space.

too many nonterminals, limit %d

Yacc has found more non-terminals than fit in its table.

Solution: Simplify the grammar; rebuild yacc with larger internal tables; use bison or Berkeley yacc.

too many states

An internal table overflowed.

Solution: Simplify the grammar (thus, it will take fewer states); increase the number of allowed states by recompiling yacc; use bison or Berkeley yacc.

too many terminals, limit %d

The grammar has found more tokens (terminal symbols) than fit in yacc's statically defined buffer space. The limit may be as low as 127 tokens.

Solution: Simplify the grammar; rebuild yacc with larger internal tables; use bison or Berkeley yacc.

type redeclaration of nonterminal %s

type redeclaration of token %s

The value type of the non-terminal token has been declared more than once. Sample:

```
%union{
int integer;
char *string;
}

%type <string> foo
%type <integer> foo
```

Solution: Remove one of the the offending **%type** directives.

unexpected EOF before %

The file given to yacc was empty.

Solution: Put something in the file (preferably a yacc grammar).

unterminated < ... > clause

A type name (within angle brackets) runs off the end of the file.

Solution: Put in a closing bracket.

working set overflow

An internal table overflowed.

Solution: Simplify the grammar or rebuild yacc with more working set space.

yacc state/nolook error

Internal error.

Solution: Report problem to system's software maintainer.

C

Berkeley Yacc

Berkeley yacc is a nearly exact reimplementation of AT&T yacc with few extra features.

Options

Berkeley yacc's options are the same as AT&T yacc's with these additions:

−*b* pref   Uses *pref* as the prefix for generated files instead of *y*.

−**r**   Generates separate files for code and tables. The code file is named *y.code.c*, and the tables file is named *y.tab.c*.

There is no library for Berkeley yacc; you have to provide your own versions of **main( )** and **yyerror( )**.

Error Messages

This section discusses correcting problems and errors reported by Berkeley yacc, aside from the shift/reduce and reduce/reduce errors discussed in Chapter 8, *Yacc Ambiguities and Conflicts*. Each error message starts with a letter **f** for fatal error, **e** for error, or **w** for warning. Yacc gives up as soon as it sees an error or fatal error. Most of the error message also include the input filename and line number, which we omit here.

Fatal Errors

f − cannot open *file*

Yacc couldn't open a file. If it's a name you specified, make sure the file exists and is readable. If it's one of yacc's temporary or output file, make sure that the appropriate directory is readable and there is not already a read-only version of the given file.

f - out of space

f - too many gotos

f - too many states

f - maximum table size exceeded

> An internal table overflowed, or insufficient virtual memory was available. Unless you have a stupendously huge grammar with tens of thousands of tokens and rules, this probably represents a bug in yacc. Solution: Report problem to system's software maintainer.

Regular Errors

e - unexpected end-of-file

> The input file ended in a syntactically impossible place.
> Solution: Check and fix the input.

e - syntax error

> Yacc didn't find a mandatory syntax element, e.g., after a "%" it didn't find any of the possible words allowed there.
> Solution: Check and fix the input.

e - unmatched /*

> The file ends in the middle of a comment, probably because the close comment is missing or mistyped.
> Solution: Check and fix the input.

e - unterminated string

> A string runs past the end of a line, probably because the close quote is missing.
> Solution: Add the missing quote.

e - unmatched %{

> The file ends in the literal block, probably because the "%}" is missing
> Solution: Add the missing "%}".

e - unterminated %union declaration

> The file ends in the %union declaration, probably because the closing brace is missing.
> Solution: Add the missing "}".

e - too many %union declarations

> There are multiple %union declarations. Yacc only allows one.
> Solution: Remove the extra one, or combine them.

e – illegal tag

> Value type tags must be valid C identifiers, e.g.:
>
> ```
> %token <ab&z> foo
> ```
>
> The tag ab&z is illegal.
>
> Solution: Change the tag name.

e – illegal character

> An octal or hex escape sequence represents a value too large to fit in a *char* variable.
>
> Solution: Use character values between 0 and 255.

e – illegal use of reserved symbol %s

> The symbol names $accept, $end, any names of the form $$*N* where N is a number, and the name consisting of a single dot are reserved for yacc's internal use.
>
> Solution: Pick another name.

e – the start symbol %s cannot be declared to be a token

> A token appears in the **%start** declaration.
>
> Solution: Don't do that.

e – the start symbol %s is a token

> The start symbol appears in a **%token** declaration.
>
> Solution: Don't do that.

e – no grammar has been specified

> The rules section of the grammar contains no rules, probably because of a missing or extra %% line.
>
> Solution: Correct the error.

e – a token appears on the lhs of a production

> The left-hand side of every rule must be a non-terminal, not a token.
>
> Solution: Correct the error.

e – unterminated action

> The grammar file ends in the middle of an action, probably because of a mising close brace.
>
> Solution: Add the missing brace.

e – illegal $-name

> A value reference with an explicit tag is of an invalid form, e.g., $<foo>bar.
>
> Solution: Correct the error.

e – $$ is untyped

> An action contains a reference to $$, but the left-hand side symbol has no value type set.
>
> Solution: Remove the reference to $$, or assign a type to the symbol.

e - $%d (%s) is untyped

> An action contains a reference to $N, but the corresponding right hand side symbol has no value type set.
>
> Solution: Remove the reference to $N, or assign a type to the symbol.

e - $%d is untyped

> An out-of-range value reference, e.g., $0, needs an explicit type.
>
> Solution: Use an explicit type, e.g., "$<sym>0".

e - the start symbol %s is undefined

> There is no rule with the start symbol on its left-hand side.
>
> Solution: Add one, or correct spelling errors.

Warnings

w - the type of %s has been redeclared

> The type of symbol's value has been set more than once, inconsistently.
>
> Solution: Only declare a symbol's type once.

w - the precedence of %s has been redeclared

> A token appears in more than one **%left**, **%right**, or **%nonassoc** declaration.
>
> Solution: Only set a symbol's precedence once.

w - the value of %s has been redeclared

> The token number of a token has been declared more than once.
>
> Solution: Only declare a token's number once. Better yet, let yacc choose its own token numbers for non-literal tokens.

w - the start symbol has been redeclared

> The grammar contains multiple inconsistent **%start** declarations.
>
> Solution: Remove all but one of them.

w - conflicting %prec specifiers

> A rule contains multiple inconsistent **%prec** specifiers. You can only use a maximum of one per rule.
>
> Solution: Remove extra predecence specifiers.

w - $%d references beyond the end of the current rule

> The action contains a reference to a nonexistent right-hand side symbol, e.g., $9 when the right-hand side contains only eight symbols.
>
> Solution: Correct the error.

w – the default action assigns an undefined value to $$

In a rule with no explicit action, $$ and $1 do not have the same value type. For example:

```
%union{
        int integer;
        char *string;
}

%TOKEN <integer> int
%type <string> s
%%
        ...
int:  s ;
```

Solution: Change the types, or add appropriate action code. For example:

```
int:  s { $$ = atoi($1); } ;
```

w – the symbol %s is undefined

There is no rule with the given non-terminal on its left-hand side.
Solution: Add one, or correct spelling errors.

Informative Messages

%s: %d rules never reduced

Some rules are never used, either because they weren't used in the grammar or because they were on the losing end of shift/reduce or reduce/reduce conflicts. Either change the grammar to use the rules or remove them.

%d shift/reduce conflicts, %d reduce/reduce conflicts

The grammar contains conflicts, which you should fix if you weren't expecting them. See Chapter 8, *Yacc Ambiguities and Conflicts*, for more details.

GNU Bison

The GNU project's yacc replacement is called *bison*. Briefly, GNU (*Gnu's Not UNIX*) is the project of the Free Software Foundation and is an attempt to create a UNIX-like operating system with source code available publicly (although GNU is not public domain, it is freely available and has a license intended to keep it freely available). Hence, bison is available to anyone. For more information on how to obtain bison, GNU, or the Free Software Foundation, contact:

> Free Software Foundation, Inc.
> 675 Massachusetts Avenue
> Cambridge, MA 02139
> (617) 876-3296

Users with access to the Internet can FTP bison and all other GNU software from prep.ai.mit.edu in the directory */pub/gnu.*

Parsers generated with some versions of bison are subject to the GNU "copyleft" software license which sets conditions on the distribution of GNU and GNU-derived software. If you plan to use bison to develop a program distributed to others, be sure to check the file *COPYING* included with the bison distribution to see if you agree to the terms.

This description reflects bison version 1.18, which was released in May 1992.

Differences

In general, bison is compatible with yacc, although there are occasional yacc grammars that do not work properly with bison. Bison is derived from an early version of Berkeley yacc, but each has been developed independently for several years and there are now many small differences. Nevertheless, bison can often be a boon when trying to deal with some of the problems associated with yacc, notably yacc's use of internal static buffers.

Bison uses dynamic memory rather than static memory, so it can often accept a yacc grammar that AT&T yacc will not.

Further, bison offers some minor enhancements that can prove to be of value:

- **%expect** in the definition section tells bison to expect a certain number of shift/reduce conflicts. Bison refrains from reporting the number of shift/reduce conflicts if it is exactly this number.

- **%pure_parser** in the definition section tells bison to generate a reentrant parser (one without global variables). This lets you use the parser in a multi-threaded environment, and allows the parser to call itself recursively. In a reentrant parser, the interface to **yylex( ) is slightly different**, and the code in the actions and supporting routines must also be reentrant.

- **%semantic_parser** and **%guard** are used in a *semantic parser,* one that attempts more sophisticated error recovery based upon the meaning (or contents) of the token, rather than the type of the token. Such a parser is more complex but provides more functionality. Bison is distributed with two model parser internals, one called *bison.simple* and the other *bison.hairy.* The latter is used for the semantic parser. "Guards" control the actions of the parser, handling reductions and errors. This feature is rarely used and not documented in the online bison manual.

- **@N** in actions maintains information about the source file line and column numbers of tokens in the current rule, which can be useful in error messages. This information must be provided by the lexer. For a more detailed explanation, see the bison manual.

- Bison does not write out names to *y.tab.c.* Instead it writes to *filename.tab.c* for the file *filename.y.* Command-line flag let you specify other filenames, or use the traditional yacc names.

- Bison has command-line options to change the prefixes of the symbols in the generated parser from the default "yy." This lets you include more than one parser in the same program.

We've noted most of the places where bison and yacc differ, but bison comes with about 100 pages of online documentation which quite completely explain the differences between bison and yacc.

E

Flex

A freely available version of lex is *flex.* It is the version of lex distributed with 4.4BSD and by the GNU project. Internet users can also FTP it from ftp.ee.lbl.gov. The most significant advantages of flex are that it is much more reliable than AT&T lex, generates faster lexical analyzers, and does not have lex's limitations upon table size. Flex may be redistributed with no requirements other than reproducing the authors' copyright and disclaimer, and there are no distribution restrictions at all on flex scanners.

Flex is highly compatible with lex. Some AT&T lex scanners will need to be modified to work with flex, as detailed below.

This description reflects flex version 2.3.7, released in March 1991.

Flex Differences

We've noted differences between flex and other versions of lex throughout the text. Here is a summary of the most important differences:

- Flex does not need an external library (AT&T lex scanners must be linked with the lex library by using *–ll* on the command line). The user, however, must supply a **main** function or some other function which calls **yylex**. For POSIX compatibility, flex 2.4 will change the default **yywrap()** from a macro to a library routine, so scanners that do not define their own **yywrap()** will need to be linked with the library.

- Flex has a different, nearly useless, version of lex's translation tables (the %t or %T declaration in the lex specification file).

- Flex expands pattern definitions slightly differently than lex. Whenever it expands a pattern, it places parentheses, "()", around the expansion. For example, the flex documentation lists the following:

```
NAME    [A-Z][A-Z0-9]*
%%
foo{NAME}?      printf( "Found it\n" );
%%
```

Lex will not match the string "foo" in this example but flex will. Without the grouping, the last parameter of the expansion is the target of the question mark operator. With the grouping, the entire expansion is the target of the "?" operator.

- Flex doesn't support the undocumented internal lex variable **yylineno**.
- Flex doesn't let you redefine the macros **input** and **output**. See "Input from Strings" in Chapter 6, for details. As in lex, **ECHO** output may be redirected by modifying the flex file pointer **yyout**. Similarly, input may be redirected by modifying the flex file pointer **yyin**.
- Flex lets scanners read from multiple nested input files. See "Include Operations" in Chapter 6.

Flex offers the following additional features:

- Flex offers *exclusive start conditions*, that is, conditions which exclude all other conditions when in that state.
- The special pattern "<<EOF>>" matches at the end of a file.
- Flex dynamically allocates tables, so table directives are not necessary and are ignored if present.
- The name and arguments of the scanning routine are taken from the macro YY_DECL. You can redefine the macro to give the scanner a different name than **yylex** or to have it take argument, or return a value other than an *int*.
- Flex lets you write multiple statements on the same action line without braces, "{}", although it is dreadful style to do so.
- Flex allows "%{" and "%}" in actions. When it sees "%{" in an action, it copies everything up to the "%}" to the generated C file, rather than attempting to match braces.
- Flex scanners can be compiled by C++ as well as by C, although they take no advantage of the object-oriented features of C++.

Options

Flex has a lot more options than AT&T lex.

−*b*   Generates a report in *lex.backtrack* of the rules which required backtracking. Rules that backtrack are slow and you can usually adjust your rules to avoid it. The online flex documentation discusses the use of this option in considerable depth

−*d*   Generates debugging code in the generated scanner.

–f   Generates uncompressed "full" tables which are faster but larger.

–i   Generates a case-insensitive scanner, one which matches upper and lowercase characters regardless of the case of the letters in the patterns in rules.

–p   Produces a report of features used in the scanner that have a performance impact.

–s   Suppressses the default rule that echoes unmatched input, so the generated scanner instead aborts with an error on unmatched input.

–v   Produces a summary report of scanner statistics.

–Cx Controls the degree of table compression. Possible values for *x* are efmF. See the flex documentation for details.

–F   Generates "fast" tables which may be faster or smaller than full tables.

–I   Generates an interactive scanner, one which matches tokens immediately on reading each input line rather than looking one character ahead.

–L   Does not put #*lines* in the generated C code.

–Sx Use the given lexer skeleton rather than the default. Of use mostly for debugging flex itself.

–T   Runs in trace mode, useful mostly for debugging flex itself.

–8   Generates a scanner that is 8-bit clean even if the local default is 7-bit characters.

Error Messages

This section discusses correcting problems and errors reported by flex.

unrecognized '%' directive

In the definitions section, a % must be followed by "{" or "}" to bracket user C code, one of the letters "s" or "x" to declare a start state, one of "anpek" for an (ignored) table size declaration, or one of "otcu" which are obsolete.

Solution: Remove or correct the directive.

illegal character

An illegal character appears in the definitions section

Solution: Remove or correct the character.

incomplete name definition

A name definition (substitution) doesn't contain a pattern.

Solution: Add one.

unrecognized %used/%unused construct

The definition section contained an invalid form of the obsolete *%used* or *%unused* declarations.

Solution: Remove it.

bad row in translation table

Each line in the translation table must start with a number.

Solution: Remove or correct the row.

undefined {name}

A reference to a named pattern (substitution) in braces refers to a name that is not defined.

Solution: Change the reference or define the name.

bad start condition name

A start condition prefix in < > has an invalid name. Names must be valid C identifiers.

Solution: Correct the name.

missing quote

A quoted pattern runs past the end of a line.

Solution: Add the missing quote.

bad character inside { }'s

Repeat counts in patters must consist only of digits, perhaps separated by commas.

Solution: Correct the count.

missing }

A repeat count runs to the end of a line, presumably because the closing brace is missing.

Solution: Add the missing brace.

bad name in { }'s

A pattern name (substitution) must consist of letters, digits, underscores, and hyphens.

Solution: Correct the name

missing }

A pattern name in braces runs to the end of a line, presumably because the closing brace is missing.

Solution: Add the missing brace.

EOF encountered inside an action

An action runs to the end of the file, presumably because the closing brace is missing.

Solution: Add the missing brace.

warning - %used/%unused have been deprecated

These obsolete declarations no longer do anything.

Solution: Remove them.

fatal parse error

The yacc parser that parses the input found an unrecoverable syntax error.

Solution: Correct the error.

multiple <<EOF>> rules for start condition %s

You can only have one EOF rule per start condition.

Solution: Remove all but one of them.

warning - all start conditions already have <<EOF>> rules

If all start states already have EOF rules, an EOF rule with no start state can never match.

Solution: Remove the rule, or correct the state states.

start condition %s declared twice

Each start state may only be declared once.

Solution: Remove the duplicate declaration.

undeclared start state %s

A start state prefix in < > refers to an unknown state.

Solution: Declare the state or correct the spelling.

scanner requires -8 flag

The lexer spec contains 8-bit characters, but the local default is 7 bits.

Solution: Remove the 8-bit characters or use the *-8* flat.

REJECT cannot be used with -f or -F

The *-f* and *-F* flags generate lexers that cannot handle the backtracking required by REJECT.

Solution: Either don't use REJECT or don't use those flags.

could not create lex.backtrack

The file couldn't be created, probably because the directory or a previous version of the file is read-only.

Solution: Remove any previous version of the file, change directory permissions, or change to another directory.

read( ) in flex scanner failed

I/O error on the input file.

Solution: Either your disk is broken or there is an error in flex.

-C flag must be given separately

You cannot combine the *-C* flag with any others in the same argument.

Solution: Don't do that.

full table and –Cm don't make sense together

full table and –I are (currently) incompatible

full table and –F are mutually exclusive

These are inconsistent table compression options.

Solution: Specify one or the other.

–S flag must be given separately

You cannot combine the *–S* flag with any others in the same argument.

Solution: Use separate arguments.

fatal error - scanner input buffer overflow

fatal flex scanner internal error — end of buffer missed

fatal flex scanner internal error — no action found

flex scanner jammed

flex scanner push-back overflow

out of dynamic memory in yy_create_buffer( )

unexpected last match in input( )

These are fatal internal errors in the flex scanner that flex itself uses. All indicate an internal error of some sort.

Solution: Report problem to system's software maintainer.

attempt to increase array size by less than 1 byte

attempt to increase array size failed

bad state type in mark_beginning_as_normal( )

bad transition character detected in sympartition( )

consistency check failed in epsclosure( )

consistency check failed in symfollowset

could not create unique end-of-buffer state

could not re-open temporary action file

dynamic memory failure building %t table

dynamic memory failure in copy_string( )

dynamic memory failure in copy_unsigned_string( )

dynamic memory failure in snstods( )

empty machine in dupmachine( )

error occurred when closing backtracking file

error occurred when closing output file

error occurred when closing skeleton file

error occurred when closing temporary action file

error occurred when closing temporary action file

error occurred when deleting output file

error occurred when deleting temporary action file

error occurred when writing backtracking file

error occurred when writing output file

error occurred when writing skeleton file

error occurred when writing temporary action file

found too many transitions in mkxtion( )

memory allocation failed in allocate_array( )

request for < 1 byte in allocate_array( )

symbol table memory allocation failed

too many %t classes!

These all represent internal errors in flex. The file errors sometimes mean that you are out of disk space.

Solution: Free up some disk space, or report problem to system's software maintainer.

Flex Versions of Lexer Examples

Two of the lex examples in Chapter 2 used code specific to AT&T lex to take input from a string instead of from a file. Flex uses different methods to change the input source. Examples E-1 and E-2 are the same examples written for flex.

Example E-1: Flex specification to parse a command line ape-05.l

```
%{
unsigned verbose;
char *progName;

int myinput(char *buf, int max);
#undef YY_INPUT
#define YY_INPUT(buf,result,max) (result = myinput(buf,max))
%}

%%

-h      |
"-?"    |
-help { printf("usage is: %s [-help | -h | -? ] [-verbose | -v]"
       " [(-file| -f) filename]\n", progName);
       }
-v      |
-verbose { printf("verbose mode is on\n"); verbose = 1; }

%%
char **targv;     /* remembers arguments */
char **arglim;    /* end of arguments */

main(int argc, char **argv)
{
```

Example E-1: Flex specification to parse a command line ape-05.l (continued)

```
        progName = *argv;
        targv = argv+1;
        arglim = argv+argc;
        yylex();
}


static unsigned offset = 0;

/* provide a chunk of stuff to flex */
/* it handles unput itself, so we pass in an argument at a time */
int
myinput(char *buf, int max)
{
        int len, copylen;

        if (targv >= arglim)
                return 0;    /* EOF */
        len = strlen(*targv)-offset; /* amount of current arg */
        if(len >= max)
                copylen = max-1;
        else
                copylen = len;
        if(len > 0)
                memcpy(buf, targv[0]+offset, copylen);
        if(targv[0][offset+copylen] == '\0') {    /* end of arg */
                buf[copylen] = ' ';
                copylen++;
                offset = 0;
                targv++;
        }
        return copylen;
}
```

Example E-2: Flex command scanner with filenames ape-06.l

```
%{
unsigned verbose;
unsigned fname;
char *progName;

int myinput(char *buf, int max);
#undef YY_INPUT
#define YY_INPUT(buf,result,max) (result = myinput(buf,max))
%}

%s FNAME

%%
[ ]+            /* ignore blanks */ ;
<FNAME>[ ]+  /* ignore blanks */ ;
```

Example E-2: Flex command scanner with filenames ape-06.l (continued)

```
-h      |
"-?"    |
-help { printf("usage is: %s [-help | -h | -? ] [-verbose | -v]"
        " [(-file| -f) filename]\n", progName);
      }
-v      |
-verbose { printf("verbose mode is on\n"); verbose = 1; }


-f      |
-file { BEGIN FNAME; fname = 1; }

<FNAME>[^ ]+ { printf("use file %s\n", yytext); BEGIN 0; fname = 2;}

[^ ]+ ECHO;
%%
char **targv;      /* remembers arguments */
char **arglim;     /* end of arguments */

main(int argc, char **argv)
{
      progName = *argv;
      targv = argv+1;
      arglim = argv+argc;
      yylex();
      if(fname < 2)
            printf("No filename given\n");
}

static unsigned offset = 0;

/* provide a chunk of stuff to flex */
/* it handles unput itself, so we pass in an argument at a time */
int
myinput(char *buf, int max)
{
      int len, copylen;

      if (targv >= arglim)
            return 0;   /* EOF */
      len = strlen(*targv)-offset; /* amount of current arg */
      if(len >= max)
            copylen = max-1;
      else
            copylen = len;
      if(len > 0)
            memcpy(buf, targv[0]+offset, copylen);
      if(targv[0][offset+copylen] == '\0') {   /* end of arg */
            buf[copylen] = ' ';
            copylen++;
            offset = 0;
            targv++;
```

Example E-2: Flex command scanner with filenames ape-06.l (continued)

```
    } else offset += copylen;
    return copylen;
}
```

MKS lex and yacc

Mortice Kern Systems has a *lex* and *yacc* package that runs under MS-DOS and OS/2. It includes an excellent 450 page manual, so in this discussion concentrates on the differences between MKS and other implementations. It is available from:

> Mortice Kern Systems
> 35 King Street North
> Waterloo, ON N2J2W9
> Canada
>
> Phone: +1 519 884 2251
>   or in the U.S. (800) 265-2797
> E-mail: inquiry@mks.com

Differences

Most of the differences are due to running under MS-DOS or OS/2 rather than UNIX.

- The output files have different names: *lex_yy.c*, *ytab.c*, *ytab.h*, and *y.out.* rather than *lex.yy.c*, *y.tab.c*, *y.tab.h*, and *y.output.*

- MKS lex has its own method for handling nested include files. See "Include Operations" in Chapter 6 for details.

- MKS lex has its own method for resetting a lexer into its initial state. See "Returning Values from yylex( )" in Chapter 6.

- MKS lex uses the macro **yygetc( )** to read input. You can redefine it to change the input source. See "Input from Strings" in Chapter 6.

- The standard lex token buffer is only 100 characters. You can enlarge it by redefining some macros. See "yytext" in Chapter 6.

- The internal yacc tables are generated differently. This makes error recovery slightly different; in general MKS yacc will perform fewer reductions than will UNIX yacc before noticing an error on a lookahead token.

New Features

- MKS lex and yacc can generate scanners and parsers in C++ and Pascal as well as in C.
- MKS provides the *yacc tracker*, a screen-oriented grammar debugger that lets you single step, put breakpoints into, and examine a parser as it works.
- MKS lex and yacc both let you change the prefix of symbols in the generated C code from the default "yy," so you can include multiple lexers and parsers in one program.
- MKS yacc can allocate its stack dynamically, allowing recursive and reentrant parsers.
- MKS yacc has *selection preferences* which let you resolve reduce/reduce conflicts by specifying lookahead tokens that tell it to use one rule or the other.
- The MKS lex library contains routines that skip over C style comments and handle C strings including escapes.
- MKS yacc documents many more of its internal variables than do AT&T or Berkeley yacc. This lets error recovery routines get access and change much more of the parser's internal state.
- The package includes sample scanners and parsers for C, C++, dBASE, Fortran, Hypertalk, Modula-2, Pascal, pic (the *troff* picture language), and SQL.

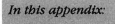
G

Abraxas lex and yacc

Abraxas Software offers pcyacc, which contains pcyacc and pclex, MS-DOS and OS/2 versions of yacc and lex. It is available from:

> Abraxas Software
> 7033 SW Macadam Avenue
> Portland OR 97219
> Phone: +1 503 244 5253

Pclex is based on flex, so much of what we have said about flex also applies to pclex.

Differences

- The output files have different names: *lex_yy.c*, *yytab.c*, *yytab.h*, and *yy.lrt*. rather than *lex.yy.c*, *y.tab.c*, *y.tab.h*, and *y.output*.
- The standard lex input buffer is only 256 characters. You can enlarge it by redefining some macros. See "yytext" in Chapter 6.

New Features

- An option lets you just check the syntax of a yacc specification rather than waiting for it to generate a complete parser.
- Each time it reduces a rule, a parser can write a line with the symbols in that rule into a file. (Abraxas refers to this as the parse tree option.)
- An optional extended error recovery library allows more complete error reporting and recovery.

- The package includes sample scanners and parsers for ANSI and K&R C, C++, Cobol, dBase III and IV, Fortran, Hypertalk, Modula-2, Pascal, pic (a demo language unrelated to *troff*), Postscript, Prolog, Smalltalk, SQL, and yacc and lex themselves.

H

POSIX lex and yacc

The IEEE POSIX P1003.2 standard will define portable standard versions of lex and yacc. In nearly all cases the standards merely codify long-standing existing practice. POSIX lex closely resembles flex, minus the more exotic features. POSIX yacc closely resembles AT&T or Berkeley yacc. The input and output filenames are identical to those in flex and AT&T yacc.

Options

The syntax of the POSIX lex command is:

lex [*options*] [*file* ...]

If multiple input files are specified, they are catenated together to form one lexer specification.

The *options* are as follows:

−*c*   Writes actions in C (obsolescent).

−*n*   Suppresses the summary statistics line.

−*t*   Sends source code to standard output instead of to the default file *lex.yy.c.*

−*v*   Generates a short statistical summary of the finite state machine. This option is implied when any of the tables sizes are specified in the definitions section of the lex specification.

The syntax of the yacc command is:

yacc [*options*] *file*

where *options* are as follows:

−*b*xx Uses "xx" rather than the default "*yy*" as the prefix in generated filenames.

−*d*   Generates header file *y.tab.h* that contains definitions of token names for use by lexical analyzer routine.

-*l*   Does not include **#line** constructs in the generated code. These constructs help identify lines in the specification file in error messages.

-*p*xx Uses "xx" rather than the default "*yy*" as the prefix in symbols in the generated C code. This lets you use multiple parsers in one program.

-*t*   Includes runtime debugging code when *y.tab.c* is compiled.

-*v*   Produces the file *y.output*, which is used to analyze ambiguities and conflicts in the grammar. This file contains a description of parsing tables.

Differences

The main differences are due to POSIX internationalization.

- POSIX doesn't standardize features that aren't implemented in a consistent way in most existing versions. Hence POSIX specifies no way to change the lex input source (other than assigning to **yyin**) or to change the size of internal buffers. It has no version of lex translation tables. A POSIX-compliant implementation may offer any of these as an extension.

- As in AT&T lex, **yywrap()** is a function which you can redefine, not a macro.

- You can force **yytext** to be an array or a pointer by using a **%array** or **%pointer** declaration. In the absence of such a declaration, an implementation may use either.

- POSIX lex defines extra character regular expressions which handle extended non-English character sets. See "Regular Expression Syntax" in Chapter 6.

- POSIX yacc has a library with the standard versions of **main()** and **yyerror()**. You can (and probably should) write your own versions of both.

I

MGL Compiler Code

Chapter 4, *A Menu Generation Language,* presented the lex and yacc grammars for the MGL. Here we present the entire code of the MGL, including runtime support code not shown in the chapter. Many improvements to the runtime code are possible, such as:

- Screen clearing after improper input.

- Better handling of the **system()** call, particularly saving and restoring terminal modes and screen contents.

- Automatic generation of a **main** routine. Currently, it must be defined outside the calling program. Furthermore, it must call the routine **menu_cleanup** before exiting.

- More flexible command handling, e.g., allowing unique prefixes of commands rather than requiring the whole command.

- Taking keyboard input a character at a time in *cbreak* mode rather than the current line at a time.

- More flexible nesting of menus.

See the Preface for information on obtaining an online copy of this code.

MGL Yacc Source

This is file *mglyac.c.*

```
%{
#include <stdio.h>
#include <string.h>
#include <stdlib.h>

int screen_done = 1; /* 1 if done, 0 otherwise */
char *act_str;    /* extra argument for an action */
char *cmd_str;    /* extra argument for command */
char *item_str;   /* extra argument for
                   * item description */
%}
```

```
%union {
    char    *string;     /* string buffer */
    int     cmd;         /* command value */
}

%token <string> QSTRING ID COMMENT
%token <cmd> SCREEN TITLE ITEM COMMAND ACTION EXECUTE EMPTY
%token <cmd> MENU QUIT IGNORE ATTRIBUTE VISIBLE INVISIBLE END

%type <cmd> action line attribute command
%type <string> id qstring

%start screens

%%

screens:  screen
        | screens screen
        ;
screen:   screen_name screen_contents screen_terminator
        | screen_name screen_terminator
        ;

screen_name: SCREEN id { start_screen($2); }
           | SCREEN    { start_screen(strdup("default")); }
           ;

screen_terminator: END id { end_screen($2); }
                 | END { end_screen(strdup("default")); }
                 ;

screen_contents: titles lines
               ;

titles: /* empty */
      | titles title
      ;

title: TITLE qstring { add_title($2); }
     ;

lines: line
     | lines line
     ;

line: ITEM qstring command ACTION action attribute
        { item_str = $2;
          add_line($5, $6);
            $$ = ITEM;
          }
        ;

command: /* empty */ { cmd_str = strdup(""); }
       | COMMAND id { cmd_str = $2; }
```

```
            ;

action: EXECUTE qstring
            { act_str = $2;
            $$ = EXECUTE;
            }
      | MENU id
            { /* make "menu_" $2 */
            act_str = malloc(strlen($2) + 6);
            strcpy(act_str,"menu_");
              strcat(act_str, $2);
            free($2);
            $$ = MENU;
          }
      | QUIT   { $$ = QUIT; }
      | IGNORE { $$ = IGNORE; }
      ;

attribute: /* empty */    { $$ = VISIBLE; }
          | ATTRIBUTE VISIBLE { $$ = VISIBLE; }
          | ATTRIBUTE INVISIBLE { $$ = INVISIBLE; }
          ;

id: ID
    { $$ = $1; }
  | QSTRING
    { warning("String literal inappropriate",
             (char *)0);
      $$ = $1;   /* but use it anyway */
    }
  ;

qstring: QSTRING { $$ = $1; }
       | ID
          { warning("Non-string literal inappropriate",
                   (char *)0);
          $$ = $1;      /* but use it anyway */
          }
        ;
%%

char *progname = "mgl";
int lineno = 1;

#define DEFAULT_OUTFILE "screen.out"

char *usage = "%s: usage [infile] [outfile]\n";

main(int argc, char **argv)
{
     char *outfile;
     char *infile;
     extern FILE *yyin, *yyout;
```

297

```
        progname = argv[0];

        if(argc > 3)
        {
              fprintf(stderr,usage, progname);
              exit(1);
        }
        if(argc > 1)
        {
              infile = argv[1];
              /* open for read */
              yyin = fopen(infile,"r");
              if(yyin == NULL) /* open failed */
              {
                    fprintf(stderr,"%s: cannot open %s\n",
                          progname, infile);
                    exit(1);
              }
        }

        if(argc > 2)
        {
              outfile = argv[2];
        }
        else
        {
                    outfile = DEFAULT_OUTFILE;
        }

        yyout = fopen(outfile,"w");
        if(yyout == NULL) /* open failed */
        {
                    fprintf(stderr,"%s: cannot open %s\n",
                          progname, outfile);
              exit(1);
        }

        /* normal interaction on yyin and
           yyout from now on */

        yyparse();

        end_file(); /* write out any final information */

        /* now check EOF condition */
        if(!screen_done) /* in the middle of a screen */
        {
              warning("Premature EOF",(char *)0);
              unlink(outfile); /* remove bad file */
              exit(1);
        }
        exit(0); /* no error */
}
```

```
warning(char *s, char *t) /* print warning message */
{
        fprintf(stderr, "%s: %s", progname, s);
        if (t)
                fprintf(stderr, " %s", t);
        fprintf(stderr, " line %d\n", lineno);
}
```

MGL Lex Source

This is file *mgllex.l.*

```
%{
#include "mglyac.h"
#include <string.h>

extern int lineno;
%}

ws        [ \t]+
comment   #.*
qstring   \"[^\"\n]*[\"\n]
id        [a-zA-Z][a-zA-Z0-9]*
nl        \n


%%

{ws}        ;
{comment}   ;
{qstring}   { yylval.string = strdup(yytext+1); /* skip open quote */
              if(yylval.string[yyleng-2] != '"')
                  warning("Unterminated character string",(char *)0);
          else /* remove close quote */
              yylval.string[yyleng-2] = '\0';
              return QSTRING;
          }
screen    { return SCREEN; }
title     { return TITLE; }
item      { return ITEM; }
command   { return COMMAND; }
action    { return ACTION; }
execute   { return EXECUTE; }
menu      { return MENU; }
quit      { return QUIT; }
ignore    { return IGNORE; }
attribute { return ATTRIBUTE; }
visible   { return VISIBLE; }
invisible { return INVISIBLE; }
end       { return END; }
{id}      { yylval.string = strdup(yytext);
              return ID;
          }
```

```
{nl}        { lineno++; }
.           { return yytext[0]; }
%%
```

Supporting C Code

This is file *subr.c.*

```c
/* subr.c */

/*
 * Supporting subroutines for the menu generation
 * language (MGL)
 *
 * Tony Mason
 * November 1988
 * Completed by John Levine, August 1992
 */

/* includes */
#include <stdio.h>
#include <stdlib.h>
#include <string.h>
#include "mglyac.h"
#include "mgl-code"        /* contains definitions of
                    * skeleton file to be built */

extern FILE *yyin, *yyout;

/* imports */
extern int screen_done;
extern char *cmd_str, *act_str,*item_str;

/* exports */

/* local */
static char current_screen[100]; /* reasonable? */
static int done_start_init;
static int done_end_init;
static int current_line;
struct item {
        char            *desc;          /* item description */
        char            *cmd;           /* command */
        int             action;         /* action to take */
        char            *act_str;       /* action operation */
        int             attribute;      /* visible/invisible */
        struct item     *next;          /* next member of list */
} *item_list, *last_item;

/* macros */
#define SCREEN_SIZE 80
```

```
      void cfree(char *);      /* free if not null */

/* code */

/*
 * start_screen:
 * This routine begins preparation of the screen.  It
 * writes the preamble and modifies the global state
 * variable screen_done to show that a screen is in
 * progress (thus, if a screen is in progress when EOF
 * is seen, an appropriate error message can be given).
 */

start_screen(char *name)   /* name of screen to create */
{
      long time(),tm = time((long *)0);
      char *ctime();

      if(!done_start_init)
      {
            fprintf(yyout,
                "/*\n * Generated by MGL: %s */\n\n",
                ctime(&tm));
            dump_data(screen_init);
            done_start_init = 1;
      }
      if(check_name(name) == 0)
            warning("Reuse of name",name);
      fprintf(yyout, "/* screen %s */\n", name);
      fprintf(yyout, "menu_%s()\n{\n",name);
      fprintf(yyout,
          "\textern struct item menu_%s_items[];\n\n",
          name);
      fprintf(yyout, "\tif(!init) menu_init();\n\n");
      fprintf(yyout, "\tclear();\n\trefresh();\n");

      if(strlen(name) > sizeof current_screen)
          warning("Screen name is larger than buffer",(char *)0);
      strncpy(current_screen, name, sizeof(current_screen) - 1);

      screen_done = 0;
      current_line = 0;

      return 0;
}

/*
 * add_title:
 * Add centered text to screen code.
 */
add_title(line)
char *line;
{
      int length = strlen(line);
```

```
            int space = (SCREEN_SIZE - length) / 2;

            fprintf(yyout, "\tmove(%d,%d);\n",current_line, space);
            current_line++;
            fprintf(yyout, "\taddstr(\"%s\");\n",line);
            fprintf(yyout, "\trefresh();\n");
      }


      /*
       * add_line:
       * Add a line to the actions table.  It will be written
       * out after all lines have been added.  Note that some
       * of the information is in global variables.
       */

      add_line(action, attrib)
      int action, attrib;
      {
            struct item *new;

            new = (struct item *)malloc(sizeof(struct item));

            if(!item_list)
            {     /* first item */
                  item_list = last_item = new;
            }
            else
            {     /* already items on the list */
                  last_item->next = new;
                  last_item = new;
            }

            new->next = NULL;  /* mark end of list */

            new->desc = item_str;
            new->cmd = cmd_str;
            new->action = action;

            switch(action)
            {
            case EXECUTE:
                  new->act_str = act_str;
                  break;
            case MENU:
                  new->act_str = act_str;
                  break;
            default:
                  new->act_str = 0;
                  break;
            }
            new->attribute = attrib;

      }
```

```
/*
 * end_screen:
 * Finish screen, print out postamble.
 */

end_screen(char *name)
{

        fprintf(yyout, "\tmenu_runtime(menu_%s_items);\n",name);

        if(strcmp(current_screen,name) != 0)
        {
                warning("name mismatch at end of screen",
                    current_screen);
        }
        fprintf(yyout, "}\n");
        fprintf(yyout, "/* end %s */\n",current_screen);

        process_items();

        /* write initialization code out to file */
        if(!done_end_init)
        {
                done_end_init = 1;
                dump_data(menu_init);
        }

        current_screen[0] = '\0';     /* no current screen */

        screen_done = 1;

        return 0;
}


/*
 * process_items:
 * Walk the list of menu items and write them to an
 * external initialized array.  Also defines the symbolic
 * constant used for the run-time support module (which
 * is below this table).
 */
process_items()
{
        int cnt = 0;
        struct item *ptr;

        if(item_list == 0)
                return; /* nothing to do */
        fprintf(yyout, "struct item menu_%s_items[]={\n",current_screen);
        ptr = item_list;

        /* climb through the list */
        while(ptr)
        {
```

```
                struct item *optr;

                if(ptr->action == MENU)
                        fprintf(yyout,
                                "{\"%s\",\"%s\",%d,\"\",%s,%d},\n",
                                ptr->desc,ptr->cmd, ptr->action,
                                ptr->act_str,ptr->attribute);
                else
                        fprintf(yyout,
                                "{\"%s\",\"%s\",%d,\"%s\",0,%d},\n",
                                ptr->desc,ptr->cmd, ptr->action,
                                ptr->act_str ? ptr->act_str : "",
                                ptr->attribute);

                cfree(ptr->desc);
                cfree(ptr->cmd);
                cfree(ptr->act_str);
                optr = ptr;
                ptr = ptr->next;
                free(optr);
                cnt++;
        }
        fprintf(yyout,
            "{(char *)0, (char *)0, 0, (char *)0, 0, 0},\n");
        fprintf(yyout, "};\n\n");
        item_list = 0;

        /* next the run-time module that does all the "work" */;
}


/*
 * This routine takes a null-terminated list of strings
 * and prints them on the standard out.  Its sole purpose
 * in life is to dump the big static arrays making up the
 * runtime code for the menus generated.
 */

dump_data(array)
char **array;
{
        while(*array)
                fprintf(yyout, "%s\n",*array++);
}



/*
 * this routine writes out the run-time support
 */

end_file()
{

        dump_data(menu_runtime);
}
```

```
/*
 * Check a name to see if it has already been used.  If
 * not, return 1; otherwise, return 0.  This routine also
 * squirrels away the name for future reference.  Note
 * that this routine is purely dynamic.  It would be
 * easier to just set up a static array, but less flexible.
 */

check_name(name)
char *name;
{
        static char **names = 0;
        static name_count = 0;
        char **ptr,*newstr;

        if(!names)
        {
                names = (char **)malloc(sizeof(char *));
                *names = 0;
        }

        ptr = names;
        while(*ptr)
        {
                if(strcmp(name,*ptr++) == 0) return 0;
        }

        /* not in use */
        name_count++;
        names = (char **)realloc(names, (name_count+1) * sizeof(char *));
        names[name_count] = 0;
        newstr = strdup(name);
        names[name_count-1] = newstr;
        return 1;
}

void
cfree(char *p)
{
        if(p)
                free(p);
}
```

This is file *mgl-code*, the supporting code copied by the MGL into the generated C file.

```
/*
 * MGL Runtime support code
 */

char *screen_init[] = {
"/* initialization information */",
"static int init;\n",
"#include <curses.h>",
```

```
"#include <sys/signal.h>",
"#include <ctype.h>",
"#include \"mglyac.h\"\n",
"/* structure used to store menu items */",
"struct item {",
"\tchar *desc;",
"\tchar *cmd;",
"\tint  action;",
"\tchar   *act_str;      /* execute string */",
"\tint (*act_menu)();    /* call appropriate function */",
"\tint  attribute;",
"};\n",
0,
};

char *menu_init[] = {
"menu_init()",
"{",
"\tvoid menu_cleanup();\n",
"\tsignal(SIGINT, menu_cleanup);",
"\tinitscr();",
"\tcrmode();",
"}\n\n",
"menu_cleanup()",
"{",
"\tmvcur(0, COLS - 1, LINES - 1, 0);",
"\tendwin();",
"}\n",
0,
};

char *menu_runtime[] = {
"/* runtime */",
"",
"menu_runtime(items)",
"struct item *items;",
"{",
"\tint visible = 0;",
"\tint choice = 0;",
"\tstruct item *ptr;",
"\tchar buf[BUFSIZ];",
"",
"\tfor(ptr = items; ptr->desc != 0; ptr++) {",
"\t\taddch('\\n'); /* skip a line */",
"\t\tif(ptr->attribute == VISIBLE) {",
"\t\t\tvisible++;",
"\t\t\tprintw(\"\\t%d) %s\",visible,ptr->desc);",
"\t\t}",
"\t}",
"",
"\taddstr(\"\\n\\n\\t\"); /* tab out so it looks nice */",
"\trefresh();",
"",
"\tfor(;;)",
```

```
"\t{",
"\t\tint i, nval;",
"",
"\t\tgetstr(buf);",
"",
"\t\t/* numeric choice? */",
"\t\tnval = atoi(buf);",
"",
"\t\t/* command choice ? */",
"\t\ti = 0;",
"\t\tfor(ptr = items; ptr->desc != 0; ptr++) {",
"\t\t\tif(ptr->attribute != VISIBLE)",
"\t\t\t\tcontinue;",
"\t\t\ti++;",
"\t\t\tif(nval == i)",
"\t\t\t\tbreak;",
"\t\t\tif(!casecmp(buf, ptr->cmd))",
"\t\t\t\tbreak;",
"\t\t}",
"",
"\t\tif(!ptr->desc)",
"\t\t\tcontinue;\t/* no match */",
"",
"\t\tswitch(ptr->action)",
"\t\t{",
"\t\tcase QUIT:",
"\t\t\treturn 0;",
"\t\tcase IGNORE:",
"\t\t\trefresh();",
"\t\t\tbreak;",
"\t\tcase EXECUTE:",
"\t\t\trefresh();",
"\t\t\tsystem(ptr->act_str);",
"\t\t\tbreak;",
"\t\tcase MENU:",
"\t\t\trefresh();",
"\t\t\t(*ptr->act_menu)();",
"\t\t\tbreak;",
"\t\tdefault:",
"\t\t\tprintw(\"default case, no action\\n\");",
"\t\t\trefresh();",
"\t\t\tbreak;",
"\t\t}",
"\t\trefresh();",
"\t}",
"}",
"",
"casecmp(char *p, char *q)",
"{",
"\tint pc, qc;",
"",
"\tfor(; *p != 0; p++, q++) {",
"\t\tpc = tolower(*p);",
"\t\tqc = tolower(*q);",
```

```
"",
"\t\tif(pc != qc)",
"\t\t\tbreak;",
"\t}",
"\treturn pc-qc;",
"}",
0
};
```

J

SQL Parser Code

Here we display the complete code for the embedded SQL translator, including the lexer, the parser, and the supporting C code. Since the parser is so long, we have numbered the lines and included a cross-reference of all of the symbols by line number at the end.

The **main()** and **yyerror()** routines are at the end of the lex scanner.

Yacc Parser

In this printed listing, some of the lines have been split in two so they fit on the page. The line numbers correspond to the original lines in the grammar file.

```
          /* symbolic tokens */

      %union {
          int intval;
5         double floatval;
          char *strval;
          int subtok;
      }

10    %token NAME
      %token STRING
      %token INTNUM APPROXNUM

          /* operators */
15

      %left OR
      %left AND
      %left NOT
      %left <subtok> COMPARISON /* = <> < > <= >= */
20    %left '+' '-'
      %left '*' '/'
      %nonassoc UMINUS

          /* literal keyword tokens */
```

```
25
      %token ALL AMMSC ANY AS ASC AUTHORIZATION BETWEEN BY
      %token CHARACTER CHECK CLOSE COMMIT CONTINUE CREATE CURRENT
      %token CURSOR DECIMAL DECLARE DEFAULT DELETE DESC DISTINCT
             DOUBLE
   .  %token ESCAPE EXISTS FETCH FLOAT FOR FOREIGN FOUND FROM GOTO
30    %token GRANT GROUP HAVING IN INDICATOR INSERT INTEGER INTO
      %token IS KEY LANGUAGE LIKE NULLX NUMERIC OF ON OPEN OPTION
      %token ORDER PARAMETER PRECISION PRIMARY PRIVILEGES PROCEDURE
      %token PUBLIC REAL REFERENCES ROLLBACK SCHEMA SELECT SET
      %token SMALLINT SOME SQLCODE SQLERROR TABLE TO UNION
35    %token UNIQUE UPDATE USER VALUES VIEW WHENEVER WHERE WITH WORK


      %%

      sql_list:
40          sql ';' { end_sql(); }
        |   sql_list sql ';' { end_sql(); }
        ;


45      /* schema definition language */
      sql:       schema
        ;


      schema:
50          CREATE SCHEMA AUTHORIZATION user
          opt_schema_element_list
        ;

      opt_schema_element_list:
            /* empty */
55      |   schema_element_list
        ;

      schema_element_list:
            schema_element
60      |   schema_element_list schema_element
        ;

      schema_element:
            base_table_def
65      |   view_def
        |   privilege_def
        ;

      base_table_def:
70          CREATE TABLE table '(' base_table_element_commalist ')'
        ;

      base_table_element_commalist:
            base_table_element
75      |   base_table_element_commalist ',' base_table_element
        ;
```

```
     base_table_element:
             column_def
80      |    table_constraint_def
        ;

     column_def:
             column data_type column_def_opt_list
85      ;

     column_def_opt_list:
             /* empty */
        |    column_def_opt_list column_def_opt
90      ;

     column_def_opt:
             NOT NULLX
        |    NOT NULLX UNIQUE
95      |    NOT NULLX PRIMARY KEY
        |    DEFAULT literal
        |    DEFAULT NULLX
        |    DEFAULT USER
        |    CHECK '(' search_condition ')'
100     |    REFERENCES table
        |    REFERENCES table '(' column_commalist ')'
        ;

     table_constraint_def:
105          UNIQUE '(' column_commalist ')'
        |    PRIMARY KEY '(' column_commalist ')'
        |    FOREIGN KEY '(' column_commalist ')'
                 REFERENCES table
        |    FOREIGN KEY '(' column_commalist ')'
110              REFERENCES table '(' column_commalist ')'
        |    CHECK '(' search_condition ')'
        ;

     column_commalist:
115          column
        |    column_commalist ',' column
        ;

     view_def:
120          CREATE VIEW table opt_column_commalist
             AS query_spec opt_with_check_option
        ;

     opt_with_check_option:
125          /* empty */
        |    WITH CHECK OPTION
        ;

     opt_column_commalist:
130          /* empty */
        |    '(' column_commalist ')'
```

```
               ;

       privilege_def:
135            GRANT privileges ON table TO grantee_commalist
               opt_with_grant_option
               ;


       opt_with_grant_option:
140            /* empty */
           |   WITH GRANT OPTION
               ;


       privileges:
145            ALL PRIVILEGES
           |   ALL
           |   operation_commalist
               ;

150    operation_commalist:
               operation
           |   operation_commalist ',' operation
               ;

155    operation:
               SELECT
           |   INSERT
           |   DELETE
           |   UPDATE opt_column_commalist
160        |   REFERENCES opt_column_commalist
               ;


       grantee_commalist:
165            grantee
           |   grantee_commalist ',' grantee
               ;

       grantee:
170            PUBLIC
           |   user
               ;

           /* cursor definition */
175    sql:
               cursor_def
               ;


180    cursor_def:
               DECLARE cursor CURSOR FOR query_exp
           opt_order_by_clause
               ;

       opt_order_by_clause:
```

```
185             /* empty */
        |   ORDER BY ordering_spec_commalist
        ;


    ordering_spec_commalist:
190             ordering_spec
        |   ordering_spec_commalist ',' ordering_spec
        ;


    ordering_spec:
195             INTNUM opt_asc_desc
        |   column_ref opt_asc_desc
        ;


    opt_asc_desc:
200             /* empty */
        |   ASC
        |   DESC
        ;


205     /* manipulative statements */

    sql:            manipulative_statement
        ;

210 manipulative_statement:
                close_statement
        |   commit_statement
        |   delete_statement_positioned
        |   delete_statement_searched
215     |   fetch_statement
        |   insert_statement
        |   open_statement
        |   rollback_statement
        |   select_statement
220     |   update_statement_positioned
        |   update_statement_searched
        ;


    close_statement:
225             CLOSE cursor
        ;


    commit_statement:
                COMMIT WORK
230     ;


    delete_statement_positioned:
                DELETE FROM table WHERE CURRENT OF cursor
        ;
235
    delete_statement_searched:
                DELETE FROM table opt_where_clause
        ;
```

```
240  fetch_statement:
             FETCH cursor INTO target_commalist
       ;

     insert_statement:
245          INSERT INTO table opt_column_commalist
         values_or_query_spec
       ;

     values_or_query_spec:
             VALUES '(' insert_atom_commalist ')'
250    |     query_spec
       ;

     insert_atom_commalist:
             insert_atom
255    |     insert_atom_commalist ',' insert_atom
       ;

     insert_atom:
             atom
260    |     NULLX
       ;

     open_statement:
             OPEN cursor
265    ;

     rollback_statement:
             ROLLBACK WORK
       ;
270
     select_statement:
             SELECT opt_all_distinct selection
             INTO target_commalist
             table_exp
275    ;

     opt_all_distinct:
             /* empty */
       |     ALL
280    |     DISTINCT
       ;

     update_statement_positioned:
             UPDATE table SET assignment_commalist
285          WHERE CURRENT OF cursor
       ;

     assignment_commalist:
       |     assignment
290    |     assignment_commalist ',' assignment
       ;
```

```
        assignment:
                column COMPARISON scalar_exp
295      |      column COMPARISON NULLX
         ;

        update_statement_searched:
                UPDATE table SET assignment_commalist opt_where_clause
300      ;

        target_commalist:
                target
         |      target_commalist ',' target
305      ;

        target:
                parameter_ref
         ;
310
        opt_where_clause:
                /* empty */
         |      where_clause
         ;
315
         /* query expressions */

        query_exp:
                query_term
320      |      query_exp UNION query_term
         |      query_exp UNION ALL query_term
         ;

        query_term:
325             query_spec
         |      '(' query_exp ')'
         ;

        query_spec:
330             SELECT opt_all_distinct selection table_exp
         ;

        selection:
                scalar_exp_commalist
335      |      '*'
         ;

        table_exp:
                from_clause
340             opt_where_clause
                opt_group_by_clause
                opt_having_clause
         ;

345 from_clause:
                FROM table_ref_commalist
```

```
              ;

      table_ref_commalist:
350           table_ref
      |       table_ref_commalist ',' table_ref
              ;


      table_ref:
355           table
      |       table range_variable
              ;


      where_clause:
360           WHERE search_condition
              ;


      opt_group_by_clause:
              /* empty */
365   |       GROUP BY column_ref_commalist
              ;


      column_ref_commalist:
              column_ref
370   |       column_ref_commalist ',' column_ref
              ;


      opt_having_clause:
              /* empty */
375   |       HAVING search_condition
              ;


      /* search conditions */

380 search_condition:
      |       search_condition OR search_condition
      |       search_condition AND search_condition
      |       NOT search_condition
      |       '(' search_condition ')'
385   |       predicate
              ;


      predicate:
              comparison_predicate
390   |       between_predicate
      |       like_predicate
      |       test_for_null
      |       in_predicate
      |       all_or_any_predicate
395   |       existence_test
              ;


      comparison_predicate:
              scalar_exp COMPARISON scalar_exp
400   |       scalar_exp COMPARISON subquery
```

```
        ;

    between_predicate:
            scalar_exp NOT BETWEEN scalar_exp AND scalar_exp
405     |   scalar_exp BETWEEN scalar_exp AND scalar_exp
        ;

    like_predicate:
            scalar_exp NOT LIKE atom opt_escape
410     |   scalar_exp LIKE atom opt_escape
        ;

    opt_escape:
            /* empty */
415     |   ESCAPE atom
        ;

    test_for_null:
            column_ref IS NOT NULLX
420     |   column_ref IS NULLX
        ;

    in_predicate:
            scalar_exp NOT IN '(' subquery ')'
425     |   scalar_exp IN '(' subquery ')'
        |   scalar_exp NOT IN '(' atom_commalist ')'
        |   scalar_exp IN '(' atom_commalist ')'
        ;

430 atom_commalist:
            atom
        |   atom_commalist ',' atom
        ;

435 all_or_any_predicate:
            scalar_exp COMPARISON any_all_some subquery
        ;

    any_all_some:
440         ANY
        |   ALL
        |   SOME
        ;

445 existence_test:
            EXISTS subquery
        ;

    subquery:
450         '(' SELECT opt_all_distinct selection table_exp ')'
        ;

        /* scalar expressions */
```

```
455  scalar_exp:
            scalar_exp '+' scalar_exp
        |   scalar_exp '-' scalar_exp
        |   scalar_exp '*' scalar_exp
        |   scalar_exp '/' scalar_exp
460     |   '+' scalar_exp %prec UMINUS
        |   '-' scalar_exp %prec UMINUS
        |   atom
        |   column_ref
        |   function_ref
465     |   '(' scalar_exp ')'
        ;


    scalar_exp_commalist:
            scalar_exp
470     |   scalar_exp_commalist ',' scalar_exp
        ;


    atom:
            parameter_ref
475     |   literal
        |   USER
        ;


    parameter_ref:
480         parameter
        |   parameter parameter
        |   parameter INDICATOR parameter
        ;


485  function_ref:
            AMMSC '(' '*' ')'
        |   AMMSC '(' DISTINCT column_ref ')'
        |   AMMSC '(' ALL scalar_exp ')'
        |   AMMSC '(' scalar_exp ')'
490     ;


    literal:
            STRING
        |   INTNUM
495     |   APPROXNUM
        ;


        /* miscellaneous */


500  table:
            NAME
        |   NAME '.' NAME
        ;


505  column_ref:
            NAME
        |   NAME '.' NAME    /* needs semantics */
        |   NAME '.' NAME '.' NAME
```

```
     ;
510
          /* data types */

     data_type:
          CHARACTER
515  |    CHARACTER '(' INTNUM ')'
     |    NUMERIC
     |    NUMERIC '(' INTNUM ')'
     |    NUMERIC '(' INTNUM ',' INTNUM ')'
     |    DECIMAL
520  |    DECIMAL '(' INTNUM ')'
     |    DECIMAL '(' INTNUM ',' INTNUM ')'
     |    INTEGER
     |    SMALLINT
     |    FLOAT
525  |    FLOAT '(' INTNUM ')'
     |    REAL
     |    DOUBLE PRECISION
     ;

530  /* the various things you can name */

     column:   NAME
          ;

535  cursor:   NAME
          ;

     parameter:
          PARAMETER   /* :name handled in parser */
540  ;

     range_variable: NAME
          ;

545  user:     NAME
          ;

     /* embedded condition things */
     sql:      WHENEVER NOT FOUND when_action
550  |    WHENEVER SQLERROR when_action
          ;

     when_action:   GOTO NAME
          |    CONTINUE
555  ;
     %%
```

Cross-reference

Since the parser is so long, we include a cross-reference of all of the symbols by line number. For each symbol, lines where it is defined on the left-hand side of a rule are in bold type.

A

ALL (**26**)

   145, 146, 279, 321, 441, 488

all_or_any_predicate (**435**)

   394

AMMSC (**26**)

   486, 487, 488, 489

AND (**17**)

   382, 404, 405

ANY (**26**)

   440

any_all_some (**439**)

   436

APPROXNUM (**12**)

   495

AS (**26**)

   121

ASC (**26**)

   201

assignment (**293**)

   289, 290

assignment_commalist (**288**)

   284, 290, 299

atom (**473**)

   259, 409, 410, 415, 431, 432, 462

atom_commalist (**430**)

   426, 427, 432

AUTHORIZATION (**26**)

   50

B

base_table_def (**69**)

   64

base_table_element (**78**)

   74, 75

base_table_element_commalist (**73**)

   70, 75

BETWEEN (**26**)

   404, 405

between_predicate (**403**)

   390

BY (**26**)

   186, 365

C

CHARACTER (**27**)

   514, 515

CHECK (**27**)

   99, 111, 126

CLOSE (**27**)

   225

close_statement (**224**)

   211

column (**532**)

   84, 115, 116, 294, 295

column_commalist (**114**)

   101, 105, 106, 107, 109, 110, 116, 131

Lex Scanner

This is file *scn2.l.*

```
%{
#include "sql2.h"
#include <string.h>

int lineno = 1;
void yyerror(char *s);

        /* macro to save the text of a SQL token */
#define SV save_str(yytext)

        /* macro to save the text and return a token */
#define TOK(name) { SV;return name; }
%}
%s SQL
%%

EXEC[ \t]+SQL    { BEGIN SQL; start_save(); }


        /* literal keyword tokens */

<SQL>ALL            TOK(ALL)
<SQL>AND            TOK(AND)
<SQL>AVG            TOK(AMMSC)
<SQL>MIN            TOK(AMMSC)
<SQL>MAX            TOK(AMMSC)
<SQL>SUM            TOK(AMMSC)
<SQL>COUNT          TOK(AMMSC)
<SQL>ANY            TOK(ANY)
<SQL>AS                  TOK(AS)
<SQL>ASC            TOK(ASC)
<SQL>AUTHORIZATION       TOK(AUTHORIZATION)
<SQL>BETWEEN             TOK(BETWEEN)
<SQL>BY                  TOK(BY)
<SQL>CHAR(ACTER)? TOK(CHARACTER)
<SQL>CHECK          TOK(CHECK)
<SQL>CLOSE          TOK(CLOSE)
<SQL>COMMIT         TOK(COMMIT)
<SQL>CONTINUE            TOK(CONTINUE)
<SQL>CREATE         TOK(CREATE)
<SQL>CURRENT             TOK(CURRENT)
<SQL>CURSOR         TOK(CURSOR)
<SQL>DECIMAL            TOK(DECIMAL)
<SQL>DECLARE           TOK(DECLARE)
<SQL>DEFAULT          TOK(DEFAULT)
<SQL>DELETE        TOK(DELETE)
<SQL>DESC         TOK(DESC)
<SQL>DISTINCT           TOK(DISTINCT)
<SQL>DOUBLE       TOK(DOUBLE)
```

```
<SQL>ESCAPE          TOK(ESCAPE)
<SQL>EXISTS          TOK(EXISTS)
<SQL>FETCH           TOK(FETCH)
<SQL>FLOAT           TOK(FLOAT)
<SQL>FOR             TOK(FOR)
<SQL>FOREIGN             TOK(FOREIGN)
<SQL>FOUND           TOK(FOUND)
<SQL>FROM            TOK(FROM)
<SQL>GO[ \t]*TO          TOK(GOTO)
<SQL>GRANT           TOK(GRANT)
<SQL>GROUP           TOK(GROUP)
<SQL>HAVING          TOK(HAVING)
<SQL>IN                  TOK(IN)
<SQL>INDICATOR           TOK(INDICATOR)
<SQL>INSERT          TOK(INSERT)
<SQL>INT(EGER)?           TOK(INTEGER)
<SQL>INTO            TOK(INTO)
<SQL>IS                  TOK(IS)
<SQL>KEY             TOK(KEY)
<SQL>LANGUAGE            TOK(LANGUAGE)
<SQL>LIKE            TOK(LIKE)
<SQL>NOT             TOK(NOT)
<SQL>NULL            TOK(NULLX)
<SQL>NUMERIC             TOK(NUMERIC)
<SQL>OF                  TOK(OF)
<SQL>ON                  TOK(ON)
<SQL>OPEN            TOK(OPEN)
<SQL>OPTION          TOK(OPTION)
<SQL>OR                  TOK(OR)
<SQL>ORDER           TOK(ORDER)
<SQL>PRECISION           TOK(PRECISION)
<SQL>PRIMARY         TOK(PRIMARY)
<SQL>PRIVILEGES          TOK(PRIVILEGES)
<SQL>PROCEDURE           TOK(PROCEDURE)
<SQL>PUBLIC          TOK(PUBLIC)
<SQL>REAL            TOK(REAL)
<SQL>REFERENCES          TOK(REFERENCES)
<SQL>ROLLBACK            TOK(ROLLBACK)
<SQL>SCHEMA          TOK(SCHEMA)
<SQL>SELECT          TOK(SELECT)
<SQL>SET             TOK(SET)
<SQL>SMALLINT            TOK(SMALLINT)
<SQL>SOME            TOK(SOME)
<SQL>SQLCODE             TOK(SQLCODE)
<SQL>SQLERROR             TOK(SQLERROR)
<SQL>TABLE           TOK(TABLE)
<SQL>TO                  TOK(TO)
<SQL>UNION           TOK(UNION)
<SQL>UNIQUE          TOK(UNIQUE)
<SQL>UPDATE          TOK(UPDATE)
<SQL>USER            TOK(USER)
<SQL>VALUES          TOK(VALUES)
<SQL>VIEW            TOK(VIEW)
<SQL>WHENEVER            TOK(WHENEVER)
```

```
<SQL>WHERE         TOK(WHERE)
<SQL>WITH          TOK(WITH)
<SQL>WORK          TOK(WORK)

        /* punctuation */

<SQL>"="    |
<SQL>"<>"   |
<SQL>"<"    |
<SQL>">"    |
<SQL>"<="   |
<SQL>">="          TOK(COMPARISON)

<SQL>[-+*/(),.;]  TOK(yytext[0])


        /* names */
<SQL>[A-Za-z][A-Za-z0-9_]*    TOK(NAME)

        /* parameters */
<SQL>":"[A-Za-z][A-Za-z0-9_]*{
                   save_param(yytext+1);
                   return PARAMETER;
              }

        /* numbers */

<SQL>[0-9]+ |
<SQL>[0-9]+"."[0-9]* |
<SQL>"."[0-9]*            TOK(INTNUM)

<SQL>[0-9]+[eE][+-]?[0-9]+    |
<SQL>[0-9]+"."[0-9]*[eE][+-]?[0-9]+ |
<SQL>"."[0-9]*[eE][+-]?[0-9]+TOK(APPROXNUM)

        /* strings */

<SQL>'[^'\n]*'    {
           int c = input();

           unput(c);   /* just peeking */
           if(c != '\'') {
               SV;return STRING;
           } else
               yymore();
      }

<SQL>'[^'\n]*$    {    yyerror("Unterminated string"); }

<SQL>\n          { save_str(" ");lineno++; }
\n          { lineno++; ECHO; }

<SQL>[ \t\r]+     save_str(" ");   /* whitespace */
```

```
<SQL>"--".* ;      /* comment */

.              ECHO; /* random non-SQL text */
%%

void
yyerror(char *s)
{
     printf("%d: %s at %s\n", lineno, s, yytext);
}

main(int ac, char **av)
{
     if(ac > 1 && (yyin = fopen(av[1], "r")) == NULL) {
          perror(av[1]);
          exit(1);
     }

     if(!yyparse())
          fprintf(stderr, "Embedded SQL parse worked\n");
     else
          fprintf(stderr, "Embedded SQL parse failed\n");
} /* main */

/* leave SQL lexing mode */
un_sql()
{
     BEGIN INITIAL;
} /* un_sql */
```

Supporting Code

This is file *sqltext.c*.

```
/*
 *      Text handling routines for simple embedded SQL
 */

#include <stdio.h>
#include <string.h>
extern FILE *yyout;     /* lex output file */

char save_buf[2000];    /* buffer for SQL command */
char *savebp;           /* current buffer pointer */

#define NPARAM    20    /* max params per function */
char *varnames[NPARAM]; /* parameter names */

/* start an embedded command after EXEC SQL */
start_save(void)
{
```

```
        savebp = save_buf;
} /* start_save */

/* save a SQL token */
save_str(char *s)
{

        strcpy(savebp, s);
        savebp += strlen(s);
} /* save_str */

/* save a parameter reference */
save_param(char *n)
{
        int i;
        char pbuf[10];

        /* look up the variable name in the table */

        for(i = 1; i < NPARAM; i++) {
                if(!varnames[i]) {

                        /* not there, enter it */
                        varnames[i] = strdup(n);
                        break;
                }

                if(!strcmp(varnames[i],n))
                        break;          /* already present */
        }

        if(i >= NPARAM) {
                yyerror("Too many parameter references");
                exit(1);
        }

        /* save #n referece by variable number */
        sprintf(pbuf, " #%d", i);
        save_str(pbuf);

} /* save_param */

/* end of SQL command, now write it out */
end_sql(void)
{
        int i;
        register char *cp;

        savebp--;    /* back over the closing semicolon */

        /* call exec_sql function */

        fprintf(yyout, "exec_sql(\"");
```

```
        /* write out saved buffer as a big C string
         * starting new lines as needed
         */

        for(cp = save_buf, i = 20; cp < savebp; cp++, i++) {
            if(i > 70) {        /* need new line */
                    fprintf(yyout, "\\\n");
                    i = 0;
            }
            putc(*cp, yyout);
        }
        putc('"', yyout);

        /* pass address of every referenced variable */
        for(i = 1; i < NPARAM; i++) {
            if(!varnames[i])
                    break;
            fprintf(yyout, ",\n\t&%s", varnames[i]);
            free(varnames[i]);
            varnames[i] = 0;
        }

        fprintf(yyout, ");\n");

        /* return scanner to regular mode */
        un_sql();

} /* end_sql */
```

Glossary

A large number of technical terms are used in this manual. Many of them may be familiar; some may not. To help avoid confusion, the most significant terms are listed here.

action

> The C code associated with a lex pattern or a yacc rule. When the pattern or rule matches an input sequence, the action code is executed.

alphabet

> A set of distinct symbols. For example, the ASCII character set is a collection of 128 different symbols. In a lex specification, the alphabet is the native character set of the computer, unless you use "%T" to define a custom alphabet. In a yacc grammar, the alphabet is the set of tokens and non-terminals used in the grammar.

ambiguity

> An ambiguous grammar is one with more than one rule or set of rules that match the same input. In a yacc grammar, ambiguous rules cause shift/reduce or reduce/reduce conflicts. The parsing mechanism that yacc uses cannot handle ambiguous grammars, so it uses **%prec** declarations and its own internal rules to resolve the conflict when creating a parser.

> Lex specifications can be and usually are ambiguous; when two patterns match the same input, the pattern earlier in the specification wins.

ASCII

> *A*merican *S*tandard *C*ode for *I*nformation *I*nterchange; a collection of 128 symbols representing the common symbols found in the American alphabet: lower and uppercase letters, digits, and punctuation, plus additional characters for formatting and control of data

communication links. Most computers on which yacc and lex run use
ASCII, although some IBM mainframe systems use a different 256
symbol code called EBCDIC.

BNF (Backus-Naur Form)

*B*ackus-*N*aur *F*orm; a method of representing grammars. It is commonly used to specify formal grammars of programming languages.
The input syntax of yacc is a simplifed version of BNF.

BSD

*B*erkeley *S*oftware *D*istribution. The University of California at Berkeley issued a series of operating system distributions based upon
Seventh Edition UNIX; typically, BSD is further qualified with the version number of the particular distribution, e.g., BSD 2.10 or BSD 4.3.

compiler

A program which translates a set of instructions (a *program*) in one
language into some other representation; typically, the output of a
compiler is in the native binary language that can be run directly on a
computer. Compare to *interpreter.*

conflict

An error within the yacc grammar in which two (or more) parsing
actions are possible when parsing the same input token. There are
two types of conflicts: *shift/reduce* and *reduce/reduce.* (See also
ambiguity.)

empty string

The special case of a string with zero symbols, sometimes written ε.
In the C language, a string which consists only of the ASCII character
NUL. Yacc rules can match the empty string, but lex patterns cannot.

finite automaton

An abstract machine which consists of a finite number of instructions
(or *transitions*). Finite automata are useful in modeling many commonly occurring computer processes and have useful mathematical
properties. Lex and yacc create lexers and parsers based on finite
automata.

input

> A stream of data read by a program. For instance, the input to a lex scanner is a sequence of bytes, while the input to a yacc parser is a sequence of *tokens*.

interpreter

> A program which reads instructions in a language (a *program*) and decodes and acts on them one at a time. Compare to *compiler*.

language

> Formally, a well-defined set of strings over some alphabet; informally, some set of instructions for describing tasks which can be executed by a computer.

LALR(1)

> *L*ook*A*head *L*eft *R*ecursive; the parsing technique that *yacc* uses. The (1) denotes that the lookahead is limited to a single token.

left-hand side (LHS)

> The left-hand side or LHS of a yacc *rule* is the symbol that precedes the colon. During a parse, when the input matches the sequence of symbols on the RHS of the rule, that sequence is *reduced* to the LHS symbol.

lex

> A program for producing lexical analyzers that match patterns defined by regular expressions to a character stream.

lexical analyzer

> A program which converts a character stream into a token stream. Lex takes a description of individual tokens as regular expressions, divides the character stream into tokens, and determines the types and values of the tokens. For example it might turn the character stream "a = 17;" into a token stream consisting of the name "a", the operator "=", the number "17", and the single character token ";". Also called a *lexer* or *scanner*.

lookahead

> Input read by a parser or scanner but not yet matched to a pattern or rule. Yacc parsers have a single token of lookahead, while lex scanners can have indefinitely long lookahead.

non-terminal

Symbols in a yacc grammar that do not appear in the input, but instead are defined by *rules*. Contrast to *tokens*.

parser stack

In a yacc parser, the symbols for partially matched rules are stored on an internal stack. Symbols are added to the stack when the parser *shifts* and are removed when it *reduces*.

parsing

The process of taking a stream of *tokens* and logically grouping them into *statements* within some language.

pattern

In a lex lexer, a *regular expression* that the lexer matches against the input.

precedence

The order in which some particular operation is performed; e.g., when interpreting mathematical statements, multiplication and division are assigned higher precedence than addition and subtraction; thus, the statement "3+4*5" is 23 as opposed to 35.

production

See *rules*.

program

A set of instructions which perform a certain predefined task.

reduce

In a yacc parser, when the input matches the list of symbols on the RHS of a rule, the parser *reduces* the rule by removing the RHS symbols from the *parser stack* and replacing them with the LHS symbol.

reduce/reduce conflict

In a yacc grammar, the situation where two or more rules match the same string of tokens. Yacc resolves the conflict by reducing the rule that occurs earlier in the grammar.

regular expression

A language for specifying *patterns* that match a sequence of characters. Regular expressions consist of normal characters, which match the same character in the input, character classes which match any single character in the class, and other characters which specify the way that parts of the expression are to be matched against the input.

right-hand side (RHS)

The right-hand side or RHS of a yacc *rule* is the list of symbols that follow the colon. During a parse, when the input matches the sequence of symbols on the RHS of the rule, that sequence is *reduced* to the LHS symbol.

rule

In yacc, *rules* are the abstract description of the grammar. Yacc rules are also called *productions*. A rule is a single *non-terminal* called the LHS, a colon, and a possible empty set of symbols called the RHS. Whenever the input matches the RHS of a rule, the parser *reduces* the rule.

semantic meaning

See *value*.

shift

A yacc parser *shifts* input symbols onto the parser stack in expectation that the symbol will match one of the rules in the grammar.

shift/reduce conflict

In a yacc grammar, the situation where a symbol completes the RHS of one rule, which the parser needs to *reduce,* and is an intermediate symbol in the RHS of other rules, for which the parser needs to *shift* the symbol. Shift/reduce conflicts occur either because the grammar is ambiguous, or because the parser would need to look more than one token ahead to decide whether to reduce the rule that the symbol completes. Yacc resolves the conflict by doing the shift.

specification

A lex *specification* is a set of patterns to be matched against an input stream. Lex turns a specification into a lexer.

start state

In a lex specification, patterns can be tagged with start states, in which case the pattern

start symbol

> The single symbol to which a yacc parser reduces a valid input stream. Rules with the start symbol on the LHS are called *start rules*.

symbol table

> A table containing information about names occurring in the input, so that all references to the same name can be related to the same object.

symbol

> In yacc terminology, *symbols* are either *tokens* or *non-terminals*. In the rules for the grammar, any name found on the right-hand side of a rule is always a symbol.

System V

> After the release of Seventh Edition UNIX (upon which the BSD distributions of UNIX are based), AT&T released newer versions of UNIX, the most recent of which is called System V; newer versions bear release numbers, so it is common to refer to either System V or System V.4.

token

> In yacc terminology, *tokens* or *terminals* are the symbols provided to the parser by the lexer. Compare to *non-terminals*, which are defined within the parser.

tokenizing

> The process of converting a stream of characters into a stream of tokens is termed *tokenizing*. A lexer tokenizes its input.

value

> Each *token* in a yacc grammar has both a *syntactic* and a *semantic* value; its semantic value is the actual data contents of the token. For instance, the syntactic type of a certain operation may be INTEGER, but its semantic value might be 3.

yacc

> *Y*et *A*nother *C*ompiler *C*ompiler; a program that generates a parser from a list of rules in BNF-like format.

Bibliography

Aho, Alfred V., Ravi Sethi, and Jeffrey D. Ullman. *Compilers: Principles, Techniques, and Tools.* Addison-Wesley, 1986.

The classic compiler text. It includes detailed discussions of the theory behind yacc and lex along with sketches of their implementation.

American National Standards Institute. *Programming Language C.* X3.159-1989. ANSI, December 1989.

The definition of modern ANSI C. Also known as Federal Information Processing Standard (FIPS) 160.

Bennett, J.P. *Introduction to Compiling Techniques—A First Course Using Ansi C, Lex and Yacc.* McGraw Hill Book Co, 1990.

Deloria. "Practical yacc: a gentle introduction to the power of this famous parser generator." *C Users Journal.* Nov 1987, Dec/Jan 1988, Mar/Apr 1988, Jun/Jul 1988, and Sep/Oct 1988.

Donnely and Stallman. *The Bison Manual.* Part of the online bison distribution.

The definitive reference on bison.

Holub, Alan. *Compiler Design in C.* Prentice-Hall, 1990.

A large book containing the complete source code to versions of yacc and lex, and to a C compiler built using them.

S. C. Johnson *Yacc—Yet Another Compiler-Compiler.* Comp. Sci. Tech. Rep. No. 32. Bell Laboratories, July 1975.

The original description of yacc. Reprinted as part of the documentation with Seventh Edition UNIX and with most versions of BSD UNIX.

Kernighan, Brian W. and Dennis M. Ritchie. *The C Programming Language*. Prentice-Hall, 1978.

The standard reference for the "classic" C language.

M. E. Lesk *Lex—A Lexical Analyzer Generator*. Comp. Sci. Tech. Rep. No. 39. Bell Laboratories, October 1975.

The original description of lex. Reprinted as part of the documentation with Seventh Edition UNIX and with most versions of BSD UNIX.

Schreiner, Axel T. and H. George Friedman, Jr. *Introduction to Compiler Construction with UNIX*. Prentice-Hall, 1985.

Develops a small subset-of-C compiler using lex and yacc with a relatively theoretical approach and excellent coverage of error handling and recovery. Beware of typographical errors in the examples.

Index

F

G

About the Authors

John R. Levine writes, lectures, and consults on UNIX and compiler topics. He moderates the online comp.compilers.discussion group on Usenet. He worked on UNIX versions of Lotus 1-2-3 and the Norton Utilities, and was one of the architects of AIX for the IBM RT PC. He received a Ph.D. in Computer Science from Yale in 1984.

Tony Mason is currently a member of the AFS development team at Transarc Corporation, a small start-up company specializing in distributed systems software. Previously, he worked with the Distributed Systems Group at Stanford University in the area of distributed operating systems and data communications. He received a B.S. in Mathematics from the University of Chicago in 1987.

Doug Brown is a consultant/contractor in Beaverton, Oregon. He has been developing software for circuit simulation, synthesis, and testing since 1977. Doug coauthored *C++: The Core Language*, another O'Reilly & Associates Nutshell handbook. He received an M.S. in electrical engineering from the University of Illinois at Urbana-Champaign in 1976.

Colophon

Our look is the result of reader comments, our own experimentation, and distribution channels.

Distinctive covers complement our distinctive approach to technical topics, breathing personality and life into potentially dry subjects. UNIX and its attendant programs can be unruly beasts. Nutshell Handbooks help you tame them.

The animal featured on the cover of *lex & yacc* is a Victorian crowned pigeon, one of the largest members of the pigeon family. Unlike other birds, the crowned pigeon drinks water by immersing its bill and sucking. Incubation of the eggs (generally two) is shared by these monogamous birds, the male warming them by day, the female by night.

Other Titles Available from O'Reilly

Scripting Languages

Programming Python, 2nd Edition

By Mark Lutz
2nd Edition March 2001
1256 pages, Includes CD-ROM
ISBN 0-596-00085-5

Programming Python, 2nd Edition, focuses on advanced applications of Python, an increasingly popular object-oriented scripting language. Endorsed by Python creator Guido van Rossum, it demonstrates advanced Python programming techniques, and addresses software design issues such as reusability and object-oriented programming. The enclosed platform-neutral CD-ROM has book examples and various Python-related packages, including the full Python Version 2.0 source code distribution.

Learning Python

By Mark Lutz & David Ascher
1st Edition April 1999
384 pages, ISBN 1-56592-464-9

Learning Python is an introduction to the increasingly popular Python programming language— an interpreted, interactive, object-oriented, and portable scripting language. This book thoroughly introduces the elements of Python: types, operators, statements, classes, functions, modules, and exceptions. It also demonstrates how to perform common programming tasks and write real applications.

Python in a Nutshell

By Alex Martelli
1st Edition February 2003
654 pages, ISBN 0-596-00188-6

This book offers Python programmers one place to look when you need help remembering or deciphering the most important tools and modules of this open source language. The book deals with the most frequently used parts of the standard library, and the most popular and important third party extensions. Python is an easy scripting language with a huge library that is enormously rich. *Python in a Nutshell* presents the highlights of all modules and functions, which cover well over 90% of a programmer's practical needs.

Python Cookbook

David Ascher & Alex Martelli,
Editors
1st Edition July 2002
608 pages, ISBN 0-596-00167-3

The *Python Cookbook* is a collection of problems, solutions, and practical examples written by Python programmers in the style of the popular *Perl Cookbook*. Its potential audience includes both Python programmers and experienced programmers who are new to Python and want to evaluate whether or not the language is suitable for their intended applications. Anyone interested in Python programming will want this wealth of practical advice, snippets of code, and patterns of program design that can be directly lifted out of the book and applied to everyday programming problems.

Exploring Expect

By Don Libes
1st Edition December 1994
602 pages, ISBN 1-56592-090-2

Written by the author of Expect, this is the first book to explain how this part of the Unix toolbox can be used to automate Telnet, FTP, passwd, rlogin, and hundreds of other interactive applications. Based on Tcl (Tool Command Language), Expect lets you automate interactive applications that have previously been extremely difficult to handle with any scripting language.

Jython Essentials

By Noel Rappin & Samuele
Pedroni
1st Edition March 2002
300 pages, ISBN 0-596-00247-5

Jython is an implementation of the Python programming language written in Java, allowing Python programs to integrate seamlessly with any Java code. The secret to Jython's popularity lies in the combination of Java's libraries and tools with Python's rapid development capabilities. *Jython Essentials* provides a solid introduction to the language, numerous examples of Jython/Java interaction, and valuable reference material on modules and libraries of use to Jython programmers.

O'REILLY®

To order: 800-998-9938 • *order@oreilly.com* • *www.oreilly.com*
Online editions of most O'Reilly titles are available by subscription at *safari.oreilly.com*
Also available at most retail and online bookstores.

Scripting Languages

Ruby in a Nutshell

By Yukihiro Matsumoto
With translated text by
David L. Reynolds Jr.
1st Edition November 2001
218 pages, ISBN 0-59600-214-9

Written by Yukihiro Matsumoto ("Matz"), creator of the language, *Ruby in a Nutshell* is a practical reference guide covering everything from Ruby syntax to the specifications of its standard class libraries. The book is based on Ruby 1.6, and is applicable to development versions 1.7 and the next planned stable version 1.8. As part of the successful "in a Nutshell" series *Ruby in a Nutshell* is for readers who want a single desktop reference for all their needs.

Python Pocket Reference, 2nd Edition

By Mark Lutz
2nd Edition November 2001
128 pages, ISBN 0-596-00189-4

This book is a companion volume to two O'Reilly animal guides: *Programming Python* and *Learning Python*. It summarizes Python statements and types, built-in functions, commonly used library modules, and other prominent Python language features.

Programming PHP

By Rasmus Lerdorf &
Kevin Tatroe
1st Edition March 2002
528 pages, ISBN 1-56592-610-2

Programming PHP is a comprehensive guide to PHP, a simple yet powerful language for creating dynamic web content. Filled with the unique knowledge of the creator of PHP, Rasmus Lerdorf, this book is a detailed reference to the language and its applications, including such topics as form processing, sessions, databases, XML, and graphics. Covers PHP 4, the latest version of the language.

Python & XML

By Christopher A. Jones &
Fred Drake
1st Edition December 2001
378 pages, ISBN 0-596-00128-2

This book has two objectives: to provide a comprehensive reference on using XML with Python and to illustrate the practical applications of these technologies (often coupled with cross-platform tools) in an enterprise environment. Loaded with practical examples, it also shows how to use Python to create scalable XML connections between popular distributed applications such as databases and web servers. Covers XML flow analysis and details ways to transport XML through a network.

Python Standard Library

By Fredrik Lundh
1st Edition May 2001
300 pages, ISBN 0-596-00096-0

Python Standard Library, an essential guide for serious Python programmers, delivers accurate, author-tested documentation of all the modules in the Python Standard Library, along with over 300 annotated example scripts using the modules. This version of the book covers all the new modules and related information for Python 2.0, the first major release of Python in four years.

PHP Pocket Reference, 2nd Edition

By Rasmus Lerdorf
2nd Edition November 2002
144 pages, ISBN 0-596-00402-8

Simple, to the point, and compact, the second edition of PHP Pocket Reference is thoroughly updated to include the specifics of PHP 4, the language's latest version. It is both a handy introduction to PHP syntax and structure, and a quick reference to the vast array of functions provided by PHP. The quick reference section organizes all the core functions of PHP alphabetically so you can find what you need easily.

O'REILLY®

To order: *800-998-9938* • *order@oreilly.com* • *www.oreilly.com*
Online editions of most O'Reilly titles are available by subscription at *safari.oreilly.com*
Also available at most retail and online bookstores.

How to stay in touch with O'Reilly

1. Visit our award-winning web site

http://www.oreilly.com/

★ "Top 100 Sites on the Web"—PC Magazine
★ CIO Magazine's Web Business 50 Awards

Our web site contains a library of comprehensive product information (including book excerpts and tables of contents), downloadable software, background articles, interviews with technology leaders, links to relevant sites, book cover art, and more. File us in your bookmarks or favorites!

2. Join our email mailing lists

Sign up to get email announcements of new books and conferences, special offers, and O'Reilly Network technology newsletters at:

http://elists.oreilly.com

It's easy to customize your free elists subscription so you'll get exactly the O'Reilly news you want.

3. Get examples from our books

To find example files for a book, go to:

http://www.oreilly.com/catalog

select the book, and follow the "Examples" link.

4. Work with us

Check out our web site for current employment opportunites:

http://jobs.oreilly.com/

5. Register your book

Register your book at:

http://register.oreilly.com

6. Contact us

O'Reilly & Associates, Inc.
1005 Gravenstein Hwy North
Sebastopol, CA 95472 USA
TEL: 707-827-7000 or 800-998-9938
        (6am to 5pm PST)
FAX: 707-829-0104

order@oreilly.com
For answers to problems regarding your order or our products. To place a book order online visit:

http://www.oreilly.com/order_new/

catalog@oreilly.com
To request a copy of our latest catalog.

booktech@oreilly.com
For book content technical questions or corrections.

corporate@oreilly.com
For educational, library, government, and corporate sales.

proposals@oreilly.com
To submit new book proposals to our editors and product managers.

international@oreilly.com
For information about our international distributors or translation queries. For a list of our distributors outside of North America check out:

http://international.oreilly.com/distributors.html

adoption@oreilly.com
For information about academic use of O'Reilly books, visit:

http://academic.oreilly.com

O'REILLY®

To order: 800-998-9938 • *order@oreilly.com* • *www.oreilly.com*
Online editions of most O'Reilly titles are available by subscription at *safari.oreilly.com*
Also available at most retail and online bookstores.

Notes

O'REILLY®

To order: *800-998-9938* • *order@oreilly.com* • *www.oreilly.com*
Online editions of most O'Reilly titles are available by subscription at *safari.oreilly.com*
Also available at most retail and online bookstores.